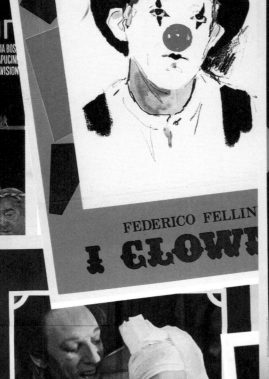

FEDERICO FELLINI
The Films

Tullio Kezich

FEDERICO FELLINI

The Films

Edited by Vittorio Boarini

RIZZOLI
NEW YORK

New York · Paris · London · Milan

PHOTOGRAPHY CREDITS

Agenzia Cekap: 251 top, 264 bottom

Archivio Fondazione Federico Fellini: 16, 21 top, 23 (posters), 35, 39, 43 bottom, 46, 47 (poster), 49, 50, 52-53, 54, 64, 70, 71 top, 75 top, 76, 85 (poster), 90 top, 96, 97, 102, 107, 109 bottom, 111 top, 125, 127, 137 (poster), 141, 149 top left and bottom right, 165 (posters), 168 top, 171, 173, 174, 175, 186 top, 191 (poster), 195, 200, 201, 207 inset, 213, 217 right (courtesy Titta Benzi), 218 top and middle, 219 middle, 225 (drawings), 229, 235, 241 (poster), 245, 248, 250 bottom (photograph Riccardo Gallini), 251 (poster), 252, 256, 260, 262 (drawing), 265, 267, 271 third from the top, 272, 275, 277, 289, 291, 295 bottom, 298, 300, 301, 303, 306, 312 (posters), 313, 314 top, 315 top, 317 top and middle
For drawings © Fondazione Federico Fellini; from *Federico Fellini: The Book of Dreams*, Rizzoli, 2008: 22, 32, 66, 89, 111, 114, 132, 155, 162, 181, 209, 238, 276, 296

Archivio Giancolombo: 46 bottom

Archivio Storico Barilla, Parma, Italy: 314 bottom

Archivio RCS: 8-9, 105

Nicola Arresto: 91 top, 92 top, 93

Gideon Bachmann: 146

Deborah Beer: 255, 261, 262, 282 top left, 283 top and middle, 288

Bettmann/Corbis: 254

Cameraphoto/Bianconero: 75 bottom, 191 bottom left

Angelo Caligaris: 282

Elisabetta Catalano: 243, 246 bottom, 247 bottom, 249, 311 second and third from the top

Mimmo Cattarinich: 167, 168 bottom, 173 top, 269, 270, 271 top, 273, 274, 315, 316, 317

Ampelio Ciolfi: 37, 38 top, 40, 41, 45

Osvaldo Civirani: 15, 20, 21 bottom, 23 top, 25, 26, 28 bottom, 33 middle and bottom

Collezione Antonello Geleng: 317 bottom

Collezione Vincenzo Mollica: 62, 281, 286 (drawing), 294, 295 top right, 299, 305

Collezione Renzo Renzi: 27, 32 top, 38 bottom, 59, 68, 81, 169, 170, 172, 197, 205, 219 top and bottom, 227

Courtesy Carla Del Poggio: 33 top

Courtesy Dante Ferretti: 246 top

Ferruzzi: 71 bottom

Emilio Lari: 291, 292, 295 top left

A. Piatti: 63, 69

Franco Pinna: 153, 154, 159, 161, 178, 183, 184, 187, 189, 190, 193, 194, 199, 204, 211, 231, 232, 233, 234, 236, 237, 240

GB. Poletto: 80 right, 84

Pierluigi Praturlon: 109 top and middle, 120, 123 bottom, 215, 222, 223, 271 second from the top

Vittoriano Rastelli: 137 right, 185

Reporters Associati/Cineteca di Bologna: 2, 12-13, 19 (Civirani), 30 (Civirani), 34 (Civirani), 57 (Piatti), 58 (Piatti), 65 (Piatti), 73 (Poletto), 74 (Poletto), 77 (Poletto), 78 (Poletto), 80 left (Poletto), 83 (Poletto), 87 (Arresto), 88 (Arresto), 90 bottom (Arresto), 91 bottom (Arresto), 92 bottom (Arresto), 94 (Arresto), 95 insets (Arresto), 98 (Arresto), 99 (Arresto), 100 (Arresto), 106 (Praturlon), 108 (Praturlon), 110 (Praturlon), 113 (Praturlon), 115 (Praturlon), 117 (Praturlon), 118 (Praturlon), 119 (Praturlon), 121 (Praturlon), 122 (Praturlon), 124 (Praturlon), 126 (Praturlon), 129 (Ronald), 133 bottom (Ronald), 134 (Ronald), 135 (Ronald), 156 (Pinna), 157 (Pinna), 158 (Pinna), 163 (Pinna), 164 (Pinna), 196 (Pinna), 202, 207, 208-209, 216, 218 bottom (Praturlon), 220 (Praturlon), 220-221 (Praturlon), 224 (Praturlon), 225 (Praturlon), 241 bottom (Praturlon), 244 (Praturlon), 246-247 (Praturlon), 257 (Praturlon), 258 (Praturlon), 258-259 (Praturlon), 268 (Praturlon), 271 bottom (Praturlon), 279 (Praturlon), 280 (Praturlon), 282 top right (Praturlon), 283 bottom (Praturlon), 285 (Praturlon), 287 (Praturlon), 304, 307, 308-309, 311

Reporters Associés: 103 bottom

Paul Ronald: 130, 131, 133 top, 142, 144, 145, 148, 149 top right and bottom left

Chiara Samugheo: 132 right, 137 bottom left and bottom center

Tazio Secchiaroli: 139, 140, 147, 177, 179, 181

Every effort has been made by the publisher to identify and contact the copyright holder for all images in this book. Any inaccuracies brought to our attention will be corrected for future editions.

Page 2: *Federico Fellini on the set of* City of Women.
Pages 8-9: *Federico Fellini gives instructions to the actors on the set of* Nights of Cabiria.
Pages 12-13: *Studio shoot for the transatlantic voyage of* SS Rex *for* Amarcord

Thanks to Franco Grattarola, Luca Pallanch, Roberto Poppi

Photo Research and Index
Giuseppe Ricci

Editorial Coordination
Giulia Dadà

Layout
Paola Polastri

Production Coordination
Sergio Daniotti

First published in the United States of America in 2010 by Rizzoli International Publications, Inc.
300 Park Avenue South
New York, NY 10010
www.rizzoliusa.com

Originally published in Italian in 2009 as *Federico Fellini: Il libro dei film* by Rizzoli Libri Illustrati

© 2009 RCS Libri Spa, Milan

ISBN: 978-0-8478-3269-9

Library of Congress Control Number: 2009936368

2010 2011 2012 2013 / 10 9 8 7 6 5 4 3 2 1

Printed in Italy by Centro Poligrafico Milano S.p.a. - Casarile (MI)

CONTENTS

INTRODUCTION

by Vittorio Boarini

Following the extraordinary event that took place in 2007 with the publication of *The Book of Dreams*—which might just as easily have been entitled *The Book of My Dreams*, imagining Fellini himself sent it in for publication—Rizzoli and the Fondazione Federico Fellini are now publishing *The Films*: Fellini's entire cinematic universe. The book is a phantasmagoria narrated by Tullio Kezich, the Italian film director's biographer par excellence. He passed away soon after finishing work on this volume, to which he dedicated himself with enthusiasm and passion.

Kezich opens each film chapter with a quote by Fellini, almost as if it were once again Fellini himself handing the work directly to the publisher. This is a *summa* with which the publishers intend to pay homage to the Maestro, a gift for the fiftieth anniversary of *La Dolce Vita*, the film that landed Fellini on the international map of cinema. But it is also an opportunity to provide scholars and enthusiasts of his movies with a reasonably definitive reference book. It is a very ambitious project and an impassioned challenge for the Fondazione Federico Fellini and its Honorary President, Tullio Kezich.

The Fondazione Federico Fellini's primary institutional goal is to safeguard and to share the filmmaker's oeuvre, and it was enthusiastic about the opportunity to entrust this task to Kezich, a grand protagonist of cinema, especially since this book represents a perfect epilogue to a lifetime of study that Kezich has dedicated to the career and figure of this great and much beloved Italian film director.

All of Federico Fellini's works are discussed in an engaging way, with a blend of reportage and history that is as lively as it is factual, describing events that the author often witnessed firsthand with the objectivity of a documentary filmmaker. The genesis of each movie is discussed in detail; then each film plot is outlined; finally, a summary of how audiences and critics reacted to the work, as well as the film festivals Fellini's movies participated in.

I'd like to spend a little time considering the plot descriptions, the main body of each chapter, precisely because they constitute the element that allows the recording of events to become a story. The generally accepted opinion that a film's plot is also its critical interpretation can without doubt be linked to the summaries Kezich makes for each movie, with a further specification that, in my opinion, seems fundamental. The implicit judgment in the narration is not a "critique" in the sense we usually intend with this term, that is, a film review such as those that appear in newspapers or magazines. Nor is it ideological judgment, which inevitably sifts through the content of a work of art at the expense of its expressive form. Kezich's judgment respects the text and the reader (I hope they will also watch the films), who is free to formulate his or her own opinion without feeling excessively conditioned by this book or in disagreement with its contents. At heart, Kezich's descriptions of the movies are critical in the classic philosophical sense; a process that transforms a nebula, as a film appears to a viewer watching it for the first time, into a decipherable text that can be understood even in its less obvious aspects. In other words, the viewer is offered—in a light, eloquent form—the foundation needed to formulate a critical judgment: an objective understanding of the cinematic text.

Furthermore, the reader is provided with a long series of details that, contrary to what may seem at first glance, ultimately prove to be important, and at times even exceptional, annotations. A perfect example of this is when Kezich indicates, wherever possible, the names of the films' dubbing artists—in other words, the men and women who lent their voices to most of the actors who appeared in Fellini's movies. If we consider the essential expressive role that dubbing played in the filmmaker's work, we cannot help but acknowledge the importance of what might otherwise seem to be mere philological adornment.

Toward the end of the book, the stories of the films all blend together into a single tale, one that coincides with Fellini's cinematographic cosmos and includes an important part of his own personal history, creating an unicum of art and life: a new, extraordinary "moviebook" enriched with more than nine hundred images that accompany and illustrate all the key points of Kezich's narration, thereby constituting an integral, fundamental part of the text itself.

Photographs, stills, drawings, posters, billboards, and other documents (which already enjoy a certain notoriety or are universally considered icons belonging to the history of cinema) are accompanied by rare and previously unpublished illustrations. Things that have "never been seen before," that normally remain hidden from view, not only in the individual stills that make up the movies (the audience in the theater doesn't see the filmmaker, nor the scriptwriter, nor the producer, and so forth), but also in the vast visual documentation provided by everything that comes before and after a film's release (ad brochures, newspapers, magazines, etc.). The image of Anita Ekberg splashing around in the Fontana di Trevi in an evening gown, for example, is familiar even to people who have not seen the movie, but very few know that underneath that evening gown Ekberg was wearing fishing boots that ran all the way up to her hips. Iconographic research for the book, a considerable group effort headed by Giuseppe Ricci, the Fondazione Federico Fellini's archivist, went well beyond the backstage, involving Fellini's friends, collaborators, technicians, and even those people incorrectly considered as playing a "minor" role in his films, seeing that cinema is an enormous machine in which every single gear, no matter how small, plays an important part (the pebble the Crazy Man speaks of in *La Strada*). And finally, it further expands the scope of the research to include Fellini's drawings, preparatory sketches for each film that were in some way connected with their production: facts, situations, and characters bound together by invisible bonds to the films that helped to suggest, offer details, or even inspire the filmmaker to realize his movies, characters, stories, and fantasies.

Earlier, I defined this publication as a "moviebook," and I wish to specify that unlike the historical ones Fellini himself considered in *The White Sheik*, this text entirely reveals the events and circumstances that preceded, accompanied, and followed each of the Maestro's films. It is a complex account, one teeming with quotations from other movies, other filmmakers, and a vast range of characters, unveiling the complexity of the events relating to Fellini's career and his life. I also used the word summa. I did so precisely because like medieval summa, this book contains everything one needs to know about the filmmaking of one of the finest representatives of the art of cinema.

INSIDE A LABYRINTH WITH TWENTY-FIVE STATIONS

HOW MANY FILMS DID FELLINI MAKE? Twenty-four? No, twenty-nine. Or shall we say twenty-five? We counted and recounted a hundred times with our friends at the Fondazione Fellini, who oversaw the publication of this book, but it's a tough task. Our intent is to establish a rigorous and definitive survey of his work, assigning a specific number to each film. For example, something similar was done with Wolfgang Amadeus Mozart and the Köchel catalogue, in which each piece of music was designated with the initials KV, followed by a number. But there was a pitfall awaiting us: a problem that Fellini himself came across when he gave the title *8 ¹/₂* to one of his films, when instead it should have been called *9 ¹/₂*, at least. The problem is how to count *Luci del varietà* (*Variety Lights*), a joint effort, and the two episodes *Agenzia matrimoniale* (*Matrimonial Agency*) and *Le tentazioni del dottor Antonio* (*The Temptations of Doctor Antonio*). If we give each of these half a point, the total would be 6 films, plus one half (*Variety Lights*) plus 2 half films (the episodes). Total: 7 ¹/₂, and not 8 ¹/₂. But if we count the movie he made with Alberto Lattuada—which Fellini finished a little too arbitrarily to be considered his work alone—as an entire film, and the two episodes that seem like films, but with shorter running times, we reach 10.

Once we overcome the difficulties of counting the first part, we find yet another problem toward the end: How should we count the advertisements he shot for Campari, Barilla, and Banca di Roma? Numbering them one by one would total five, but would it be fair to assign a whole number to films that last mere two minutes each? It seemed more reasonable to group them together into a single number—twenty-five—entitled "Advertisement Films." But we immediately knew that our decision would be the subject of controversy.

Twenty-five films in forty-three years. Is that a lot? It doesn't sound like much when compared to the 143 titles by John Ford. But it's enough when compared to Fellini's Italian peers: Luchino Visconti made around eighteen movies, as did Francesco Rosi; Michelangelo Antonioni filmed exactly eighteen (not including his documentaries); Vittorio De Sica made some thirty-odd movies, though over a much longer period of time. Others made fewer, skipping the documentaries: Elio Petri made twelve; Valeria Zurlini made nine; Gillo Pontecorvo made six. Among the group of director/filmmakers who were unable to work under contract and on request, Fellini is one of the most prolific. And this despite the slowdown he experienced during his final years due to the precarious circumstances in which Italian cinema found itself and the indifference of both public and private producers, in addition to his own personal doubts and unexpected reluctance, which reached its apex in his escape from the scheduled *Il viaggio di G. Mastorna* (*The Voyage of G. Mastorna*). Even though we will mention the most important projects and works among those Fellini never finished, this catalogue aims to deal exclusively with films that were completed and presented to the public.

Taken as a whole, these twenty-five films (or however many we want them to be) narrate the story of an artist's life over a period of more than forty years, from Fellini's youth to the final curtain call. What are they like? Were they all successful? Are all his movies interconnected? Are they similar to one another, or decidedly different? All are true. In order to have a better idea, I propose—for once—the risky game of an academic ranking system.

Drawing inspiration from the way Julius Caesar divided Gaul *in partes tres* (in three parts), I'll risk dividing this Fellini filmography into six parts, giving each numbered part its own title in order to clarify the system I've chosen.

GOOD-BYES Federico Fellini was born in 1920 in a small town. He grew up in a world still rooted in late nineteenth-century life. When he was nineteen, Fellini moved to Rome. He found the Eternal City to be a complementary mother, an affectionate and maternal metropolis, willing to embrace, envelop, and never abandon her children. In fact, he never left. Ironically aware that he lived under a dictatorship sustained by rhetoric, Fellini fought back in his own way, avoiding all political commitments or resistance efforts in order to carefully poke fun at the dictatorship in magazines, variety shows, on the radio, or writing for the cinema. Like everyone, Fellini was anxious to see something new and different appear on the horizon, even if that meant a dangerous war. But nonetheless, he hoped to keep many things from the past he held dear. Unfortunately, this "Baby Italy" was destined to disappear little by little, as a new country took shape amid countless uncertainties, plunging headlong toward an unknown future. The chronicle of this transformation can be found in his first films, shot between 1950 and 1957, including *Variety Lights*, *Lo sceicco bianco* (*The White Sheik*), *I Vitelloni*, *Matrimonial Agency*, *La Strada*, *Il bidone* (*The Swindle*), and *Le notti di Cabiria* (*Nights of Cabiria*). This is a chapter in the filmmaker's life that can be summed up with a single word: "good-bye." Due to production difficulties he encountered along the way, two important moments are however missing: the celebration of madness as a refuge from an unacceptable reality (*Le libere donne di Magliano*, or *The Loose Women of Magliano*) and that adieu par excellence that is the death of a father figure (*Viaggio con Anita*, or *Journey with Anita*).

THE TURNING POINT A time for change had arrived. When he was forty years old, Fellini felt in tune with the transformations taking place across the globe: religious ecumenism, détente between rival power blocks, and new frontiers. Within this group, I'll include a series of works of grand, short-lived illusions (1960–1964): four movies, starting with the film/manifesto *La Dolce Vita*, a tragicomic reflection of the impending changes. This film was followed by *Le tentazioni del dottor Antonio*, or *Boccaccio '70*, which was a short Swift-esque vendetta on the cabal of bigots who opposed freedom of expression, then by *8 ½*, or the discovery of a psychoanalytical backdrop to the "interior foreign land" (Freud), and by *Giulietta degli spiriti* (*Juliet of the Spirits*), an exploration of the world of women that was as chivalrous as it was misunderstood.

ANGUISH Fellini reached a difficult and crucial moment in his career, characterized by films abandoned right as they were born (precisely the danger experienced by the "I" character in *8 ½*). Thanks to a mix of shyness and cowardice, Fellini's descent into the circles of hell—a voyage that had illuminated both Virgil and Dante—was put off. Fellini emerged from a sudden illness after having experienced firsthand the anxiety of death he feared was at his doorstep: *Toby Dammit*. The risk of looking back at a distant past in *Satyricon* expressed all the anxiety and weight of a tradition that was completed in an anguished state and at the price of happiness. This was the way things went from 1967 to 1969.

A REAWAKENING Better times returned (fortunately, every once in a while, life affords good times as well), and along with them came the ability and willingness to have fun, the joy of telling the story of things we've experienced and emphasizing our moments of serenity: *I clowns* (*The Clowns*), *Roma* (*Fellini's Roma*), and above all, *Amarcord*.

DISENCHANTMENT Anyone who has tasted the bitter fruits of existential disillusionment is destined to try them again. Thus came *Il Casanova* (*Fellini's Casanova*), *Prova d'orchestra* (*Federico Fellini's Orchestra Rehearsal*), in which Fellini ran the risk of suggesting that Italy was becoming unlivable; *La città delle donne* (*City of Women*), or the impossibility of being normal amid wounded males and wild and uncontrollable females; and *E la nave va* (*And the Ship Sails On*)—how can we ever forget that we survive with war constantly on our doorstep?

MELANCHOLY This last phase was characterized by a powerful and desolate melancholy. But then the grand art exhibition held in Berlin in 2005 by Jean Clair was entitled *Melancholie*, epitomized by a lapidarian motto of Raymond Klybansky: "A heavy man is melancholy." In *Intervista* (*Fellini's Intervista*), we see once again the remorse for that which has come and gone; in *La voce della luna* (*The Voice of the Moon*), Fellini began to glimpse the first feeble signs of redemption. After this, he pragmatically agreed to apply his art to advertising, transforming his dreams—the most jealous part of himself—into commercials.

I hope that anyone who wants to read further, to study and reexamine these six chapters of Fellini's extraordinary artistic career and life, will find a common thread running through the labyrinth of pages that follow.

*"The film was born from
an idea I had or felt was mine,
interwoven with memories
that are sometimes real
and sometimes make-believe."*

VARIETY LIGHTS

LUCI DEL VARIETÀ

WHY DON'T WE DIRECT IT TOGETHER?

As a young man in his native Rimini, Federico Fellini certainly couldn't have imagined that one day he would become a movie director. He wasn't particularly interested in cinema; in fact, he preferred reading comics or spying on the legs of local dancers. At home, in school, or with his friends, he enjoyed telling stories and drawing. Just after he turned nineteen he moved to Rome—where his mother Ida was born—with the aim of becoming a lawyer, but he never set foot near the law department at the university. Instead, he began collaborating with a biweekly magazine *Marc'Aurelio*, contributing short stories and illustrations. Using just the name "Federico," he quickly gained a certain notoriety that guaranteed him a small income. He went to interview the popular leader of a theater company, Aldo Fabrizi, and they quickly became friends. Federico began writing jokes and drafting monologues for Fabrizi. The young man got some time on the air at a radio station and wrote a vast number of short scenes that were nothing less than dramaturgical mini-essays. Fabrizi got him involved in screenwriting, asking the young Fellini to help with the script of his first film, *Avanti c'è posto* (*Before the Postman*, 1942), as well as those that followed soon thereafter, all of which were successful. From that point on, Fellini, who in the meantime dodged military service and during World War II married the young, promising actress Giulia Masina, whom he called "Giulietta," dedicated himself almost entirely to screenwriting. He realized that there was a lot more money in cinema, and that it got him involved in a much more enjoyable milieu. Still following Fabrizi, Fellini contributed to the script for *Roma città aperta* (*Rome Open City*), fraternized with Roberto Rossellini, working for him as factotum in *Paisá* (*Paisan*, 1946). As part of a joke, Fellini grew a beard at Rossellini's request and impersonated a false Saint Joseph in the episode *Il miracolo* (*The Miracle*, 1948) alongside Anna Magnani. Beginning in 1946, Fellini worked together with Tullio Pinelli, a lawyer from Piedmont who had already made a name for himself as a comedy writer. The pair produced a number of scripts for various directors, including Pietro Germi. But the collaboration that would prove significant for Fellini's future was the one he established with Alberto Lattuada, working on *Il Delitto di Giovanni Episcopo* (*Flesh Will Surrender*), *Senza pietà* (*Without Pity*, 1948), and *Il mulino del Po* (*The Mill on the Po*, 1949).

Lattuada and Fellini had little in common. Lattuada was Milanese, the oldest of seven brothers, and son of the well-known musician Felice Lattuada. He got a degree in architecture from Milan's Politecnico and was a passionate classic-movie buff, so much so to have numbered among the founders of the Cineteca Italiana. But most importantly, he enjoyed a reputation as a thoroughly prepared and technically savvy cinematographer. Mario Soldati, who had worked as Lattuada's assistant on *Piccolo mondo antico* (*Old-Fashioned World*, 1941), described him as "a passionate nitpicker." In other words, he was the complete opposite of Fellini, who was born in the countryside, the son of a modest traveling salesman, and who had gone about his own education in an incomplete and disordered manner. Furthermore, the young Fellini limited his reading almost exclusively to newspapers, didn't like music, had seen very little cinema, and had never taken a photograph in his entire life. Lattuada, on the other hand, had actually published a small book of his photographs entitled *Occhio quadrato* (*Square Eye*). But Lattuada and Fellini had one thing in common: they had married show biz women. Even though Carla Del Poggio was very young, she was already a diva who had moved from the minor comedy roles of her debut to playing important dramatic female characters caught up in the misadventures common to

Page 15: *Peppino De Filippo (Checco) and Giulietta Masina (Melina).*

Below: *A clipping of the column on Vaudeville Theater that Federico Fellini penned in the biweekly publication,* Marc'Aurelio.

many immediately after World War II. In *Without Pity*, she played a *signorina* who had fallen in love with a black soldier in the hell that was the pine forest outside Tombolo. She insisted on involving her new friend Masina in the production, offering her a stand-in role in a scene that was a guaranteed tearjerker and which earned her open applause when the film was screened at the IX Venice Film Festival in 1948.

So it was somewhat surprising that Lattuada would ask Fellini to be a second director by his side. Fellini was sorely tempted. Their dream project, which they soon shared, was to direct a film together and produce it on their own. Lattuada was tired of arguing with producers and had lost many months preparing projects that missed the mark, not through any fault of his own. He wanted to become the master of his own destiny. But unfortunately this would never happen.

Below top: *Federico Fellini, Giulietta Masina, Carla Del Poggio, and Alberto Lattuada.*

Below bottom: *Alberto Lattuada chats with the ballerinas during a break in filming. One of the ballerinas is Sofia Lazzaro (center), later known as Sophia Loren.*

Lattuada had been drawn by Fellini's short stories and his experiences in variety theater when Fellini was still working with Fabrizi, even though they were embellished with fantastical tales of imaginary artistic jaunts around the countryside that the Roman comic—who had never actually experienced such squalid adventures—continued to deny. In reality, Fellini, though never becoming a true "traveling troubadour" and never once actually heading out into the countryside, had spent a great deal of time in this milieu, establishing friendships. He was particularly struck by a thoroughly unsuccessful comic, Vittorio Sezani, who was forever searching for a place to live and something to eat, and who eventually died destitute in a Milanese hostel immediately after World War II.

The script for *Variety Lights* began taking shape. It was brilliant, if not particularly original. In truth, it wasn't that different from an earlier film, *Sidewalks of London* (1938), in which Charles Laughton became infatuated with Vivien Leigh; not to mention *Limelight* (1952), in which Charlie Chaplin saves Claire Bloom from a suicide attempt and turns her into a famous dancer. The plot is the same: a successful, over-the-hill comic falls in love with a beautiful young girl, promotes her artistic career, and winds up woefully empty-handed for his efforts. Even Mario Monicelli's *Vita da cani* (*It's a Dog's Life*, 1950)—filmed together with Steno, although he never actually participated—narrates a similar story: after falling head over heels for Gina Lollobrigida, Fabrizi becomes yet another disappointed Pygmalion. Fabrizi convinced Carlo Ponti to produce the film because he claimed that his former disciple, Fellini, had stolen the idea of telling a tale of the end of local theater, threatened by production costs and the looming advent of the gigantic, immobile screens of CinemaScope. There was also the newly established "cooperative between husbands and wives," as the newspapers called it, making a film that the big corporation that consisted of Italian cinema producers perceived as a threat. If the autarchic formula invented by Lattuada and Fellini took hold, wouldn't the producer risk becoming obsolete? Their initiative was even considered problematic in political circles. The film was small and unassuming enough, but didn't this precedent run the risk of inspiring spontaneous, uncontrollable, and therefore dangerous initiatives?

Completely undisturbed by these negative signs, they decided to follow their own course. They convinced the expert Mario Inghirami to head production and added Janus Film and Fincine Distribution to the name of their cooperative: Capitolium. Lattuada and

Fellini had fun on the job: hanging out surrounded by dancers, including future divas Sofia Lazzaro (soon to become Sophia Loren) and Giovanna Ralli, was appealing to both. Almost immediately they had to face the question of whether the film would be considered Lattuada's or Fellini's. But those watching the troupe, in Rome or in the immediate environs, sensed that while Lattuada held the reins, his partner became less and less shy about commenting on the acting, improvised jokes, and details of the set. Among the actors, Peppino De Filippo did his best to keep the troupe upbeat; and Del Poggio was enjoying her onstage activities so much that she was ready to take it up seriously. The film proceeded quickly,

with outdoor shots and inside locations filmed within the old Scalera buildings. The general atmosphere was so euphoric that Lattuada's sister, Bianca, was having trouble imposing a little seriousness on the set, despite her role as a hard-as-nails production director. It was as though working in this manner represented a sort of authorized leave of absence from the barracks of cinema. It was all too beautiful to be true. Most of all, it was too beautiful to last. The music was composed by Felice Lattuada, and the variety songs were written by Roman Vatro and De Angelis. The cameraman, who would remain by Fellini's side for more than a decade, was the very talented Otello Martelli.

Above: *Fanny Marchiò (left) with Carla Del Poggio in the Wanda Osiris-style review.*

PYGMALION LEFT EMPTY-HANDED

Nighttime in a small town in Italy's Lazio region. No one is around, but the local movie theater is packed with people who have come to see the variety show *Tutti a Bikini* (*Everybody in Bikini*). Onstage the comic Checco Dalmonte (Peppino De Filippo) is singing "I've lost my parrot. . . ." Among the audience is a beautiful girl, Liliana (Carla Del Poggio), who's watching the show, lost in rapture. The show ends with the troupe lined up onstage, singing:

Luci del varietá	Show lights
sorrisi e sguardi audaci	smiles and audacious glances
nuvole di baci	clouds of kisses
fate pur sognar	go ahead and make us dream!
Questa é la felicitá	This is truly happiness
Fe-li-ci-taaaa	Hap-pi-nessss

The chorus includes Checco's wife, Melina L'Amour (Giulietta Masina), the older soubrette Valeria del Sole (Gina Mascetti), the Neapolitan singer and head comedian Remo (Dante Maggio), the Roman fakir Edison Will (Giulio Calì), and the dancing girls. But the happiness is only an illusion. Behind the stage curtains, Achille (Enrico Piergentili), Melina's father and the boss, is fighting with the hotel owner, who has taken the night's earnings.

Pressed and penniless, the troupe is forced to take a night train. The crew has only ten tickets, and some of them are forced to ride in the toilets. Dragging her luggage behind her, Liliana also climbs on board. She has decided to grab the chance of joining the theater. Checco wakes up, and the girl shows him some photo-graphs and her résumé: she won a seventy-hour dance marathon and was elected beach queen. To complete her presentation, the girl lifts up her skirt and shows off her legs. Now awake and a little aroused, Checco leads her off to the side and makes a pass at her, but gets nothing more than a slap in the face.

The next morning, the troupe has to walk all the way to their next "gig," but Liliana arrives in a carriage and tries to win them over by offering them all a ride. The ambitious young girl is more than met halfway by the rough theater manager (Checco Durante), who needs to present a fresh young face to the audience. During the show, the audience boos impartially at the singer, the Spanish dance performed by Checco and Melina, and the "scientific wizard" (who eats light bulbs), but as soon as Liliana, shaking and squirming to the best of her ability, lets her skirt drop to the floor, the audience's enthusiasm skyrockets. Promoted to soubrette despite the other girls' envy, the newcomer is sent back onstage to sing "Me gusta un bel muchacho" ("I love a handsome muchacho").

Once the show is over, a lawyer named La Rosa (Carlo Romano, accompanied by Silvio Bagolini and Giacomo Furia) shows up backstage. He's clearly interested in Liliana and invites everyone out to dinner. Euphoric, the troupe heads out en masse to La Rosa's villa, singing the refrain to *The Barber of Seville* (sung by Riccardo Billi). Located just outside the town, the house is filled with all kinds of food, and the actors, jubilant over such abundance, happily prepare dinner. They discover that there are more than enough rooms in the house and that they can spend the night. But Melina, a worldly woman who immediately understands what's going on, keeps Liliana alone in her room where there is a large queen-sized bed

Below left: Giulietta Masina and Carla Del Poggio.

Below right: Carla Del Poggio and Carlo Romano.

in which two can sleep comfortably. And, in fact, immediately after Liliana shows up in a nightgown, the lawyer makes a crude attempt to hit on her but is interrupted by Checco. All hell breaks loose: annoyed, La Rosa insults Checco ("Fool, beggar, good-for-nothing!") and throws them all out of the house, even though it is four in the morning. What follows is a retreat at dawn, the first of many that would appear in Fellini's films. Along the tree-lined street that leads to the train station, the camera takes in the tired troupe of actors while a farmer working out in the fields follows their progress. Melina's old man doesn't feel well, but there's no point in asking Checco for help. He's too busy being the dreamy knight in shining armor for Liliana, who's clinging languidly to his arm.

The second half of the film takes place in Rome. Checco acts as a mentor for Liliana as they walk down Galleria Colonna: we immediately understand that his bragging is unfounded, and nobody's paying any attention to what he says. He decides it would be a good idea to put on a coat and tails and take Liliana to the nightclub, La Boite, where he hopes to meet the important entertainment entrepreneur Palmisano. But it's an unlucky night for Checco: during the talking parrot act (a true rival to Dalmonte's "Lost Parrot"), the two star comedians of the "Hunchback Theater"—Vittorio Caprioli and Alberto Bonucci—are washouts, and Liliana is disappointed: "You said you knew all kinds of important people, but. . . ." "They'll be here later." Up onstage the ladies are riding knights, who are down on all fours, and Liliana triumphantly rides Checco's back as well. Checco catches sight of the powerful entrepreneur Palmisano from afar and chases him, but it's no use. In the meantime, one of the entrepreneur's partners, Adelmo Conti (Folco Lulli, voiced by Michele Malaspina in Italian) is drawn to Liliana and approaches and introduces himself. One thing leads to another and he quickly takes Liliana away, leaving Checco to pay the pricey bill for the lobsters and champagne they've had. At dawn, Checco meets up with his colleague Remo, who warns him that he's been passed over, to which the old comedian responds, "Italy's entire entertainment industry will find out about our success." Then he goes to wait for Liliana at the front door of the house. He has decided to take his revenge by going to bed with her. But instead, the talented faker manages to twist him around her little finger, once again.

Attempting to create a small variety show—*Saette e scintille (Outlines and Sparks)*—for his protégé, the poor man's colleagues no longer support him. He's kicked out of the house by the landlord, who is tired of not getting paid, and as he is wandering around the town at night, he has a se-

ries of almost magical encounters: a black trumpet player (John Kitzmiller, who had already starred in *Without Pity*), an American gunslinger (Joe Falletta), who is staying at a night halfway house, and a young Brazilian guitarist (Vania Orico). Is it perhaps a flashback to the fake "stars" brought in from the American co-producer of *Paisan*? Anything but enchanted by his new colleagues, Liliana is working on something better and moves out of the furnished room and into a hotel. Melina, on the other hand, performs as a quick-change artist in a show. She interprets famous historical figures: Napoleon, Verdi, and Garibaldi, who is the only character the audience likes, an element that harks back to the fact that the General was the symbol of a people's party that ran in the 1948 Italian

Above top: *Peppino De Filippo wandering around at dawn.*

Above bottom: *Peppino De Filippo and John Kitzmiller at the nighttime locale.*

Above: *Aldo Fabrizi in* Vita da cani *(A Dog's Life).*

Right: *Carlo Ponti who produced* Vita da cani *to compete directly with* Variety Lights.

Below: *Aldo Fabrizi in a dream Fellini had in 1974.*

elections. Melina is moved by Checco's requests, and gives him all her savings. The troupe has by now reunited under an extravagant Hungarian choreographer (Franca Valeri). Still not satisfied, Liliana asks that her name be placed at the top of the bill, above Checco's. The key to the performance is a cancan entitled *One Night in Paris,* but during rehearsal Liliana shows up late ("I've got great news . . . I'll never be able to thank you enough. . . .") and announces that she's been given a part in an important variety show. Checco tries to act like he's above the situation ("Bravo, you've done the right thing . . . Go on . . . Get the hell out of here. . . ."), but as soon as she leaves, he faints and falls to the floor.

Liliana debuts in the variety show, where the audience can catch glimpses of Lattuada and the film's screenwriter, Aldo Buzzi, among the frantic stage technicians. The young woman appears at the top of the stairs alongside the feathered diva (Fanny Marchiò in a clear parody of Wanda Osiris), who sings:

Angosciosamente	Anxiously
tu mi piaci ancor	I'm still attracted to you
risplendentemente	splendidly
resti nel mio cuor	stay close to my heart

When it's time for the curtain call, the audience's applause is all for Liliana: she's certainly not talented, but she has the gift of enchanting young people, unlike the diva, who skewers her with an envious eye.

The scene moves to Rome's central train station, Stazione Termini, which is a recurrent location in Fellini's cinematic universe. Two trains are headed in opposite directions. Liliana is going to Milan in a sleeper car, along with Adelmo, who has taken over the semicomical role as her protector. Meanwhile, in a third-class car, the other poor souls are headed toward a small town in southern Italy. There's a brief encounter at the window between Liliana and Checco, who is outside on the platform. She's headed north, full of hope. He is headed south, weighed down with disappointment. Once he's back in his seat next to Melina, the "crafter of hilarity" doesn't even have the time to become sad. A young girl has taken the seat in front of his, and he strikes up a conversation with her. It all starts over again. The ending plays down the atmosphere, bringing the film back to the level of costumed frivolity and pleasant comedy.

A WAVE OF BILLS IN ITS WAKE

Although it was clearly a superior film, the success of *Variety Lights* at the box office when it was released on December 6, 1950, was negligible: little over 117 million lira. The film was given a final coup de grâce when its distributor—Fincine—went bankrupt. Aside from generally favorable reviews from the press and a small audience, only a few movie theaters screened the film, with half-empty halls. Unfortunately, another film—*It's a Dog's Life*—had been released just a few weeks earlier, and in these cases the first one off the block wins the race. Among the actors, Peppino was unperturbed by the fiasco, and his position remained solid. Even in future productions, Fellini would continue to rely on his talents, preferring him over his brother, Eduardo De Filippo. Del Poggio kept feeling somewhat nostalgic about her work as a showgirl, until she was written into the variety show *Tutte donne meno io* (*All Women Except Me*), penned by the comedian Macario. The former violinist Gaetano Masina, Giulietta's father, was able to glue a series of glowing newspaper reviews celebrating her performance into the family scrapbook. But the entire adventure left behind in its wake a series of unpaid bills that the film's young producers would have to keep paying off for years, amidst much disagreement and discussion. The fact is the friendship was damaged: after *Variety Lights* Lattuada and Fellini rarely saw one another, and when they did, it was almost always by chance. Lattuada boasted, based on Fellini's rapid rise to fame, that he was responsible for giving a grand talent his first real break; Fellini, on the other hand, was responsible for even less gracious statements, and would eventually come to claim full credit for the film they had created together. But the movie was "a film by Lattuada and Fellini," just as the title credits state.

"Just as I was about to shoot the first scene of the film, I suddenly became a demanding director, capricious and meticulous about details, along with all the defects and merits that I had always envied in true film directors."

THE WHITE SHEIK

LO SCEICCO BIANCO

LET NO COMIC CAUSE STRIFE TWIXT HUSBAND AND WIFE

After the unsuccessful *Variety Lights,* Fellini's career as a film director could easily have come to a close. But the established producer Luigi Rovere felt just the opposite and willingly offered him a second chance. Fellini was perplexed, and at one point declared that he would rather face the challenge along with someone else, asking Tullio Pinelli, who was a theater expert, to oversee the actors' performances. But Pinelli couldn't stand the confusion of the movie set and preferred to keep at his desk. The film in question was based on a story by Michelangelo Antonioni, who was making documentaries at the time and had written the screenplay with the idea of making a foray into narrative film: *Caro Ivan* (*Dear Ivan*). In the version rewritten by Fellini and Pinelli, all that was left of Antonioni's original plot was the name of the protagonist: Ivan Cavalli.

Cavalli is a newlywed who has just arrived in Rome on his honeymoon, only to experience the terrible surprise of having his wife disappear. A semicinematic variant of comic books (popular novels such as *Bolero Film,* which Carla is holding in her hand when she introduces herself to Peppino at the beginning of *Variety Lights*) had been popular for some time in Italy, and are now precisely the target of this new film's satire. Even the title of the film is based on an imaginary star of these novels: the white sheik. Fellini ignored Masina's tacit candidacy to play the young bride. She had to settle for a marginal part, a prostitute named Cabiria. Instead, Fellini chose Brunella Bovo, the twenty-something actress who had been catapulted to fame a year earlier in Vittorio De Sica's *Miracolo a Milano* (*Miracle in Milan,* 1951). Fellini's favorite actor, Peppino, was not available for the film, and the choice for Ivan fell on a young playwright, Leopoldo Trieste.

There are various versions of the story of how Fellini and Trieste met. According to one, they met at Caffé Berardo in Galleria Colonna (today named after Italian actor Alberto Sordi), where Trieste liked to go because he was courting a young dancer named Olga there. According to another version, Fellini spied Trieste by chance while peeking through the tiny window in the sound studio, as Trieste donned an enormous sombrero and was impersonating a Mexican priest condemned to die by gunshot. This image apparently split the director's sides in two, and he was quickly informed that the broad face under the sombrero belonged to Leopoldo Trieste, a part-time actor who had played a role in the drama *Sulla via di Guadalupe* (*On the Way to Guadalupe*). Trieste had written the film himself, but the production had been interrupted halfway through when the producer suddenly found himself strapped for cash. No matter how they met, the two immediately clicked, and a very close relationship began. Extraordinarily erudite, capable of reading Aeschylus at first glance and speaking in ancient Greek, Trieste confessed to his newfound friend that he had gleaned nothing but disappointment from his intense studying. His true goal, he admitted, was to impress women. In fact he had always played the part of Casanova and would continue to do so for the rest of his long life as an eternal bachelor, even though the path he had chosen wasn't the right one for him. Fellini convinced him that becoming the star of a film would be a much more effective route to success. When Trieste hesitated at the opportunity of transforming himself from serious dramatic auteur into comic actor, Fellini was quick to share his own convictions: "You

Page 25: *Alberto Sordi.*

Opposite: *Brunella Bovo and Alberto Sordi in one of Fellini's early takes for the film.*

Below: *A drawing of the White Sheik, Alberto Sordi, by Fellini.*

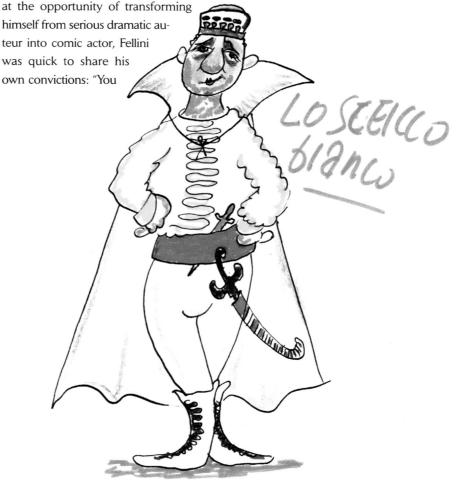

LO SCEICCO bianco

Above: *Movie producer Luigi Rovere, the first one to believe in Fellini.*

are talented, you are a grand intellectual, you write extremely well, but you are first and foremost a clown."

At the end of a perfect screen test—the police station interrogation—Trieste accepted the challenge to change his profession, "just this once." But it would prove to be the first step that would lead the man to perform in more than one hundred films. However, he drew the line when Fellini asked him to call himself "Poldino," the way comic actors traditionally did. Naturally, the director insisted on including Sordi, one of the long-standing members of the Roman bohemians, who had made a name for himself as a character actor on radio, but who had failed at the cinema, in the film *Mamma mia, che impressione!* (*Mamma Mia, What a Shock!,* 1951), produced and supervised by De Sica. Aroldo Tieri was also given a chance at *The White Sheik.* Fellini finalized the script together with Pinelli and Ennio Flaiano, a trio that would remain together all the way up to *Juliet of the Spirits* (1964). The cameraman was the veteran Arturo Gallea, whose valuable advice the director often failed to take advantage of. Most importantly, *The White Sheik* marked the first, definitive appearance of the musician Nino Rota alongside Fellini. Rota would become an essential component of Fellini's cinematic opus. Production management was taken over by Enzo Provenzale, who immedi-

ately began fighting with the director, who already on his own tended to take extra time in creating the film, always inventing new situations. In the end, Provenzale no longer showed up on the set, preferring to keep tabs on the situation from a little table in a bar not far away in the Hotel Ginevra on Via della Vita, where a number of the scenes would eventually be shot. Hesitant in the beginning—after an initial disastrous day in Fiumicino, during which Fellini directed Brunella in a sailboat with Sordi the Sheik on Mastino's autumn beach in Fregene, which would later become a favorite restaurant for movie folks—Fellini discovered the pleasure of filming, much to his great surprise. Once his initial crisis was over, the newborn director started filming quickly and deftly, always able to guess where the camera should be, and establishing right from the start a marvelous relationship with his actors. From this moment on, his destiny was set.

During the shooting, the distribution company realized that the title was misleading because it led people to think of an adventure film rather than what *The White Sheik* really was: a comedy. Some of the alternative titles put forth included: *Miss, May I?*; *No Comics Between Husband and Wife*; *S.O.S. Commissioner*; and *Comics, What Joy.* One after the other, they were all, fortunately, tossed.

Above: *The bride after her suicide attempt.*

Right: *The boat trip off the beaches of Fregene.*

THE HUSBAND, THE WIFE, AND THE PAPER HERO

T he *White Sheik* narrates the story of two newlyweds on their honeymoon. The couple is also a pair of mythomaniacs. Upon their arrival in Rome (once again at Stazione Termini!) from their hometown, Altavilla Marittima, both Wanda (Brunella Bovo, voiced over by Rina Morelli) and Ivan Cavalli (Leopoldo Trieste, voiced over by Carlo Romano) believe their dreams have come true. He plans to get his uncle, a Vatican employee, to help him land a job as municipal secretary. She has decided to seek out and meet the White Sheik, Fernando Rivoli, in person. He is the star of her beloved pop novels, and she's written countless letters to him, all signed "Passionate Baby Doll." As soon as they get to the Tre Fiori Hotel, where they are welcomed by the doorman (Giulio Moreschi, an accomplished singer and the father-in-law of Riccardo Fellini, voiced over by Checco Durante), Ivan shares the schedule he has "down to the last minor detail," including a visit to the Catacombs, another to the Vittorio Emmanuele Monument, and, *dulcis in fundo*, to see the Pope ("there will be two hundred couples there"). While the hot water is running for the bath and her consort is taking a nap, Wanda slips out of the hotel and dashes over to the nearby Via XXIV Maggio to the "Incanto blu" publishing house. She's brought along a sheaf of papers that contain a portrait of the Sheik she drew herself. The ingenuous young woman is given a kind welcome by the director, Marliena Alba Velardi (Fanny Marchiò, voiced over by Tina Lattanzi), who seems to appreciate Wanda's compliments and says: "The truth lies in dreams!" Then she invites Wanda to come down into the courtyard, where she can meet the Sheik.

Startled awake by doors slamming and other clients of the hotel complaining, Ivan realizes that the bath water has overflowed and is flooding the room and the hallway, raising up infernal clouds of steam. A letter floats past on the water, which the young husband picks up and puts in his pocket. One of the porters (Enzo Maggio) tells him that the signora went to Via XXIV Maggio.

Before Wanda's wide-open and incredulous eyes, an extraordinary event is taking place in the courtyard of the building on Via XXIV Maggio. The scene marks the grand entrance of ragamuffin fantasy into Fellini's filmmaking. From the top of the stairs, several characters in costume are walking down to a little marching tune— the first of many different versions that Rota would invent based on Julius Fučik's "Entrance of the Gladiators." The group includes Felga the mysterious Greek (Lilia

Right: A theatrical Leopoldo Trieste in the unfinished film Sulla via di Guadalupe *(On the Road to Guadalupe), in which Fellini discovered the actor's comedic talents.*

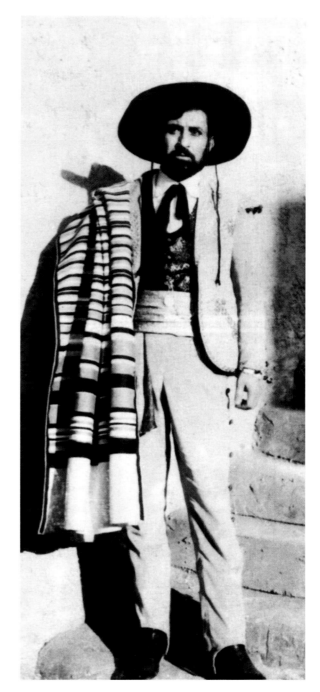

Landi, voiced over by Andreina Pagnani), Omar the Bedouin, and a variety of Moors. There is a great deal of movement around the trucks, orders overlapping one another, all the confusion of an active stage set, and Wanda follows the others around as if in a trance. She gets up into a little truck headed for where filming is taking place and drives off, passing right by Ivan. However, they don't see one another.

It seems that there's nothing there, on Via XXIV Maggio, right in front of the Quirinale. Finally Ivan reads the letter, discovering that it's from the Sheik. The Sheik has invited Wanda to come meet him in person. Distraught, the poor man feels as if he's about to faint when,

just like Wanda before him, he seemingly hears captivating music in the distance. This time, however, it is the very real fanfare of an Italian military band, which arrives and marches past quickly amid applause. Out of instinct, the young groom dashes off like a rabbit under fire. Upon arriving at the hotel, he finds all his relatives lined up. They have been waiting there for an hour: his pompous, solemn uncle (Ugo Attanasio), his cruel-looking aunt (Anna Primula), his saucy cousin Rita with her boyfriend, and the little Aroldino. It's hard to convince them that Wanda has a tremendous headache and can't come down, and even more difficult to stop his aunt, who immediately sets off upstairs to visit the sick girl in her room.

When the truck stops near the seaside, Wanda is stunned upon seeing the sign "Rome: 26 kilometers." The group she's arrived with has spread out on the beach, and a rather elderly director (Ernesto Almirante, voiced over by Lauro Gazzolo) shouts at them: "Anybody who goes swimming won't get paid a single lira!" While she's wandering around, lost among the Mediterranean pines along the beach, the young bride hears the Sheik singing. Fernando Rivoli appears, dressed in costume, high up on a rise between two pine trees. When he leaps down, the star gallantly invites his admirer for a drink, and they dance at the little bar on the beach.

Before long, the director is back giving orders to the troupe. The wind picks up, the men's capes and the women's veils lift up and flutter, even the beach umbrellas are about to take flight. A mustachioed, nosy little fellow (Mimmo Billi) wearing shorts and a tank top has to be chased away from the set. Wanda is already wrapped in the veils of Fatma, the loyal slave.

On the telephone at the restaurant in Santa Maria in Trastevere, where he is having lunch with his relatives, Ivan pretends to talk to Wanda, sending the confused porter on the other end a kiss. Prodded by his uncle, the groom is forced to recite a sonnet dedicated to his Wanda. The poem begins: "She is gracious, sweet, and small. . . ." (At Fellini's request, the verse was improvised by Trieste during rehearsal). The groom is interrupted by the arrival of their meal and a Neapolitan parking attendant who sings a song made up of just a few words: "O' sole . . . o' mare . . . o' sole . . ." ("O' sun . . . o' sea . . .").

We move to the sun and the sea at Fregene, where Fernando is inviting Wanda to go out with him in a boat. Once they are far from show, he pretends he is married to a mean woman who managed to separate him from his beloved Milena. Just as he is about to kiss the young bride, a sudden gust of wind knocks the sailboat spar into his head.

Opposite: *Alberto Sordi as the heroic romance novel character, the White Sheik.*

Cabiria Matilde e il Mangiafuoco

Above: *A drawing by Fellini that anticipates Ivan's nighttime encounters.*

Right: *A drawing by Fellini. Together with Michelangelo Antonioni, they dream of the final explosion in Zabriskie Point.*

At the Teatro dell'Opera (the scene was filmed at the Teatro Nuovo in Spoleto), another Don Giovanni is singing "Là ci darem la mano" ("There We Will Take One Another by the Hand") and Ivan slips out of his seat next to his uncle and goes to make another phone call: Wanda hasn't come back, and at this point there is nothing left to do but go to the police. Ivan presents himself to the police commissioner (Antonio Acqua, voiced over by Aldo Silvani) in a sugary manner, having written "for delicate reasons" on a piece of paper. But the expert policeman pulls the truth out of him little by little, leaving Ivan extremely remorseful for having rendered his shame official in a police report. As soon as he is alone, Ivan runs away, fleeing down Kafka-esque hallways filled with paperwork.

"I made you and I can destroy you!" the director is yelling at the Sheik, now back from his unfortunate jaunt in the sailboat. "You'll go back to being a barber, the butcher's errand boy!" Fernando is helped by his wife (Gina Mascetti). As soon as the wife catches sight of the loyal slave, she screams "You slut!" and jumps on the poor bride. Fernando is on his knees crying in the sand, displaying the same total surrender that we will see in other Fellini heroes from Zampanò to Augusto and Marcello.

It is almost night, and Wanda, half naked and trembling, finally retrieves her jacket from the camel guardian. The others have all gone back to Rome. Fernando the Coward, dressed in a blue suit, has made peace with his shrewish wife and the two drive off in his Lambretta.

Taking leave of his family, Ivan pretends to go back to the hotel. Really he heads out into Rome. Sitting on the edge of a fountain in Piazza Campitelli, two prostitutes, one large and one small, approach. The second is Cabiria, who will play an important role in Fellini's films. For the moment, the two try to console the poor man, and in an attempt to get his mind off his worries, they convince a passing fire-eater to perform for them. But Ivan needs more substantial comfort and loses himself in the embraces of the gigantic prostitute (Jole Silvani, voiced over by Marina Dolfin).

The nosy man in the tank top has brought Wanda back to Rome in the hopes of having a little tryst with her. When he is rejected, he brutally dismisses her: "Take a hike, tramp." Still wrapped in her veils, the young bride doesn't dare appear before the doorman. She calls the porter from a nighttime pharmacy and confides in him that she wishes she were dead. She has chosen to throw herself into the river, just in front of Castel Sant'Angelo, but there the Tiber is only a few centimeters deep and we see the swimmer from *Er Ciriola* (whose real name

Left: *Carla Del Poggio as a young girl with her father, Ugo Attanasio, who plays the uncle in* The White Sheik.

Below: *Giulietta Masina in the scene that is a precursor to* Nights in Cabiria.

is Guglielmo Leoncini), a specialist in lifesaving. At dawn the city rings with the wailing siren of an ambulance.

After the night with the prostitute (the segment in which Ivan wakes up in her house was cut from the film and only rediscovered more than fifty years later), Ivan finds his whole family waiting for him back at the hotel. At that very moment, the local police station calls him and the groom faints. Carried upstairs, he suddenly comes back to his senses and, making up lies too far-fetched to be believable, manages to get his uncle to give him another half an hour. Ivan finds his wife, still dressed up as a slave girl, in an insane asylum rife with the classic characters one might find in a cartoonish depiction of a mental hospital. (During the key scene of their reunion, Fellini had the extraordinary idea of abolishing the dialogue, putting Ivan's shoulders to the camera and having him hiccup at the same time as Wanda: a solution that would

clarify once and for all to Trieste the difference between theater and cinema.) After a few moments of dejection, their sense of family honor prevails: at eleven they are scheduled to meet the Pope, their best clothes are immediately unpacked, and they move quickly.

The bells are ringing in Saint Peter's Square, where Ivan's uncle is nervously pacing back and forth. Aroldino first sees Ivan and Wanda get out of a taxi. There is momentary embarrassment, then everyone's discomfort dissolves in an embrace. The newlyweds lead the small group toward the entrance to St. Peter's. Wanda tries to explain what has happened in the cropped sentences of a popular novel. Ivan is so beside himself that he almost admits he has been with a prostitute. But Wanda interrupts him: "Now . . . you are my White Sheik." And the group moves forward to the ringing of the bells, almost marching along toward their personal papal apotheosis.

NO SEQUEL IN SIGHT

In terms of box office earnings, *The White Sheik* (released on September 20, 1952) did much worse than *Variety Lights*: 42 million lira, which was another devastating blow for a young director just getting his start in the business. A potential candidate for the Cannes Film Festival, the movie was tossed aside at the last minute. It was presented again at the Venice Film Festival, where on the afternoon of September 6, 1952, it earned lukewarm reception from audiences, followed by an overwhelming avalanche of negative reviews from film critics. Some even went so far as to claim that the results of this first attempt at movie directing precluded any second effort. The few enthusiastic reviews could be counted on the fingers of one hand, though these critics were quick to personally congratulate the film's creator. When the film finally hit public movie theaters, the situation worsened considerably as the distribution company that had cost Rovere, the film's producer, so much money went bankrupt. For his part, Rovere, who was now in trouble but still kept his eye on the long term, insisted that before long, people's opinions would change. He believed that people would be talking about Fellini again, and in vastly different tones, even though he would no longer act as Fellini's loyal producer and was not lucky enough to share the filmmaker's future successes.

"I think that the film's triumph at the Venice Film Festival was due to the fact that it wasn't the right film for a festival. In other words, it wasn't bleak, serious, and intimidating."

I VITELLONI

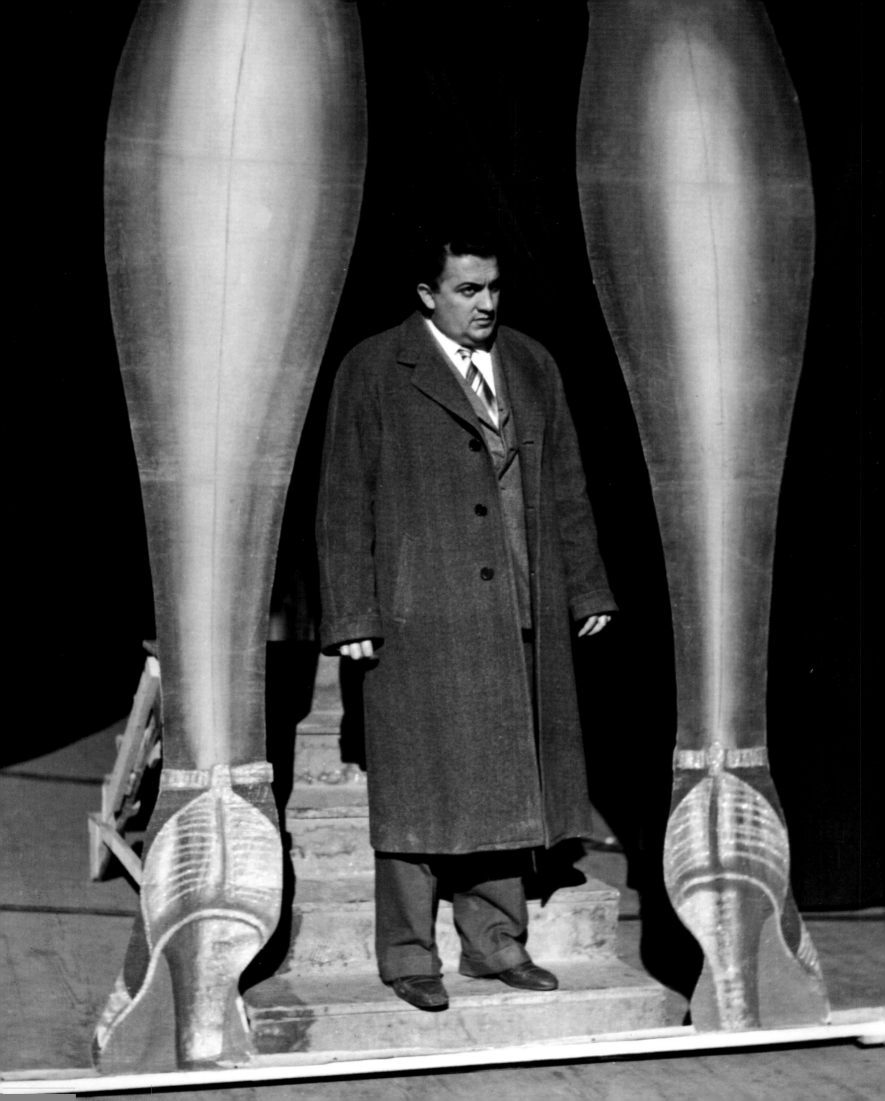

F. Mellou.

1

MAKE WAY FOR THE VITELLONI

Fellini's first major success was the unexpected outcome of a compromise. The young director wasn't the least bit offset by the troubles he encountered with his previous films. He had discovered he was a cineaste, born to follow the career he preferred above all others. Fellini enjoyed filmmaking more than drawing and writing. He had many ideas, but one stood out: a film entitled *La Strada*, which he shared with those few critics who had separated themselves from the generally critical reviewers who had spoken up in the wake of *The White Sheik*, talking to them on the terrace of the Hotel Des Bains on the Lido. Fellini's new friends heard him out, filled with compunction, respectful, but not particularly convinced. In fact, they were rather afraid that this dramatic tale about circus wanderings was, with respect to the prevailing neorealist style at the time, a step in the wrong direction. The producers had the same doubts, expressed first by Lorenzo Pegoraro, with whom Fellini had signed on to make a movie. No one wanted to do *La Strada*, and especially not with Giulietta Masina, who had little market appeal. Instead, Pegoraro proposed that Fellini make a comedy, the kind that almost always worked. Fellini hedged, consulting Tullio Pinelli, then Ennio Flaiano, who had earned a permanent position in his circle of screenwriters. Finally, he decided to accept the idea of making a film about the young men known as *vitelloni* (layabouts) in Italy's Romagna region: young men raised in the provinces who had a hard time being adults. Even though the film has autobiographical connotations, especially in the character Moraldo, whose solitary separation in the finale is an echo of Fellini's escape from Rimini in January of 1939, the events do not reflect the director's personal experiences. Fellini, precisely because he left before he was old enough to join this kind of group, never managed to find a place among the vitelloni, who were all older than him.

In his search for the right actors, the director displayed his customary open-mindedness. Franco Interlenghi (Moraldo) had played the older of the two street urchins in De Sica's *Sciuscià* (*Shoe-Shine*). Franco Fabrizi was a former variety showboy who had done next to nothing in cinema, Leonora Ruffo had very little experience, and Riccardo Fellini was his younger brother and would soon give up his acting and singing ambitions and start dreaming of getting behind the camera. For the other characters, Fellini made do with the various actors the French co-producers sent his way, and picked up a couple of old national stars such as Enrico Viarisio and Paola Borboni. He also drew Carlo Romano into the project and was respectfully curious to see what the ever-pleasant Lida Baarová would do. She had been exiled from Germany, where she was persecuted as Goebbels's ex-lover. Trieste, now an intimate friend, came back to participate, as did Sordi, even though the distributors were increasingly opposed to his presence and didn't even want his name to appear in the credits. But Fellini refused to do without his "Big Alberto." When the making of the film extended into its fourth month, the schedule was adapted to fit with the places and performance dates of the variety show *Gran baraonda* by Giovannini and Garinei, in which Sordi was starring alongside Wanda Osiris. This is why, for example, the carnival party is set in an old theater in Florence and the neighborhood street scenes were shot in Viterbo. Even though it is tacitly understood that the film takes place in Rimini, Fellini did not shoot—and never would—a single scene on the streets of his hometown. All the scenes are set elsewhere. The sea that the vitelloni look out at from the dock in the most famous scene is not the Adriatic Sea, but the Tyrrhenian Sea.

Fellini made an attempt to get De Sica to play the role of the beggar, but to no avail. Some said it failed because De Sica asked for too much money, while others maintained that he didn't want to play a gay molester. Fellini instead went with the famous stage actor Achille Majeroni, who only after the film was over intuited the character's murky, questionable nature, protesting: "I have a wife . . . I'm a serious actor!"

Page 37: *Fellini on the stage that will host the Faville d'amore (Love Sparks).*

Opposite: *A drawing by Fellini of the vitelloni, facing the sea. (In reality the Tyrrhenian Sea; in the film the Adriatic Sea).*

FAUSTO, ALBERTO, MORALDO, AND THE REST

The 104 minutes of film in *I Vitelloni* illustrate the handiwork of a director who is experimenting with a novel, rhapsodically refreshing way of telling a story. Fellini created the story together with Pinelli and Flaiano, and wrote the screenplay together with just Flaiano. More than simply narrating, he described an environment through a story divided into large episodic blocks that take place over the course of one year: from the end of summer to the beginning of the following summer. The film is divided into four main chapters, subdivided into a large number of secondary situations, and closes with the youngest of the protagonists from the neighborhood leaving home: Moraldo's farewell to his own adolescence.

The first chapter tells the tale of Fausto's rushed wedding, after Fausto had gotten Sandra, his friend Moraldo's sister, pregnant. The second chapter describes the life the other vitelloni are leading during Fausto and Sandra's honeymoon. In the third chapter, we watch Fausto's failed attempts to get and keep a job. Finally, in the fourth chapter, we watch as a traveling theater company blows through town, as well as Fausto cheating on his wife for the umpteenth time, provoking a matrimonial crisis that is more serious than the others. Although everything ends for the best, it is clear that nothing will change for those who remain.

As the film opens, five cocky young rascals are running together through the nighttime streets of an old Italian town, singing some devilish tune. We then see the waiter Antonio (the operetta comic Gondrano Trucchi) worriedly scrutinizing a cloudy sky. On the terrace of the Kursaal (a precursor to the Grand Hotel we will soon see in *Amarcord*), the last party of the summer season is underway, including the competition to elect Miss Mermaid 1953. A narrator (the sixth *vitellone* in the group, invisible and never identified, although the voice-over artist Riccardo Cucciolla imitates the director's accent and speaking cadence) is busy presenting the characters: Alberto (Alberto Sordi), Leopoldo (Leopoldo Trieste, voiced over by Adolfo Geri), Moraldo (Franco Interlenghi, the character's name comes from Moraldo Rossi, who was initially cast to play the role), and Riccardo (Riccardo Fellini), who sings "Vola nella notte" ("Fly into the Night," a song by Rota taken from the musical score of *La notte porta consiglio* [*The Night Brings Good Counsel*]). Introduced as "our boss and spiritual leader," Fausto (Franco Fabrizi, voiced over by Nino Manfredi) is behind the changing booths, trying to steal a kiss from a girl. Riccardo announces that Sandra Rubini (Eleonora Ruffo, voiced over by Deddi Savagnone), Moraldo's sister, has won the beauty pageant and been elected "Miss." Suddenly the wind picks up and it starts to rain. Everybody runs inside where the newly elected Miss faints in the middle of the crowd. Mrs. Rubini (Paola Borboni, voiced over by Giusi Raspani

Right: Moraldo (Franco Interlenghi) and the small train station man.

Above: *Fausto (Franco Fabrizi) attempts to seduce Signora Giulia (Lida Baarová).*

Left: *Sergio Natali (Achille Majeroni) attempts to seduce Leopoldo.*

Above: *Alberto Sordi and Wanda Osiris in the variety show* Gran baraonda.

aunts left in his room, gets ready to start working once again, even tonight, on his new comedy. . . ." (This is Fellini's playful allusion to Trieste, who was an unrepentant night owl.) But rather than start working, the writer begins chatting from his window with the housemaid Caterina. Accustomed to staying up all night, Moraldo wanders around the train station, listening to the night train whistles. He chats for a moment with Guido, a short railway man who gets up when he heads off to bed.

Life goes on just as it always has. Alberto scrounges five hundred lira from Olga so he can go to Bologna and bet on the races. At this point, the screenplay calls for a long episode during which the vitelloni try to sell a broken-down car to a guy who proves to be less of a fool than he seems (anticipating the plot of *The Swindle*). Out on the wharf, our five heroes (the fifth, selected to substitute Fausto, is a mustachioed fellow who is never identified) are busy contemplating the winter sea. Walking down the deserted beach, Alberto leaves the group in order to follow a running dog, and discovers Olga with her lover. When he gets back to the house, he attacks his sister: "That guy's got a wife . . . He's married!"

Alberto is out in the sunlight in front of the bar. Fausto returns and is merrily welcomed by the entire group. He has let his mustache grow and has brought a record player. Fausto immediately shows the others how to dance the mambo. Alberto wants to learn the dance immediately, and starts dancing along with Fausto in the middle of the street.

Fausto's father-in-law (Enrico Viarisio) accompanies Fausto to a friend's store. The store is owned by Signor Michele (Carlo Romano), who sells religious home furnishings. Fausto has been brought there to be hired as an assistant, and is anything but enthusiastic at the prospect. He is introduced to the owner's wife, Signora Giulia (Lida Baarová). When the store closes, Sandra comes to pick up her husband and go to the movies together. In the darkened theater, the young man's attention is captured by the girl sitting next to him, a dark-haired lass (Arlette Sauvage) wearing a little veil. When she gets up, Fausto mumbles an excuse to his wife and follows the stranger all the way to the door to her building, where he finally manages to kiss her. How on earth will he justify his disappearance to Sandra, who is waiting for him outside the movie theater?

Fausto has shaved his moustache, Riccardo has grown his out. Carnival celebrations have come to town, along with a long parade of allegoric floats and caravans. Riccardo is dressed up as a musketeer, while Leopoldo is disguised as a Mandarin man. They both have gone to

Dandolo) calls for a doctor, who seems to know exactly what is going on. When Sandra sees Fausto arrive she says: "I wish I were dead."

Fausto runs home in the middle of the thunderstorm. He has decided to pack his bags and make a run for it. Moraldo shows up to confront his friend and tells him that Sandra is pregnant. Francesco (Jean Brochard, voiced over by Enrico Ostermann), Fausto's widowed father, figures out what is going on and starts to shout. The noise and chaos wake up Mirella, Fausto's little sister. Outside his group of friends are hanging around and laughing at his predicament.

At the wedding, Riccardo sings Schubert's "Ave Maria" (just as he did at the real-life wedding of his brother and Masina in 1943). There are embraces, the wedding march, and picture taking. Then, at the train station, Fausto and Sandra leave for their honeymoon. Everyone is emotional, even the town idiot, Giudizio (Silvio Bagolini), a character we'll see again in *Amarcord*. While the newlyweds are traveling on their honeymoon, the group of friends spends the evening in the pool hall, talking about movie actresses or regular beachgoers they have lusted after during the summer season. After the pool hall closes, the group raises a ruckus in the town's deserted streets. Then we see them head back home, one by one.

In the thick of a tense, squalid atmosphere, Alberto encounters his mother and sister Olga (Claude Farell), who is busily typing away. Riccardo grimaces in front of the mirror; he sees he is getting fatter. "And Leopoldo," the narrator tells us, "after having finished the dinner that his

get Alberto, who has his hands full trying to dress up as a woman and is unaware of the chaos elsewhere in the house. In the big room at the Politeama, masked couples are swooning, flirting, and dancing together amid streamers and confetti. The orchestra is playing "Io cerco la Titina" ("I'm Looking for Little Titti"). Fausto, dressed in a tuxedo, is dancing with Sandra. Riccardo has gotten a hold of a floozy somewhere, while Leopoldo is flirting with a girl (Vira Silenti) who is also dressed in a Mandarin costume ("Why are you squeezing so hard?" "You know . . . that's how the Chinese do it. . . ."). Signora Giulia, a little too happy, her shoulders bare, seems much different to Fausto than she does when she is in the store.

The night feels like it is coming to an end. The old people have fallen asleep. Most of the revelers have already left and Alberto, clearly drunk, is dancing with a big papier-mâché head as an incredibly tone-deaf trumpeter follows him around playing "Yes, Sir, That's My Baby." Outside the sun is rising, and Moraldo struggles to drag off his friend, who is on the verge of being sick. But at the door to his building, they spy Olga on her way out. The man from the beach is waiting for her by his car. Alberto stops talking and starts to weep.

In the store, Fausto is unabashedly hitting on Signora Giulia. He kisses her on the neck and receives a slap in return, then the arrival of Signor Michele abruptly ends the situation. When it's time to close up shop for the day, the owner invites Fausto to come up to his apartment and join him and his wife in celebrating their wedding anniversary. Almost immediately Michele makes it clear to the young man that he knows what's going on, and fires him on the spot. Ordered off the premises, Fausto addresses the Signora with a weak defense: "Look, you know I was just kidding, right?"

After telling Moraldo that he was fired because his boss's wife had fallen in love with him, Fausto convinces his friend to join him on a walk across the rooftops that winds up at the store warehouse. Together, they carry off the statue of a big baroque angel that is worth forty thousand lira. The two petty thieves put the angel on Giudizio's cart and drag it off, first to the nuns and then to the monks, to try and sell it. When evening arrives, they turn the statue over to Giudizio who happily and enthusiastically sets it up for all to see on the beach.

"They stole an entire statue . . . And that pig bothered my friend's wife. . . ." Sandra's father bursts in on the whole family gathered around the dinner table, causing a scene. Later on, Moraldo manages to convince Sandra that Fausto is innocent. These tensions seem to be alleviated after the birth of Moraldino. Moraldo continues his

Right: *The vitelloni all together at Des Bains in Venice.*

nighttime chats with the short railway man as the two stare off at distant stars. The Narrator says: "Now the evenings were sweeter and spring was in the air." (The scene calls to mind one of the last drawings in Fellini's Book of Dreams: Fellini and Clemente Fracassi contemplating the sky as they are stretched out on the grass in Piazza Re di Roma.)

At the Politeama there is a crowd of dancers from the Faville d'amore (Love Sparks) theater company, directed by the *commendatore* (commander of an Italian order of chivalry) Sergio Natali (Achille Majeroni), an old trombone player who is Leopoldo's idol and to whom he sent a comedy to read. The vitelloni are watching the show from a balcony. The scene culminates in a performance by the commendatore, who reads the patriotic poem, *Fantasy di giovinezza* (*Fantasy of Youth*), and immediately afterward the song "Suona fanfara mia, suona fanfara" ("Play, Dear Fanfare, Play"). Six dancers in sharp military uniforms join in on the chorus. In the orchestra, the trombone player performs the flag-raising song, the curtains come up, and the Neapolitan soubrette (played by an American, Maja Nipora, voiced over by Jole Fierro) comes waddling down a few steps, dressed as Lady Italy, right up to the crown on her head. She sings "Vola, colomba" ("Fly, Dove"). Next, a comedian and singer take the stage alongside the whole company, lined up next to one another for the finale. They sing the variety show's chorus:

Faville d'amor	Sparks of love
faville del cuor	sparks from the heart
voi siete la voluttà.	you are sensual pleasure.
Faville d'amor	Sparks of love
faville del cuor	sparks from the heart
voi siete la fe -li -ci -tà . . .	you are happiness . . .

(As in *Variety Lights*, here we find ourselves once again within a sensual vision of the stage: the women, even though they are caricatures, are attractive. They would only become monstrous much later in Fellini's filmmaking.)

The chorus line marches past to the notes of "Ah, come si stava meglio prima" ("Oh, How Much Better Things Were Before"). Up on their balcony, the vitelloni erupt into enthusiastic applause.

Leopoldo anxiously takes his friends behind the curtains. Commendatore Natali welcomes them affably as he removes his makeup. Riccardo tells him that he saw the actor perform in the movie *I due Foscari* (directed by Enrico Fulchignoni in 1942). Leopoldo remembers how moved he was by a theater performance he saw in Bologna in 1943: "You revealed Ibsen to me." The com-

mendatore sighs: "You gentlemen are catching me here in a break that I would like to call a vacation. . . ." The following year, he would join Sarah Ferrati and Vittorio Gassman to perform a series of young people's works. Leopoldo is ecstatic when Natali compliments him on his screenwriting: "You have this (touches Leopoldo's forehead) and this (touches his heart)." Meanwhile, Fausto exchanges glances with the soubrette.

At the restaurant Leopoldo reads the script to the leader of the theater company, who is busy eating. The soubrette arrives, accompanied by a couple of dancing girls (the younger of the two is Franca Gandolfi). Half an hour later, Fausto, Alberto, Riccardo, and Moraldo have moved over to the girls' table. Alberto imitates Amedeo Nazzari (a famous prank phone call he performed in real life as well). Fausto and the soubrette start dancing together, while the bored commendatore heads off, dragging Leopoldo along with him. "Sea wind, night wind," proclaims Natali as soon as the two are out in the open. He compliments Leopoldo again and insists that he use the more familiar Italian "tu" form: "Come on, Leopoldo, let's go read the third act. . . ." Almost giddy with emotion, Leopoldo wants to share all his frustrations as a small town intellectual with the older showman. They arrive at the seaside. Natali invites the young man to follow him into the darkness between the changing booths. Leopoldo begins to understand what is going on only when a smile appears on the older man's face. "Come on . . . What, you're not scared of me, are you?" Hugging his script to his chest, the young writer runs away.

In the hotel, Fausto leaves the friendly soubrette he has just finished making love to. Moraldo is waiting for him downstairs, worried about Sandra. "What's Sandra got to do with it? What are you, getting all high and mighty on me?" On the stairwell at the house, Moraldo grumbles angrily: "Clean yourself up. You're all covered with lipstick. . . ." Sandra hasn't slept a wink, and from his room her brother can hear her crying through the thin walls. Early in the morning, the young wife takes Moraldino and runs off. Fausto and his friends look everywhere for her, even driving in Riccardo's father's car to the house of her nursemaid out in the countryside. A fight breaks out among them, and Fausto rides off alone on a bicycle.

Sandra hasn't come home yet, and the maid says that people are looking for her at the seaside. Desperate, Fausto runs to the beach. There he meets the beautiful woman from the movie theater, but there is no time for that now. He runs into Moraldo, and Fausto melodramatically announces that he is going to kill himself. His brother-in-law doesn't believe him: "You're not going to kill yourself. You are a coward." Not knowing where to go, Fausto ends up at the store where he used to work, his eyes wet with tears.

After having had a bite to eat at the nursemaid's house, Alberto, Leopoldo, and Riccardo drive back toward the town. They pass a few laborers who are repairing the road, and Alberto can't resist the temptation of making fun of them: "Workers . . ." followed by a rude gesture and a loud raspberry. A little further down the road, Alberto is still grumbling about the workers ("Workers my ass. . . .") when the car breaks down. Scared, the cowardly Alberto runs away on foot, chased by the furious workers who kick and pummel Riccardo and Leopoldo, too. (This is precisely what happened to Fellini and his friend from Rimini, Titta Benzi, during a misadventure in their youth.)

Signor Michele accompanies Fausto to his father's house, where they find Sandra. Fausto's father, Francesco, takes off his belt and gives his son a good whipping, as the home furnishings store owner looks on with clear satisfaction. As the couple returns home, making peace with each other, the narrator tells us: "The tale of Fausto and Sandra ends here, for the moment. The story of Leopoldo, Alberto, Riccardo, and all of us, you can imagine for yourselves. . . ." The only character who escapes this shared destiny is Moraldo, who waves good-bye to the short railway man and leaves on a train, headed for the big city. The voice that fills in for Interlenghi in order to say good-bye to the small town is Fellini's. In these lines, he is telling the tale of his own departure. He will tell the tale of his arrival in the capital twenty years later in *Fellini's Roma*.

Below: *Maja Nipora, Franca Gandolfi (left, later Domenico Modugno's wife) and Achille Majeroni.*

Right: *At the Lido in Venice for* I Vitelloni: *producer Lorenzo Pegoraro, Nino Rota, and Alberto Sordi with several lady friends.*

Below: *Alberto Sordi and Leonora Ruffo at the Lido.*

THE KISS OF SUCCESS

The Venice Film Festival, August 26, 1953. Only a year has passed since *The White Sheik* flopped, but for Fellini, the atmosphere was completely different. The entire group of vitelloni had arrived at the event, engaging in toasts, jokes, comments, and endless frivolity. Right from its first screening, the film enjoyed enormous success and emerged as the guaranteed winner of the Leone d'argento (Silver Lion Award) and various other prizes. The film's Italian box office earnings (*I Vitelloni* was released in Italy on September 17) totaled 596 million lira, signaling a success that was quickly and widely confirmed by sales outside Italy, which the producer Pegoraro wouldn't benefit from because he had sold the rights to the film early, predicting another Fellini fiasco. Sordi suddenly became one of

Italy's most in-demand actors, and the following year he would make no fewer than fourteen films, one after the other. *I Vitelloni* quickly gained a following outside Italy, was successful wherever it was shown, and inspired imitation both at home and abroad. Some people (unsuccessfully) offered Fellini the opportunity to film a female sequel, *Le vitelline*, while those working around Fellini began to toy with the idea of shooting *Moraldo in the City*, in which the filmmaker would draw upon his early experiences as a small town boy uprooted and transplanted in the capital. It was a project, as we will later see, that would come to life in an entirely different form several years later. But Fellini wouldn't rest until he finally managed, despite countless difficulties and obstacles, to work on the project he was most fond of: *La Strada*.

Above: *Fellini and the vitelloni in a caricature by Majorana.*

"*Forget cinema verité. Pinelli and I had fun sketching out a story we then described to [Cesare] Zavattini as if it were a true story in order to make him happy.*"

MATRIMONIAL AGENCY

AN EPISODE IN LOVE IN THE CITY

AGENZIA MATRIMONIALE

LO SPETTATORE
RIVISTA CINEMATOGRAFICA

DIRETTA DA
CESARE ZAVATTINI   RICCARDO CHIONE
MARCO FERRERI

"L'AMORE CHE SI PAGA"
regia di CARLO LIZZANI

"PARADISO PER 4 ORE"
regia di DINO RISI

"UN'AGENZIA MATRIMONIALE"
regia di FEDERICO FELLINI

"TENTATO SUICIDIO"
regia di MICHELANGELO ANTONIONI

"STORIA DI CATERINA"
regia di ZAVATTINI-MASELLI

"GLI ITALIANI SI VOLTANO"
regia di ALBERTO LATTUADA

AMORE in CITTÀ

DCN

DISTRIBUZIONE
CINEMATOGRAFICA
NAZIONALE

PROD. FARO FILM

RIPALTA Industrie Grafiche - Milano - Via Antossi, 17

READY-MADE KAFKA

I In the exhibition *I libri di casa mia* (*The Books of My House*), organized in Rimini in November 2008 by the Fondazione Fellini in order to present a catalogue of the books Fellini had owned and read during his lifetime, there were dozens of Franz Kafka volumes. Given that other important authors are absent or poorly represented, it is reasonable to view this fact as indicative of Fellini's profound affinity for Kafka's writing. It is an affinity that was born when the humorist Marcello Marchesi smuggled the anxiety of Kafka's *The Metamorphosis* past the daydreaming publishers of *Marc'Aurelio*. That text, together with many others later on, would deeply influence Fellini right from his debut. Just consider the nighttime walks in *Variety Lights* and *The White Sheik*. But the true Kafka-esque sequence, which many critics recognized, is the one that opens the episode *Matrimonial Agency*, in which Antonio Cifariello nearly loses himself in the hallways at the top of an old palazzo, wonderfully captured by the cameraman Gianni Di Venanzo (who would join Fellini once again on *8 ½*). It is as if all the shots were filmed in a single breath so that no one could see the editing cuts.

Amused, Fellini admitted that he was "a great big liar," but in reality he was merely an artist equipped with enormous imagination, one he couldn't contain. This irrepressible imagination often came at the expense of the truth, although people often tend to exaggerate this aspect of the filmmaker's personality. It's not true that he always told bald-faced lies. Those who knew him well understood that he was also capable of evaluating people and things with the simple yardstick of common sense. In any case, *Matrimonial Agency* was born of a true tall tale told to Cesare Zavattini. After having been invited to take part in a collective film, contributing a short, sixteen minute episode, Fellini listened to his friend Zavattini's thoughts for the project without raising a single objection. The idea was to entrust the film to different directors: Carlo Lizzani, Michelangelo Antonioni, Dino Risi, Alberto Lattuada, Fellini, and Zavattini himself—who would work alongside Francesco Maselli, a novice director). Each

would create an episode that reflected the reality of male/female relationships in the cities. This innovative undertaking lay in the hands of two young people, Riccardo Ghione and Marco Ferreri, who even went so far as to think of the project together with Zavattini as a sort of "cinematographic magazine" that would be released periodically. They entitled their first episode *Lo spettatore N. 1* (*Spectator No. 1*). Unfortunately, there would be no spectator number two. Destined to become one of the most original auteurs in Italian cinema, and perennially in playful competition with Fellini, Ferreri, twenty five years old at the time, abandoned his efforts in a range of different jobs to become a producer, organizer, and part-time actor. (In Lattuada's episode, Ferreri played a "parrot" who follows a beautiful girl up the marble stairs at the Trinità dei Monti.) Ferreri was the first to outline the fruitful partnership for Antonioni's *Cronaca di un amore* (*The Chronicles of a Love*), and was later unjustly excluded from its realization. He then created a series entitled *Documento mensile* (*Monthly Document*), which stopped after its fourth episode.

Spectator No. 1 was another intelligent but unfortunate attempt in the same direction. In an interview held a number of years later, Ferreri said: "As any good Lombard boy, I was talented at getting hold of the money . . . No, I can't say that I found Zavattini's themes particularly interesting, but it was a good idea: a bunch of episodes based on a single theme; each director was free to do what he wanted; no pay, just expenses."

Fellini liked the opportunity, so much so that he invented a short story on the spot. But in order to reassure Zavattini, he promised the man—and this was where the white lie came in—that it was based on a true story. But on the contrary, in confirmation of the anti-documentary nature of the work, the filmmaker relied on two professional actors: Antonio Cifariello (the character in the episode also had the same name) and Livia Venturini. The wonderful dialogue for the episode was written together with Pinelli. The whole thing was "a packaged deal," indicating that at that time Fellini didn't seem at all bound to the monstrous expenses and long development period that would accompany him throughout the second half of his career.

Page 49: *Federico Fellini on the set.*

Above: *Livia Venturini and Angela Pierro.*

WOULD YOU MARRY A WEREWOLF?

Matrimonial Agency is narrated in the first person by the protagonist's off-screen voice (voiced over by Enrico Maria Salerno): "What I'm about to tell you is a true story, and it happened to me. I was hired to investigate a wedding agency. I didn't know anything about it, somebody gave me an address . . . I found an enormous, extremely old building . . . in a neighborhood in old Rome. There, on the top floor, practically up on the roof. . . ." Following Antonio Cifariello—a shy journalist not unlike Marcello Mastroiani in *La Dolce Vita*, who pretends to be tough but in reality is timid and tends to pull his dark sunglasses down over his face—we join the search for the Cibele Agency. We are led through long hallways that suggest the dreamlike descriptions of Kafka's *The Trial* (the shots were taken inside the San Michele hospice on the Lungotevere Ripa, a street along the Tiber River). We hear music from a radio, a child holding her sister in her arms offers to act as a guide, and soon the journalist is being led by a group of laughing, running kids. Through half-open doors we glimpse people seated around the table and other fragments of daily life. When Antonio finally finds the offices he is looking for, he discovers that the waiting room is full of strange people, all expecting something. The owner, Signor Attilio (Ilario Maraschini, voiced over by Gaetano Verna), comes to his aid, regaling the journalist with stories that amplify the agency's successes. Despite its difficult and delicate task, the agency manages to put together five weddings per month. Without revealing to the director (Angela Pierro, voiced over by Gianna Piaz) that he is a reporter, Antonio makes up a story on the spot for her. He tells her that he needs to work something out for a childhood friend, who still lives in the countryside with his parents. The friend's family are rich landowners, but he suffers from epilepsy. According to the doctors, a wedding might be his last chance. The director leafs through her cards and says: "If I only told you the things we see in here. . . ."

Antonio has to sign a great deal of paperwork that obliges him to pay installments for the agency's services.

At home, the journalist gets a phone call setting up a meeting on a street corner. The owner, wearing dark sunglasses, arrives accompanied by a shy young woman, Rossana, who he pushes into the client's car saying: "You understand, huh? Go be a lady." Antonio tells Rossana that the candidate is a "very rich gentleman . . . he has a big villa out in the countryside." Unfortunately he's sick, a werewolf, and is sensitive to lunar cycles. The girl's comment is inspired by unexpected pity: "Poor man . . ." and immediately after that: "Is he a good man?" The journalist stops the car. Accepting a cigarette, Rossana says: "I'll give it to my brother." There are seven siblings in her family, two boys, and she is the oldest.

The two have gotten out of the car and are sitting by the side of the road, looking out over the countryside. "We are not from around here, we are from Olevano," she says. She is the daughter of country farmers. She has a sister-in-law in Rome who took her in for a little while, but then times got hard. In the past, she went as many as three days in a row without eating. Not knowing what to do next, she thought of putting an ad in the paper in order to find a husband. Even a wedding with a werewolf would be a solution. "As long as he is good, I know what I'm like, I'd start to care for him . . . And then it wouldn't be so bad, because I'd care about him." Faced with such disarming candor, and such an upsetting human situation, the journalist can't keep lying to the girl. "It would be better if you just forget the whole thing. I'm sorry." She sighs, like someone who has just received confirmation of her own inadequacy. "I knew it couldn't be for me."

They drive back into the city without talking. When they reach Piazza dei Cinquecento, Antonio lets the girl out of the car and wishes her good luck. She stands there, small and defenseless, in the middle of the city traffic.

Above: *Marco Ferreri in* L'amore in città *(Love in the City).*

Below: *Antonio Cifariello in the hallways of the San Michele hospice in Ripa.*

THE CROWD-PLEASER

Despite the skill of the various directors who contributed to the film, when *Love in the City* was released in November 1953 it failed to capture the Italian public's attention. By March 31, 1959, the film's box office earnings were a mere 132 million lira. But critics liked the movie, and especially Fellini's episode, perhaps aided in part by the wave of success that followed *I Vitelloni*. Compared with the other episodes in the film, Fellini's seemed the most personal. Abroad, the movie was released only later (André Bazin reviewed it in *Cahièrs du Cinéma* in March 1957, more than three years later), and was heavily edited because of the censorship imposed on Lizzani's episode, which featured prostitutes and was considered dishonorable for Italy's good name. In this manner, Fellini was indirectly made aware of the threatening presence that Bulgakov referred to as the "cabal of the bigots" when speaking of Molière's misadventures—which he had up until that point happily ignored. It was a rubber wall the lightheartedly apolitical Italian artist would have to grapple with just a few years later to defend his film *Nights of Cabiria*, and would be the first of many such battles.

Opposite: *Fellini during shooting of the film.*

Above: *Antonio Cifariello and Livia Venturini out in the open countryside.*

Right: *Cesare Zavattini.*

"This film is a complete catalogue
of my entire mythological world,
a dangerous representation
of my identity that was undertaken
with no precedent whatsoever."

LA STRADA

A SECRET ITALY

For Fellini, the idea for *La Strada* came very early on, even before *I Vitelloni*. As soon as Fellini understood, while filming *The White Sheik*, that cinema was the expressive medium best suited to his personal talents—much more than painting or writing—he nurtured a desire to narrate with images a story that was seemingly objective, though in reality mysteriously personal. The story that began to take shape in the director's mind was echoed in a parallel inspiration on the part of Pinelli, who had been surprised during a road trip to see a pair of vagabonds pushing their little cart along a mountain road: Why not write a short story explaining their situation? The idea didn't appeal to Flaiano very much, and he would continue to dislike it right up to the end. They divided the tasks: the story by Fellini and Pinelli, the dialogue by Pinelli, with collaboration from Flaiano. Fellini's desire was to interpret the theme in an almost metaphysical way, reminiscing about summer holidays near Gambettola and including stories of fairies, wizards, and country witches that were told years ago. In other words, he wanted to recount the impressions of a distant 1920s Italy, a secret, still primitive land inhabited by people wandering about without any fixed destination, like gypsies and other picturesque characters. Some would soon identify in this film project the typical Italian marriage, with an interweaving of male bullying and female subservience. It is tempting to connect this theme with the actual marriage of the Fellinis, but Fellini himself would forever reject any comparison to his relationship with Masina. He created a formal, definitive framework for the issue only many years later, explaining that in order to understand *La Strada*, one had to accept the fact that Fellini was, in turn and at different moments, each of the three protagonists: the anxious Gelsomina, the violent Zampanò, and the imaginative poet, the Crazy Man.

In any case, the filmmaker's inspiration would center on Masina. With great effort, he created a made-to-measure character for her: a clown in skirts, a variation on a circus trope that Fellini would repeat time and again, first with Polidor's frequent appearances and finally with an entire film dedicated to the theme: *I clowns* (*The Clowns*). There would also be repeated road trips along Via Salaria, which Federico considered, according to the actor Moraldo Rossi, "the most beautiful road in the world." These were not actual on-the-spot investigations, but rich views of settings and atmospheres.

Not at all encouraged by his experience with Pegoraro, who had produced *I Vitelloni*, Fellini took every chance he could get to shop around the project. The film was dear to him, and he offered it together with clips from Masina's screen tests. The result was that Fellini scared off every single potential producer, until Dino De Laurentiis finally read the script and immediately and enthusiastically declared: "Yes, let's do it!" But many problems, starting with Masina, still stood in the way of actually realizing the project. She didn't convince De Laurentiis, and he put off giving her a contract until long after the shooting began in the hopes of a replacement. Who did he have in mind? According to

Page 57: Giulietta Masina (Gelsomina).

Opposite: Anthony Quinn (Zampanò) and Giulietta Masina.

Below: A drawing by Fellini of Gelsomina.

people at the time, Silvana Mangano, his wife. But this was always denied by those directly involved. Furthermore, on this particular point, Fellini was not willing to budge. The film had been conceived for Masina, therefore it would be made with her or it wouldn't be made at all. In exchange, the director accepted to include—guaranteeing a certain commercial appeal for the release—a pair of important American actors. First and foremost was the grand actor Anthony Quinn as Zampanò. At the time, Quinn was filming *Attila* for De Laurentiis. Then, Fellini accepted Richard Basehart to play the Crazy Man. Basehart was a hot property after having played the aspiring suicide victim on the edge of the skyscraper in Henry Hathaway's *Fourteen Hours*. Earlier attempts to find the right person for the role within Fellini's usual circle of friends had proven fruitless: Moraldo Rossi, who had the right athletic physique and the playful personality for taking on the role, wished to continue as an assistant director. Walter Chiari wasn't right for the part, and Alberto Sordi, whose star was on the rise following the success of *I Vitelloni* and who would have done anything to land the role, flubbed the tryout "wearing a costume and with little bells on his head," as he would continue to bitterly repeat for years. This event took its toll on the friendship between Sordi and Fellini. Things would get better between them only

many years later, when, in 1983, Fellini accepted a choice role as an inspired client in Sordi's film, *Il tassinaro* (*The Taxi Driver*). With Basehart, on the other hand, Fellini would establish a cordial relationship. At the time, Basehart was married to Valentina Cortese, and he would pick up his wife on the set of *Donne proibite* (*Angels of Darkness*), where Masina was also working, and the four would all go out to dinner.

The production was supervised by veteran film pro Luigi Giacosi, known as Gigetto, who managed to pull off outright miracles, given the scarce funds and means at his disposal. He rented out the small circus owned by a certain Savitri, a circus strongman and fire-eater who would become Quinn's instructor. Then he rented a much larger circus (the Zamperla circus), where he picked up stuntmen who would play themselves. In the beginning, Quinn was irritated at not having his own dressing room and being forced to put on his costumes and makeup on the street. He even considered breaking his contract, but after just a few days of work, he became convinced that Fellini was a genius and that all the inconveniences were really a small sacrifice to ask. According to Rossi, Fellini and Quinn were fortunate enough to look upon one another with the amused, tolerant eyes of children: each believed he had to accommodate the other and both behaved rather childishly.

The film was shot in central Italy during the cold and inclement weather of the 1953–1954 winter, moving from Roccaraso to the Ovindoli plateau, Bagnoregio and Fiumicino. Gigetto's teeth chattered from the cold, but he kept at it just like everyone else. He created wintry landscapes even where there had been no snow, tossing out white sheets and chalk by the sack. And when Fellini made fun of his thaumaturgic activism by complaining "You promised me an elephant. . . ." Gigetto had one delivered two hours later right in the middle of the set. Basehart was thrilled to watch his stunt double walk the tightrope from one side of Piazza di Bangoregio to the other, impressed most of all by the proud tightrope walker's decision to flat-out refuse a net or protection of any kind. Quinn fell deeper and deeper in love with his new Italian friends (as well as his assistant, Jolanda Addolori), and insisted they call him "Antonio." Many years later at lunch on the Bolognese terrace in Piazza del Popolo after Fellini and Masina had passed away, several people would see tears appear in Quinn's eyes as he turned his gaze toward Via Margutta, where the Fellinis once lived.

But at the time, the person crying on the inside, the victim of a strange desperation, was actually Fellini. On the wharf at Fiumicino, filming one of the last scenes, Fellini was overcome by a sudden, unexpected bout of depression. What had that film aroused in the depths of his soul? He was unable to come up with the answer, even after a series of sessions held with a famous Freudian psychoanalyst, who helped him stay strong enough to finish the film. But most of all, he would be saved by a fortuitous encounter with a woman outside the doctor's office, which would keep Fellini occupied for several years. (This relationship would be echoed in the Mastroianni-Furneaux relationship in *La Dolce Vita*.) When it came time to do the voiceovers for the film, Fellini identified, after a number of attempts, the perfect voice for Zampanò in Arnoldo Foà.

Below: *Alberto Sordi, turned down for the part of the Crazy Man, with Paul Douglas and Giulietta Masina. Sordi plays a variation on Zampanò in* Fortunella, *script by Federico Fellini and Tullio Pinelli, directed by Eduardo De Filippo.*

ZAMPANÒ HAS ARRIVED!

La Strada opens, amid the beach and dunes, with a young woman dressed in rags, half priest and half clown (Giulietta Masina). The sisters run after her, calling "Gelsomina, Gelsomina. . . ." A large man on a motorcycle arrives. He is the person who took Rosa, her older sister, away. Now Rosa is dead and her mother (Anna Primula, voiced over by Franca Dominici) is selling Gelsomina to the gypsy Zampanò (Anthony Quinn, voiced over by Arnoldo Foà). The character's name is a blend of Zamperla and Saltanò, two small circuses that existed at the time.

The girl is filled with all kinds of feelings. She is pained by Rosa's death, afraid to leave her house and mother, excited about traveling in a gypsy caravan and "dancing and singing" along with that tattooed giant.

Zampanò is performing before a small town audience, puffing out his chest and snapping an iron chain. He adds a lively little speech as part of the act. Even Gelsomina applauds him.

Now they are eating soup Gelsomina prepared over an open campfire. She throws hers away when no one is looking. Zampanò eats his, commenting: "This stuff'd be good for the pigs."

Zampanò tries to give Gelsomina's wardrobe a makeover, pulling out a crushed bowler hat, a top hat, and a man's dressing gown. He also tries to teach her how to play the tambourine and to shout, "Zampanò is here!" She is clumsy and awkward, but she seems to enjoy the work. When it's time to go to bed, there is an embarrassing moment of intimacy. "Get inside," orders Zampanò. "I'll sleep outside," volunteers Gelsomina. But he shoves her inside all the same.

Zampanò has fallen asleep. Gelsomina is watching him with fear still in her eyes and half a smile on her lips.

Gelsomina debuts. While Zampanò represents the muscular vein in circus artistry, his companion interprets its comical side. Dressed as a clown with the tip of her nose painted red, "Signorina Gelsomina" performs in an "entirely laughable farce," in which she pretends to be a duck under fire. Zampanò is the hunter, taking aim at her with his rifle. Their act draws laughter and applause, and ends with an appeal to people's wallets: "My lady will walk around with a hat for collections."

The gypsy takes Gelsomina to a tavern full of wandering salespeople and farmers. The waiter (Mario Passante) offers her some roast pig or chicken. The naive girl orders both. Once every attempt at conversation has fallen flat, the girl devours her dinner until the plate is clean. Zampanò addresses a random prostitute, presenting himself as a "traveling artist" and flexing his muscles in a show of strength. Once they are back outside, the gypsy takes the woman up into his caravan and orders Gelsomina to wait outside.

Sitting on a step, humiliated and frightened, the girl sees a mysterious horse without a rider pass by.

When it is daytime again, a girl informs Gelsomina that the caravan is near a field. She runs there and finds Zampanò sleeping on the ground. She waits for him to wake up, gathering flowers together with a little girl, imitating a tree, and enjoying the surrounding nature. When the gypsy wakes up, Gelsomina tells him happily, "I planted some tomatoes." But she'll never see them grow because with Zampanò, it is always time to leave for the next town.

They are on the road again. Sitting behind Zampanò while he drives the caravan, Gelsomina asks him, "So you're the kind of man who sleeps around with women?"

They are at a wedding banquet on a farm. Some vagabonds are performing and Gelsomina dances and sings "La colpa è del bajon" ("It's the Bajon's Fault"). The women of the house invite the artists to eat some-

Left: *A drawing by Fellini of the Crazy Man.*

Above: *Fellini and Richard Basehart on the set.*

thing. On one side, the owner, who is a widow, has her eye on Zampanò; on the other, the children—who are always friendly with Gelsomina—take her inside, up narrow stairs and down long, dark corridors, to visit sick little Osvaldo. Gelsomina tries performing a few tricks in order to get him to smile, but an old lady arrives and chases everybody off. In the meantime, the widow has ensnared Zampanò by offering him some of her dead husband's clothing.

The wedding party is over (like at the end of *Amarcord*) and Zampanò shows up wearing his new clothes. Gelsomina has yet another misadventure, falling into a hay bin. When she manages to drag herself back up, she finds Zampanò sleeping. She suddenly decides, "I'm going to leave." She leaves the shoes, overcoat, and everything else. At dawn, Gelsomina runs away, shoeless and wearing her old cape.

While she is enjoying her first few hours of freedom, Gelsomina, a bit frightened, sees three musicians marching along in single file at the side of the road. She joins their group, following like a mouse after the pied piper. In the next town, there's a great deal of commotion as everyone gets ready for a festival celebrating the town's patron saint: lights, banners, and a solemn procession with the Virgin Mary that trundles slowly along to the band's music. Gelsomina is upset, and only becomes more so when she sees a tightrope walker moving back and forth along a rope strung 130 feet above the town square. He is wearing angel's wings and everyone calls him "Il Matto" (the Crazy Man).

Above: *A caricature
of Nino Rota by Fellini.*

Right: *Giulietta Masina
playing the famous theme
song for* La Strada.

64

Later on, the square has emptied and Gelsomina is lying on the ground, drunk. Zampanò comes rumbling up on his motorcycle. He has come to collect his slave. Her escape is over.

Waking up one morning, Gelsomina discovers that the gypsy caravan is parked among the bandwagons of a small circus. A melody she once heard as a young girl is played on a violin. The sound is coming from the big tent. The Crazy Man (Richard Basehart, voiced over by Stefano Sibald) is at the center of the small arena, playing the song. (The theme for the song was inspired by music of Arcangelo Corelli, used as playback during the shooting. A few critics have identified traces of Antonín Dvorák's *Serenata in sol, op. 22,* but it may be more accurate to say that the tune was nothing less than a splendid invention of Nino Rota, a musical emblem of Fellinian filmmaking.)

Zampanò presents Gelsomina to the circus owner, Signor Giraffa (Aldo Silvani, voiced over by Cesare Polacco), who hires them both. They won't be paid, but they can keep whatever they collect with their little beggar's dish. The Crazy Man intervenes with a sarcastic remark, "You did the right thing taking them in. A circus needs some animals." He enjoys making fun of Zampanò, a habit that threatens to make things unpleasant.

"Sometimes I've said that the story of Gelsomina and Zampanò is a metaphor for Italian marriage."

During a show, while Zampanò is struggling to break his chains, the Crazy Man ruins his act by shouting, "Zampanò, there's a phone call for you!" Furious, the gypsy chases after the fool, but can't catch him. The Crazy Man tries to teach a new comic act to Gelsomina, who is supposed to interrupt his violin playing with a violent, off-tune blast from a trumpet. Against the wishes of Signor Giraffa, who likes to keep everyone working together, Zampanò rebels and refuses to let his assistant work with the others, and especially with that imbecile. During the ensuing fight, the Crazy Man throws a bucket of water in Zampanò's face, the gypsy draws a knife on him, and the Italian police drag both off to jail.

Alone at night on the steps to the circus on Via di Smontaggio, Gelsomina sees the Crazy Man coming home. He has been released. She confesses to him that she can't decide whether or not to accept Signor Giraffa's offer to take her away with them. At the height of her desperation, she cries and wails, "Nobody needs me! Oh, I'm just sick and tired of living!" The Crazy Man makes light of the situation, consoling her. He admits that Zampanò "can't think," but adds "maybe he cares about you . . ." And then, "if you don't stick with him, who will?" In any event, nothing is completely useless. "Even this little stone has a use . . . Even that artichoke head of yours is useful for something." Gelsomina hatches a rebellious little plan. She wants to burn her clothing, the gypsy caravan, and everything along with it. But ultimately, she winds up doing nothing, saying, "If I don't stick with him, who will?"

The Crazy Man accompanies Gelsomina to the police station on Zampanò's motorcycle. He leaves her a

Left: *Producer Dino De Laurentiis and Fellini on the set.*

Below: *A visit by Jerry Lewis during filming.*

little medal as a parting gift, and then heads off, singing as he goes. After Zampanò is released, they take to the road again. They make it to the seaside, and Gelsomina runs toward the sea as if she is returning to something safe and familiar. "Where's my house?" she asks. Zampanò makes a vague gesture. Suddenly Gelsomina discovers she is no longer nostalgic or homesick. "Now I think my home is with you."

The two vagabonds are allowed to spend the night in a barn outside a convent. Gelsomina enchants the sisters, playing the Crazy Man's song on her trumpet. One sister (Livia Venturini) inspects the caravan with curiosity. She tells them that the sisters change convents every two years, too. It is something they do in order to keep from becoming attached to things. "We are both travelers. You are after your mates and I'm after mine."

"Why do you keep me with you?" Gelsomina asks Zampanò that night in the convent. "I don't know how to dance, I don't know how to cook, I don't know how

to do anything . . . Would you be sad if I died? . . . Do you love me, at least a little bit?" But he has fallen asleep.

Zampanò would like to "thank" the sisters for their hospitality by stealing a few silver reliquaries located behind a small grate, but he can't get close to them without Gelsomina's help. Horrified, she refuses to take part in the theft.

The following morning, when Zampanò takes leave of the sisters with a pompous display of hypocrisy, the mother superior asks Gelsomina if she would like to stay with them. But she doesn't stay at the convent, just like she didn't stay at Giraffa's circus: one has to accept one's own destiny.

While they are traveling, Gelsomina and Zampanò come across the Crazy Man's car parked at the side of the road. He has had a breakdown. The Crazy Man is relieved to see some of his colleagues arrive, but he berates Zampanò with his usual irreverent tone. Another fight breaks out and Zampanò strikes his rival so violently that he breaks the man's head open on the side of the car. The Crazy Man falls to his knees and dies. Gelsomina is thunderstruck.

The trees have lost their leaves and there's snow on the ground. It is their last trip. Gelsomina no longer plays the trumpet. She almost never speaks, and when she does, it is only to repeat with disturbing monotony, "The Crazy Man is not well." She even chants this phrase during their last show.

Zampanò can't stand being around this living reminder of remorse and decides to run away. He leaves Gelsomina the overcoat, some money, and the trumpet and runs away while she is sleeping alongside a low wall.

Some time goes by. An older Zampanò has joined the Medini circus. He has a new assistant (Yami Kamadeva).

While he is walking around town, he hears a woman sing the Crazy Man's song while she is hanging her laundry out to dry. "Where did you learn that song?" A woman who lived there four or five years ago used to sing it. She is dead now. Zampanò has learned that Gelsomina has passed away.

In an open-air arena the gypsy performer repeats his chain-busting routine. That night, drunk as a skunk, he is thrown out of the local tavern. He protests, starting a big fight. Zampanò is pressed to the ground, shouting "I don't need anybody! Nobody! . . . I just want to be left alone!" Then he faces a stormy sea topped with white foam. He falls to his knees and then down onto the sand, almost in a fetal position. For the first time Zampanò begins to cry.

Below: *Anthony Quinn.*

Screened on September 6, 1954 at the Venice Film Festival, *La Strada* obtained lukewarm success and few positive comments. Its reception confirmed a reality that has remained in place even today, more than half a century later: the Venice Film Festival has never managed to establish an expert audience, like the opera aficionados in Milan and Parma, thanks to their important theaters. Instead, it entrusts the fate of the movies to the moods and trends of the moment. Fellini was cursorily labeled an Italian right-wing, Catholic filmmaker; someone who was open to spiritualism, who denied and betrayed neorealism. He was considered the opposite of Luchino Visconti, who cemented his place in the avant-garde left with the presentation of his Risorgimento film, *Senso* (*The Wanton Countess*). A fight between the two factions broke out at the awards ceremony held on the evening of the 7th: a "Silver Lion" (albeit with a rather listless explanation) for Fellini, nothing for Visconti, and a shameful, Pontius Pilatesque "unassigned" decision for the two great actresses competing for the prize, Giulietta Masina and Alida Valli, both of whom deserved to win. A brawl broke out in the theater, while Rossi and Visconti's steadfast defender Franco Zeffirelli began punching one another as the media had a field day. This senseless contraposition led to the legendary hostility between Fellini and Visconti that would last for almost a decade before finally turning into—thanks in part to the good-hearted efforts of Masina, who had always taken pains to maintain a cordial relationship with Visconti—a relationship of deep, sincere esteem, and even affection.

De Laurentiis had staked a great deal on the film and the Venetian debut, while its respectable though low box office earnings on the national level (518 million lira by September 22, 1954) were enough to make him happy. He decided to act pragmatically, choosing the Salle Pleyel in Paris, France, as his base for launching the film once again in March 1955. The movie was a triumph. The French press, including French communists who had no trouble contradicting their Italian counterparts (whose minds were clouded by their loyalty to socialist realism), hailed the film as a masterpiece. From that moment on, *La Strada* was in demand everywhere, swept up in an avalanche of positive reviews and prizes. The entire experience culminated in an Academy Award for Best Foreign Film in April 1957. The whole winning team got to enjoy the apotheosis.

Above: *Hollywood, April 1957. From left: Dino De Laurentiis, Tullio Pinelli, George Seaton (President of the Academy), Giulietta Masina, and Fellini, holding the Academy Award.*

Right: *Fellini and Giulietta Masina at the Palazzo del Cinema in Venice for the opening night of* La Strada. *Director's assistant Paolo Nuzzi is standing behind them.*

"Augusto, in other words Monsignor Bidoni, is a character I actually met and knew. In a certain sense he is not unlike Zampanò, but more lucid, and therefore guiltier."

THE SWINDLE

IL BIDONE

FROM EASY WHISKEY TO A WINE FESTIVAL

In Italian, the expression *tirare un bidone* means to take someone for a ride, to swindle. The expression had been around a long time before Fellini's film, and could probably be traced back to the years during World War II when there were lots of shady deals underway and people were often hoodwinked into unfortunate endeavors on the black market. Therefore, the Italian word *bidonista* is synonymous with swindler, cheat, and even worse. Little by little, affairs such as these created an underground network of relationships and converging interests, spawning an actual caste of professional swindlers who in turn fostered an infamous aura on their accomplishments. After having gotten to know a few unsavory characters from this group of swindlers, Fellini tried to pass off a fake diamond on film star Osvaldo Valenti, even going to meet him on the set of *La corona di ferro* (*The Iron Crown*). The film director's curiosity pumped new life into stories told by a certain Eugenio Ricci, known as the *Lupaccio* (Bad Wolf), whom Fellini had met in a country trattoria while filming *La Strada*. Fellini was amused to discover, by chatting with Ricci, the behind-the-stage details of swindling: the setup, the pleasure of wearing disguises, and so forth. He began to intuit the destiny all swindlers who practiced this "profession" shared, with only a few rare exceptions. After practicing this art for years, ultimately they all wound up tired, disgusted, and penniless. Swindling does not guarantee survival: there can be hard times; you can wind up in serious trouble with the law; you can lose your inspiration just as artists might lose theirs; you can even begin to suffer the weight of remorse over so many poor individuals who have been taken for a ride and robbed. These ideas slowly but surely evolved into the movie's protagonist, Augusto Rocca, a timeworn fellow who is portrayed affectionately and with almost brotherly criticism, and who nurses his own hopes for redemption that are however destined to fail. He also hides a secret, masochistic inclination toward martyrdom. We find ourselves once again in Fellini's crepuscular vein, the one that drove the filmmaker to revisit the poor comedians in *Variety Lights,* the small-town dandies, the vagabond artists in *La Strada*—in short, an entire world from yesteryear that was slowly disappearing.

De Laurentiis wasn't interested in producing the movie. Goffredo Lombardo came on board in his place. Lombardo had wanted for some time to make a movie with Fellini, and joined bursting with hopes of a favorable outcome for the project. But he wouldn't give up on the idea of having a big American name for the leading role. As Fellini talked over the treatment for the film together with Pinelli and Flaiano, he continued to envision Humphrey Bogart's devastated expression. For Fellini, Bogart looked a lot like a "Calabrese swindler." But when they asked the American actor to join the production, they learned that Bogie was seriously ill. (He would die in 1957 after a long battle with cancer.) After thinking things over, the director remembered having seen Broderick Crawford, who had earned an Academy Award for Best Actor in 1949 for his work in *All the King's Men,* on the movie billboard, although he had not seen that film and never would. A deal was struck in record time. The rest of the cast included Giulietta Masina, Richard Basehart, Franco Fabrizi, and some other Fellini habitués, as well as an extremely young Lorella De Luca who was beginning to make a name for herself in television.

By the end of April, organizer Giuseppe Colizzi, a close relative of the director Luigi Zampa and future director of an "Italian Western," had everything ready to start filming in Marino, near Rome. With great enthusiasm,

Page 73: *Giulietta Masina and Broderick Crawford in a scene, later cut, from* The Swindle.

Opposite: *Richard Basehart (Picasso) dressed up as a priest.*

Below: *Goffredo Lombardo.*

Below: *Valentina Cortese, Federico Fellini, and Giulietta Masina in front of the Excelsior in Venice in 1955.*

Crawford confessed that he had just come out of an alcohol detox program. Unfortunately, the location they had chosen for the initial filming proved entirely inappropriate: a wine festival was underway and the American actor lacked the willpower to refuse the brimming glasses that were offered to him one after the other. The result was a tremendous crisis right from the start, followed by a state of permanent inebriation that barely allowed Crawford to stand on his own two feet. He forgot his lines and was deaf to the director's instructions. There was debate over whether to substitute Crawford, but everyone's fears magically dissipated once the film was up and running. Even while semiconscious, the actor proved he was strong: appropriately pathetic and extremely talented. The troupe moved on from its tormented location shooting and into the Titanus studios and the New Year's Eve swindler's apartment (June 10–17), installed by the talented Dario Cecchi, who had to swallow his pride and adapt to Fellini's precise directions. Later on, the crew had to shoot scenes in the Canova bar, the Euclide and Flaminio theaters, on the Felice aqueduct, and ultimately in Cerveteri, where the final scene of the film takes place. The close-ups of Crawford, who in the meantime had never fully recovered his senses, would be shot in the studio on July 17. At that point there remained, more or less, forty days until the Venice Film Festival, and the crew had no choice but to devote itself entirely to film editing, with high hopes.

THE RISE AND FALL
OF MONSIGNOR BIDONI

Baron Vargas (Giacomo Gabrielli) is waiting in a vast expanse of Roman country-side, reading *Il cavallo* (*The Horse*). A car arrives, driven by Roberto Tucci (Franco Fabrizi, voiced over by Mario Colli), a uniformed chauffeur. Vargas complains about the wait to Augusto Rocca (Broderick Crawford, voiced over by Arnoldo Foà) and Carlo, who is called "Picasso" (Richard Basehart, voiced over by Enrico Maria Salerno, who is, in some ways, similar to Rinaldo Geleng, one of Fellini's companions during the filmmaker's bohemian years). The two dress up as priests while the Baron pulls out a little map and the chauffeur places a "SCV" (Vatican City) license plate on the car.

Their "ecclesiastical swindle" involves fooling two peasants, Stella Fiorina (Maria Zanoli) and her sister (Sara Simoni), who live on an isolated farm. As soon as he is invited into the house, Monsignor De Filippis, aka Augusto, tells the women: "On his deathbed, a poor sinner confessed a terrible, terrible secret to me. . . ." He tells the story of a murder committed during wartime. When his accomplice was killed, the master thief buried the remains beneath a certain tree, along with their booty, a "veritable small treasure."

They find the tree. Digging near it they discover the skull, bones, and a small box. The objects it contains are laid out on the kitchen table to be inventoried. Picasso offers an estimate of their worth: six, perhaps seven million lira. The assassin's will leaves everything to the owners of the land, on the condition that they pay for 500 masses for his soul: at 1,000 lira per mass, they have to come up with 500,000 lira. The two elderly sisters dash into town and come back with 425,000 lira. It is all the money they were able to get, but "Monsignor Bidoni" is willing to offer them a discount.

Set to a rhythmic, picaresque soundtrack by Rota (which Fellini would reuse more than thirty years later for *Fellini's Interview*), the car heads back into the city. Picasso gets out in Piazza del Popolo: the painter lives on Via Margutta with his wife Iris (Giulietta Masina) and their little daughter, Silvana. Iris doesn't know what her husband does and is pressuring him to go back to painting.

Augusto and Roberto triumphantly head into the nightclub "Le grotte del piccione" (The Pigeon's Grotto). They order champagne and Roberto dances with an American. The band is playing "Coimbra en Portugal." Augusto starts talking with Maggie (Mara Werlen), an English dancer who performs together with another girl. Roberto starts bragging and boasting at the table with the Americans, while Augusto contemplates the dancer and sips his champagne.

Closing time has come and gone. Roberto is drunk and is giving the band a hard time. Augusto loses himself in bitter comments with a waiter on young people.

At dawn, a strange foursome comes walking down Via Barberini: Augusto has his arm around Maggie and Roberto is harassing the violinist to play variations on "Coimbra en Portugal."

The next scene was cut. On a rainy day, Augusto is holed up at his place, pretending not to be home while a tall, blond fellow (the man who will recognize him later on at the cinema) bangs threateningly on his door.

At the Canova bar in Piazza del Popolo (one of Fellini's favorite spots), Augusto is trying in vain to sell a small fake watch to a shrewd Milanese commendatore (Alberto Plebani, voiced over by Mario Carotenuto), who is familiar with the hustle. Vargas is waiting inside for him. He has another extraordinary idea.

This time Roberto drives the car into a small town, a typical scene in neorealist cinema. Pretending to be officials for the Italian general housing office, Augusto and Picasso are struggling to fend off a crowd of people

Below: *Broderick "Brod" Crawford standing at a wine bar at Marino.*

(including Ada Colangeli, Amedeo Trilli, and Ettore Bevilacqua, Fellini's future "gymnastics coach") shouting and demanding housing. Augusto patiently instructs the crowd: "One at a time . . . I have the contracts right here . . . You just have to sign and pay the first install-ment." The first installments range from eight to ten thousand lira, and the swindlers collect quite a few.

On New Year's Eve, Augusto and Picasso are almost run down by a Cadillac in Piazza Navona. The car is driven by Rinaldo Rossi (Alberto De Amicis, a non-ac-tor voiced over by Nino Manfredi), an old companion and accomplice who has made a fortune selling cocaine. Even though his companion Luciana (Xenia Valderi, voiced over by Elena Zareschi) doesn't like them, Rinaldo invites them to get in the car. They continue to exchange quips and friendly insults with one another. The rich swindler invites them to spend New Year's Eve with him at his house at 38 Via Archimede (Fellini lived on the same street, at number 141 A).

The rich swindler's party (the enormous apartment was constructed in the studio by architect Cecchi) is a sort of "Trimalcione's Dinner" from *Satyricon*, updated to fit in with 1950s styles. Iris is shy amid the enormous crowd of guests. Picasso has brought a fake De Pisis to sell off on Rinaldo (who would respond: "What, did you make this yourself?"). Roberto is at the party, too, to-gether with one of his foreign ladies. There's a feeling of heavy-handed joking. In an anticipation of *La Dolce Vita*, they try to get a naive girl (Irene Cefaro) to strip. Roberto tries to force Augusto to introduce him to Rinaldo, then does so himself in an awkward, inexpert manner. Augusto, who is usually careful with his words and manner, can't resist clinging to his old friend's good fortune, and proposes a series of absurd little deals to him. As midnight draws closer, the general euphoria in-creases: led by Rinaldo, a group of revelers pretends to toss a hapless soul out of a window. The dance degen-erates into bacchanalia. One of the guests brandishes a siphon and soaks everyone (the actor is "Lupaccio," the man who supposedly inspired the film). In the midst of chaos and fighting, Rinaldo, who has made up with his woman after a bout of jealousy, fires his gun off the bal-cony. Roberto takes advantage of the general confusion to pocket a gold cigarette case he has stolen from its rightful owner (Cristina Pall).

Iris and Picasso dance, dreaming of a trip to Venice. Rinaldo impatiently informs Augusto that he is no longer interested in certain kinds of trivial deals. He asks him how old he is. The answer is forty-eight. "And you're still playing with games at your age?" Warned by

Left: *Fellini behind the camera on the set.*

Left: *A girl (Irene Cefaro) surrounded by the swindler's New Year's Eve guests.*

Below: *Eugenio Ricci, aka "Lupaccio," the real inspiration for the film, sprays the other revelers.*

Luciana, Rinaldo blocks Roberto at the doorway just as he is about to leave. "Listen here. There's a young lady over there who has lost her cigarette case. . . ." When the thief pretends not to understand him, Rinaldo is explicit. "My friend, you have a lot more miles to row before you can come play around in here . . . Go on, just pretend you were joking, alright?" Roberto admits that he was only joking, the cigarette case reappears, and it's goodnight for everyone.

On the way out Augusto reproaches Rinaldo and takes off like a whipped dog. Even Iris is dejected, and upbraids her husband for his lies, fears, and humiliations. Picasso promises that he will change. Augusto crosses Piazza del Popolo at dawn. Two prostitutes call to him in vain as he walks toward the Corso, alone and with a lowered head.

In the next scene, the protagonist seeks refuge at Maggie's place, where he is happily welcomed. But he is too tired and just wants to sleep.

On a sunny day, Augusto is walking down the steps at the Trinità dei Monti. Roberto is waiting for him behind the wheel of a Fiat 1400 sports car that he has borrowed from one of the elderly ladies he spends time with as a gigolo. Picasso is waiting in Piazza del Popolo, anxious to check out the overcoats they will be using for their next swindle: a bunch of raggedy coats worth no more than 1,600 lira each. Augusto dashes over to Canova to get some cigarettes and runs into a few young students, one of whom is his daughter Patrizia (Lorella De Luca). Moved and embarrassed by the encounter, the man who has been in touch for the past year promises to give her a call.

Squeezed in together on the backseat of the Fiat 1400, the three swindlers set out to hoodwink an elderly gas station attendant in the countryside. Roberto fools him with an extremely simple trick: instead of paying the 1,300 lira they owe for a full tank of gas, he pretends he has forgotten his wallet. He gets the man to lend him 10,000 lira and leaves "a coat worth 50,000 lira" in exchange. At the next stop, it is Augusto's turn to fool a fifteen-year-old boy.

The next few scenes, all set in Marino, were cut. The three good-for-nothings wander around a small town amusement park, among the merry-go-rounds, games, and trials of strength. Roberto and Picasso go into the "rotor" and Augusto watches them from above while they are pressed, weightless, and overcome against the spinning walls of the machine. Night has fallen and the clock in the local piazza strikes ten. Picasso is drunk, flapping his tattered overcoat like a pair of wings, crying that Iris wants to leave

Below: *Drawings of swindlers by Fellini.*

"In our line of business you can't have a family . . . You have to be alone . . . If you're afraid now, just imagine what you'll feel like when you're my age."

him. He feels like he is going to be sick. Augusto helps him
and sternly warns Picasso: "With a job like ours you can't
have a family . . . You have to go it alone . . . If you are
scared now, imagine what you will feel like when you are
my age." But Picasso doesn't want to go to Florence anymore. Instead, he goes back home. Roberto has managed
to dig up Signorina Luigina, a local prostitute he has baptized Miss Frosinone, and he invites Augusto to go with
them for a ride in the countryside.

Cuts include Picasso's return to a squalid little hotel
room and the scene in which he asks for a ride to Rome
on the highway, as well as the end of Augusto and
Picasso's nighttime adventures, during which the two
take turns having sex with a prostitute in the backseat
of the car.

One Sunday, Augusto and his daughter go out together to eat at an open-air restaurant in Monte Mario,
where the parking attendants are playing "Souvenir d'I-
talie." Patrizia may have landed a job as a bank teller, but
she needs 300,000 lira to secure the position. Augusto
takes the little fake watch from New Year's Eve out of
his pocket. The girl thinks it is beautiful, and he gives it
to her as a gift.

While they are at the cinema, the father whispers to
his daughter that he will take care of the money she
needs for her job. There is a tall blond man in the audience (Tiziano Cortini, voiced over by Aldo Giuffrè)
that Augusto recognizes immediately. He tries to escape,
but the man is quicker than he is and grabs Augusto: the
whole scene takes place to the sound of a grotesque
marching tune that accompanied the cartoonists in *The
White Sheik*. There's a brief scene in the lobby, where
Augusto is arrested right before his daughter's eyes.

A scene with Augusto leaving the cinema with the
police was cut, as well as another scene with Patrizia
waiting outside the local police station.

Some time later, Augusto is released from Regina
Coeli prison. He asks a guard for a cigarette. The guard
warns him not to come back. But Augusto is an incor-
rigible swindler. He can't find Roberto in Canova;
his friend has wound up in Milan. Instead, Augusto joins
up with another guy in his line of business: Riccardo
(Riccardo Garrone).

Another cut: Augusto visits the nightclub where he
learns that Maggie has taken off without leaving any for-
warding address.

An important scene that came next was also cut. It
concluded Picasso's story, which was abruptly abandoned in the version of the film that was released for
the general public. Augusto meets Iris, who has left her

Below: *Broderick Crawford (Augusto) together with his daughter Patrizia (Lorella De Luca, the future wife of director Duccio Tessari) at a restaurant.*

"I saw Brod again in New York. He was in an all-out crisis. He warned me, 'Don't get married.' I told him, 'But I am married, you've been to my house.' He looked at me, but didn't understand."

husband and blames the people he was hanging around with for having destroyed their marriage. "But when your husband brought money home, everything was just fine . . ." counters Augusto icily. "The more a guy steals, the more women stick by him . . . Money is scared of unfortunate folks . . . And when you don't have any more money, everything is over. You're nothing then, nothing at all."

The film has now reached its final chapter, a repeat of the "ecclesiastical swindle." It is like the umpteenth version of a show the main protagonists no longer believe in. This time Monsignor is accompanied by Riccardo, a rather swinish-looking secretary (Mario Passante), and a third accomplice (Paul Grenter). Their chosen chump is an old farmer who has a paraplegic daughter. Just as the time comes for Augusto to take off with his swindled bundle of cash, he is asked to say a few words to comfort the girl. He finds Susanna (Sue Ellen Blake, voiced over by Fulvia Mammi) on a chair behind the house. She is resigned to her fate; she needs a miracle in order to be healed. Now fully into his role as a priest, Augusto tells her, "But miracles do happen. Don't you believe?" He goes on: "You don't need me . . . Our lives, the lives of lots of people that I know aren't filled with anything beautiful . . . You're not missing much. . . ." Watching him walk away, Susanna pulls herself up on her crutches and kisses his hand.

Up on a barren hill, at the top of the slope, Vargas is waiting, just as he was at the beginning of the film. Augusto has already changed out of his costume and denies having taken any money. "I've got a daughter of my own. I just couldn't do it. . . ." The situation degenerates and they begin to fight. Augusto runs away down the hill, but Vargas throws a stone at him and hits him right in the head. Augusto falls backward and breaks his back: he can't move and his accomplices take advantage of his immobility to steal everything he has. They find the money in one shoe (350,000 lira, more or less the money his daughter Patrizia needs). Augusto calls for help, but the other swindlers take off and leave him where he has fallen.

Gripped by delirium and agony (the scene was shortened in a revised version of the film), Augusto passes the whole night paralyzed on the ground. When night turns into day, the dying man manages to drag himself slowly up the hill. He sees two women walking along the road, carrying wood. Two children are following them. "Wait," murmurs Augusto, "I'll come with you." They are the last words he will ever say.

THUMBS DOWN

In the middle of August, while Fellini was working day and night to finish the film, the newspapers unexpectedly ran a series of gossip stories about his marriage. Some even went so far as to suggest that Masina, who played Basehart's wife in the film, was on the verge of running off with her on-screen partner. Others added that Fellini was attracted to Valentina Cortese, his rival's wife. The first order of business for the foursome in question upon their arrival in Venice for the closing of the film festival was to deny these reports. The entire affair ended during a spirited press conference in Venice, and the newspapers stopped printing the stories.

Meanwhile, much more important things were going on. Everyone was awaiting the screening scheduled for September 9, 1955, the last day of the festival. Unfortunately the film, against Lombardo's expectations, who was already preparing to accept the Leone d'oro (Golden Lion) award, wasn't a success. It was too long (120 minutes, later cut to 105 and ultimately to a mere 92), too dark, and too anguished. Critics blasted the movie, as happens all too often when a film comes in on the heels of a great success by the same filmmaker. Few critics had the insight to pick up on the rigorous, serious, and poetic portions of Fellini's latest creation. Naturally, *The Swindle* won no awards. A number of years would pass before the film was understood and reconsidered. The only person to earn any positive notoriety for his efforts was Crawford, whom no one suspected in the least, since he spent his time working on the film (in Fellini's words) "in an alcoholic cloud." But then, as *The Film Encyclopedia* points out, Crawford had, until then, appeared moribund. By drinking and working a little, he would continue to "live out his last years increasingly bitter and disillusioned" until his death in 1986.

Lombardo lost his faith in Fellini and wasted no time backing out of the agreements he had made to produce additional films. He even printed an unprecedented booklet entitled *Il bidone: Film umano e polemico nei giudizi positivi e negativi della critica* (*The Swindle: A Controversial and Human Film in Both Positive and Negative Critiques*). The pamphlet was a naive little cover-up the producer had excogitated in an attempt to hide his shame for the flop. But nothing could lighten the blow, which became that much more stinging when the movie was released in Italy on October 7, 1956 and earned a mere 239 million lira at the box office.

Above: *The cover of the rare booklet* Titanus, *published to defend* The Swindle *from critics in the wake of what happened in Venice.*

Left: *Federico Fellini, Giulietta Masina, Valentina Cortese, and Franco Fabrizi at opening night in Venice in 1955.*

"They criticize me because I went to a cardinal to try and save this film from the censors. But if it happened again, I'd be willing to go all the way to the Pope."

NIGHTS OF CABIRIA

LE NOTTI DI CABIRIA

LOOK WHO'S BACK: CABIRIA

The catastrophe of *The Swindle* was followed by a period of confusion. For a few weeks, Fellini toyed with the idea of shooting *La piccola suora* (*The Little Sister*), a semidocumentary about a nun who lived during the 1800s and who was capable of performing small miracles, for which she was misunderstood and persecuted by the Vatican. Thanks to her Catholic education and upbringing, Masina had always dreamed of obtaining beatification on the silver screen. So she was interested in playing the part. She also liked the fact that Basehart would be playing the priest who hears her confessions and investigates her conduct. But the idea for the film wasn't strong enough to hold its own. After reading the book *Le libere donne di Magliano* (*The Loose Women of Magliano*), a shocking real-life reportage on the Maggiano insane asylum written by doctor and man-of-letters Mario Tobino, Fellini became captivated by the idea of making a film with Montgomery Clift among a group of frenzied, possessed women. Fellini and Pinelli were particularly struck by their impressions during a visit to Tobino, who was equally excited about the project, and the story was quickly sketched out between them. But the American film star refused to take the part, and although they spent a great deal of time shopping the project around to various producers—who had already dubbed the film "the crazy ladies' movie," and someone had added: "you'd have to be crazy to make it"—the film flopped on its own. In the midst of these difficulties, Fellini and Masina, after the death of their aunt, Giulia, with whom they were living on Via Lutezia, moved into a large apartment on Via Archimede. Shortly thereafter, Fellini's father Urbano passed away. The filmmaker's precipitous trip to Rimini under these tragic circumstances would soon provide the inspiration for a movie with Sophia Loren and perhaps Gregory Peck: *Viaggio d'amore* or *Viaggio con Anita* (*Journey of Love* or *A Trip with Anita*).

Another event that resisted the various changes and transformations taking place in Fellini's life was a simple story that appeared in newspapers in 1955: the discovery of a woman's headless body, immediately baptized "the decapitated woman of Castel Gandolfo." The body was eventually traced to Antonietta Longo, a thirty-something waitress whom authorities surmised had been drawn in by a false promise of marriage and subsequently robbed and murdered by someone who would never be identified. Details of the event were general and left plenty of room for speculation, complemented by the statements of a solitary, combative prostitute named Wanda, whom Fellini had met during the filming of *The Swindle* around the Felice aqueduct. In the new film—in which Cabiria is played by Masina—Wanda will be the name of the protagonist's friend. Once again, production difficulties seemed to threaten the entire project until one evening, while driving around with Fellini, De Laurentiis had the filmmaker pull over so that he could step outside the car and read the script by the light of the headlights. He liked it and decided to back the film, entrusting the organization of the project to his brother Luigi, the family intellectual. Luigi De Laurentiis was ecstatic about working with Fellini. At first, Dino underestimated the negative impact that official opinions about the film—which connected the Eternal City with images of roadside prostitution—would have. In the meantime, the filmmaker had himself chauffeured around this "peripheral womb" of Rome, which he was barely familiar with, at turns by Piero Gherardi (the costume director and art director of Fellini's films until *Juliet of the Spirits*) and Pier Paolo Pasolini, a rising young Italian literary star whom Fellini had recently met.

Page 87: *Giulietta Masina during shooting of the film.*

Opposite: *Franca Marzi (Wanda) and Giulietta Masina (Cabiria) with cameraman Arturo Zavattini.*

Below: *In a drawing from Fellini's Book of Dreams, he dreams of visiting Pier Paolo Pasolini (in the armchair) after he has been assassinated.*

Pasolini was both personally and professionally interested in the dialects and folklore of that part of Rome and knew neighborhoods such as Guidonia, Tiburtino Terzo, Pietralata, and the Idroscalo—where some twenty-odd years later he would be brutally murdered by at least one of the young local men he so enjoyed spending time with—like the back of his hand. Over the course of these exploratory jaunts, Fellini was in touch with Mario Tirabassi—the "bag man"—a former nurse who was working as a real-life benefactor for the poor despite disapproval from Italy's religious organizations. Fellini's decision to include Tirabassi in the film led to heated debate. Together, Fellini and Pinelli also made a rather disappointing trip to visit the Italian senator Lina Merlin, who had undersigned a bill to close the halfway houses operating in that part of Rome.

Filming for *Nights of Cabiria* lasted twelve weeks, from July 9 to October 1, 1956, and took place in different locations. Gherardi re-created the protagonist's tiny home in Acilia, along Via del Mare. The troupe then moved on to film the star's villa along Passeggiata Archeologica (the entrance we see is that of the publisher Renato Angiolillo's home on Rome's ring road; the rooms were built directly in the studio), the pilgrimage to the Sanctuary of Divine Love, for which De Laurentiis had to obtain difficult-to-get ecclesiastical permits; the variety show with the hypnotist;

and the episode with the assassin accountant in Castel Gandolfo. This last episode saw the return of Otello Martelli behind the camera: for a series of incomprehensible disagreements, the expert Aldo Tonti was no longer the troupe's cameraman. Fellini wanted his friend Leopoldo Trieste to play the ignoble character, promoting him to dramatic actor status, but Trieste made the mistake of his life and chose to direct a film on his own, another "nocturnal" movie entitled *Città di notte* (*City by Night*). But before he left, Trieste advised Fellini to consider the French actor François Périer, who would give an excellent performance in the role. Although the brotherly relationship enjoyed by Fellini and Trieste remained intact, the filmmaker—who though in his heart of hearts resented the rejection—would never again call upon his old friend to act in any of his films. Amedeo Nazzari, a god of Italian cinema, willingly accepted to poke fun at himself as the actor Lazzari, and had only the displeasure of working no more than a single week on the project. Rota sat down at the piano together with Fellini underneath the screen, improvising the general outlines of the music for the film the way they did back in the days of silent movies: "Just listen to them," commented the few fortunate witnesses who were given the opportunity to peep in on their sessions. "It was at once a lesson and a party." But no sooner was the film ready that the troubles began.

Above: *A drawing by Fellini on the cover of the typed copy of the script for the film.*

Right: *Giulietta Masina, Federico Fellini, and Amedeo Nazzari.*

Above: *Cabiria is saved from drowning in the river at the beginning of the film.*

Left: *Cabiria along the Passeggiata Archelogica.*

IT MIGHT BEND,
BUT IT WON'T BREAK

Nights of Cabiria was a living portrait of a character, unfolding over five chapters like a cartoon story: Cabiria thrown in the river, Cabiria and the star, Cabiria makes a pilgrimage to the Sanctuary of Divine Love, Cabiria at the variety show, and Cabiria gets married. Her real name is Maria Ceccarelli (a claim she makes in the "bag man" scene, which was later cut), but now she is Cabiria, a prostitute living in the rundown landscape outside Acilia. Extremely proud of her little house, a cement cube that seems like something out of a child's drawing, Cabiria seems disturbed, aggressive, and petulant. But in reality, she is ingenuous, generous, and capable of hope.

The film begins near the Tiber River, between San Paolo and the Magliana neighborhood. One sunny afternoon, Cabiria, wearing a black-and-white striped outfit that makes her look like a caterpillar, is out walking with Giorgio. They chase one another, laughing and joking, and embrace: but when they are on the riverbank, the man tosses her into the water and runs off with her handbag. A few young boys jump in and save Cabiria, dragging the half-drowned woman out of the river. They bend her head down to help her cough out the water. When she reopens her eyes, Cabiria doesn't really have a clear idea of what just happened.

At home, Cabiria asks Wanda (Franca Marzi), who is hanging the laundry, if she has seen "my darling Giorgio." She can't resign herself to the bitter reality, but she is forced to admit that she doesn't have the key—it was in her handbag—and she has to climb into the house through a window.

That evening, Cabiria, still lying in bed, talks to her friend. She can't admit that Giorgio tried to kill her for forty thousand lira. Wanda says: "There are some people today who are willing to do that for just five thousand lira." Once she is alone, Cabiria gathers up Giorgio's things, including his photographs, and burns them.

That night along Passeggiata Archeologica, we discover a small crowd of prostitutes, pimps on their scooters, and hordes of clients. Marisa and Amleto (Ennio Girolami) are driving in a new Fiat 600. Everyone admires them, even Cabiria, who is just getting back from spending time with a client. Cabiria starts dancing the mambo to the music coming out of the car radio, along with a young man who calls himself "the best heel in Rome." An exchange of insults with the Atomic Bomb, a veteran streetwalker, gives rise to a brawl when the hag declares "my darling Giorgio." Some look on, entertained, while others try to separate the two. In the end, Amleto and Marisa have to drag Cabiria away in order to put an end to the incident.

The young man tries to convince the woman to get some protection but she doesn't want anything to do with pimps, and to the surprise of her companions, she gets out on Via Veneto, where the long-legged, finely dressed hookers anticipate the bird women found in *La dolce vita*. Attracted to music coming out of the "Kit Kat," a nightclub, Cabiria dances by herself on the sidewalk. Jessy (Dorian Gray, voiced over by Fulvia Mammi) comes out of the nightclub, followed by the actor Alberto Lazzari, who is wearing a white jacket and has his tie in one pocket. They've been drinking and get in a fight. After the two slap one another, the beautiful blond takes off. The actor gets into his white car, notices Cabiria, and invites her to get in with him. The car comes to a stop outside the "Piccadilly." Alberto gets out and goes into the nightclub, dragging his new companion along with him.

Below: Pier Paolo Pasolini, who was a dialect consultant for the film, and Federico Fellini on the set.

Opposite and left: (from left) the film star and the prostitute; the hypnotizer (Aldo Silvani); and the treacherous accountant (François Périer).

Below: Cabiria offers to give the accountant her life savings.

Welcomed like a regular, the actor takes a seat at the bar. The evening is gloomy, like the ones that will appear in *La Dolce Vita*, with individual females popping up here and there. The orchestra strikes up a mambo and the actor invites Cabiria to dance. The prostitute abandons herself to a sort of joyful shimmy. But Alberto drags her away again and announces that he is going to take her to his house. Incredulous at her good fortune, Cabiria makes fun of the beautiful women on Via Veneto from the window of the car: "You bunch of fools!"

The car races past the tomb of Cecilia Metella, heading south. The actor's villa on Appia Antica is a grand, luxurious house (a parody of Nazzari's sumptuous, real-life residence). They run into dogs, walking down long corridors and stairways. After having instructed the butler (Amedeo Giraud) not to put any calls from Jessy through, Alberto orders dinner for two to be sent to his bedroom. Following along after the lord of the manor, Cabiria discovers a grand aviary that houses a toucan. The actor puts on a night robe.

The sounds of a symphony drift in over the radio. Alberto is enthusiastic about the music and wants Cabiria to join in. To the notes of Beethoven, the cart with their dinner is wheeled solemnly in: caviar, lobster, champagne. Alberto asks Cabiria about her life. The woman brags about her own house. The actor turns off the radio and invites his guest to eat something. Encouraged by his behavior, she confesses that she recognized him and tells him what an admirer she is.

When they toast with the champagne, Cabiria touches the star actor as if to reassure herself that he is real, actual flesh and bones. She wants to kiss his hand. She begins to cry at the thought that no one will believe her adventure, then she asks him for a photograph with a dedication and his autograph. "Cabiria was here." The phone rings, and the butler announces that Jessy is on her way up. The actor races to hide the prostitute in his bathroom. Cabiria watches the two kiss and make up through the keyhole in the bathroom door.

Right: *Giulietta Masina
and Federico Fellini work on
the final scene of the film.*

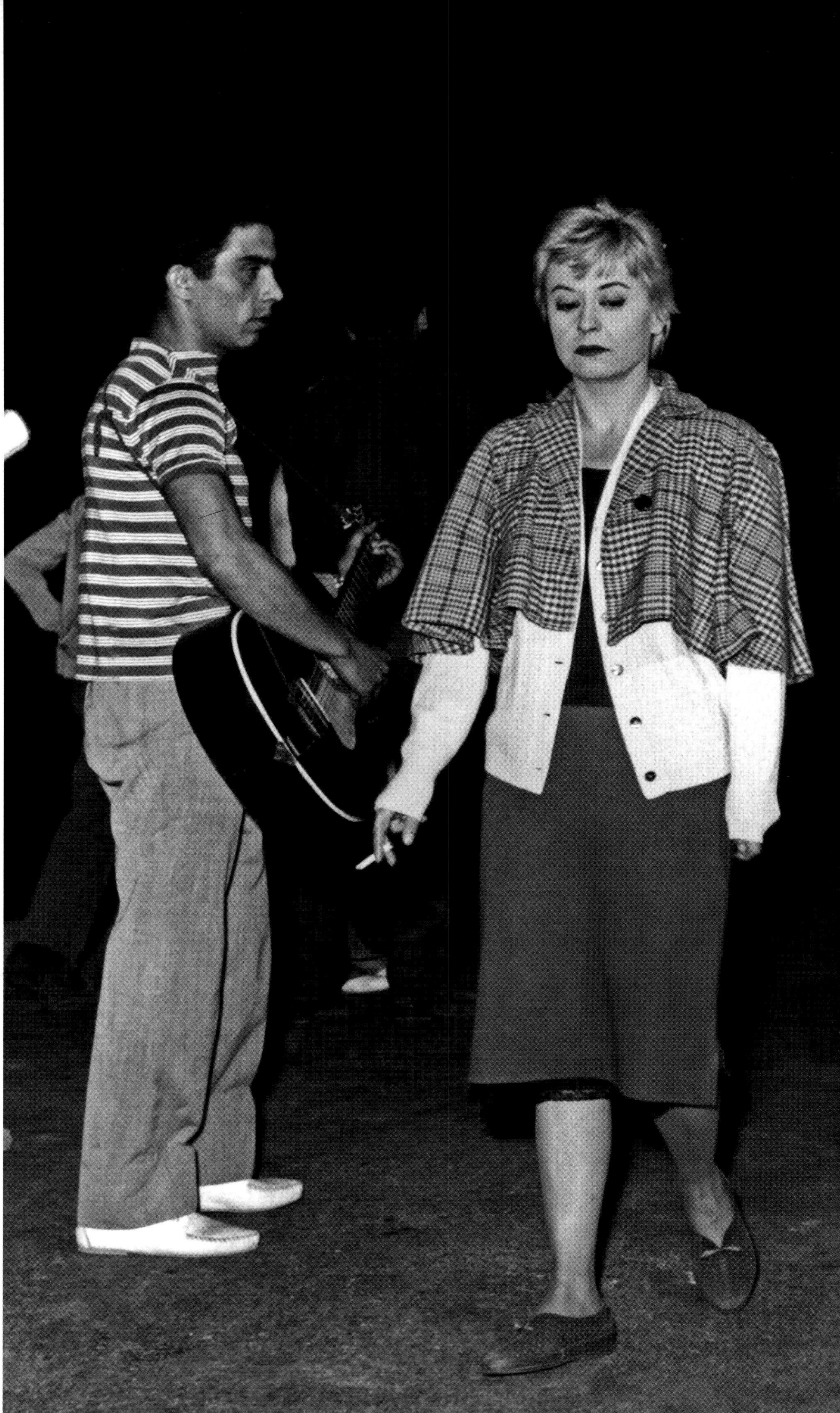

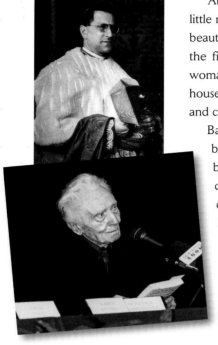

At dawn, Alberto tiptoes his guest outside. There's little more than a moment's time to glance at sleeping beauty. We see the silhouettes against the glass door as the film star insists on putting some money in the woman's hand. After finally finding her way out of the house, Cabiria walks down a drive lined with statues and cypress trees.

Back on Passeggiata Archeologica, Amleto has brought his uncle (Mario Passante), the vile pimp boss and cocaine dealer. The uncle is a cripple and can only get around with a pair of crutches. He has decided to come to ask for a miracle from the Madonna at Divine Love.

The women decide to join his pilgrimage. Only Cabiria is perplexed: "I have everything I need, what could I possibly ask the Madonna for?" The shoeless pilgrims walk through the night, led by a priest and various crosses and banners, singing a special hymn:

Above: *Cardinal Giuseppe Siri and Father Angelo Arpa.*

Mira il tuo popolo	Admire your people
bella signora	beautiful lady
che pien di giubilo	who joyful and festive
oggi ti onora…	honor you today . . .

Cabiria is so struck by the unexpected appearance of this religious procession that she almost decides to follow them.

At this point in the original screenplay, there were two episodes that never made it into the film. In the first episode, Cabiria and Matilde are drawn into the exploits of a pair of thieves. In the second, Cabiria meets the "bag man" (Leo Catozzo, the film editor), followed by a series of wanderings from one outcast to the next. At the end of this episode (which was later included in the television specials *A Director's Notebook* and *Fellini nel cestino*, or *Fellini in a Basket*), the man accompanied Cabiria back into Rome in his car.

The sacred and profane blend together at the Divine Love within the crowd of pilgrims, petitioners, and salesmen, creating the kind of noisy chaos reminiscent of a town fair. The crippled uncle offers free candles to all the women so that they can say a better prayer to heal him. Meanwhile, Cabiria has decided that she wants to pray for something, too, but she doesn't know what to ask for.

Inside the church, amid votive offerings and orthopedic instruments, there are repeated cries of "Viva Maria" ("Long live Mary"). Songs and invocations interweave with one another. Cabiria's heart starts to race as if something spectacular were really about to happen. Amleto urges his uncle to try and take a few steps without his crutches, but the man collapses to the floor.

No miracles take place. The crippled uncle is eating like a pig, stretched out in the middle of a field. All around him people are playing music, dancing, and playing soccer in a festive, bacchanalian atmosphere. Cabiria looks sad. "You haven't changed. . . ." she cries, repeating once again that she wants to take off, to leave everything behind. She even criticizes a few women on their way to communion, walking by in the middle of the field behind a banner, but she follows them with the same disconsolate gaze, like Augusto's at the end of *The Swindle*.

One evening, Cabiria goes to a movie theater on the outskirts of Rome where a variety show performance is being held. During one scene, an old conjurer (Aldo Silvani) performs the usual sawed-off head routine. Cabiria is called up on stage together with a group of young men (Franco Balducci, Ciccio Barbi, and Nino Milano) to take part in a hypnosis act: they row together on a plank, survive a storm, and battle an imaginary heat wave that forces them to get undressed. When the performance is over, the conjurer keeps Cabiria onstage. Two devil's horns spring up from his scalp as the old man takes off his top hat. He diabolically sends Cabiria into a trance, making her believe she is standing alongside a young man—Oscar—who is in love with her and wants to ask Cabiria for her hand in marriage. Within the white halo of a spotlight, a small crown of flowers on her head, Cabiria agrees to go for a walk with Oscar. She picks some little flowers for her lover, and at a nod from the conjurer dances the waltz from *The Merry Widow*. The conjurer asks her: "So you love me?" But the game is up. Cabiria faints, and when she comes back to her senses, she is in the middle of the cancan from *Orfeo all'inferno* (*Orpheus in Hell*) and the uproar that has broken out among the audience.

Later on Cabiria is afraid to leave the movie theater lobby for fear of being made fun at. There is a man waiting for her. He seems perfectly normal and introduces himself as an accountant, Signor D'Onofrio (François Périer, voiced over by Silvio Noto). The man says he was moved by the performance. His name is Oscar and he claims he has seen destiny in Cabiria's declaration of love. The man is nice, speaks kindly, and offers her a drink. He accompanies her to the bus stop and they agree to meet the following Sunday at Stazione Termini.

Cabiria goes to the station just to see if he shows up. He is there, his shirt open to his chest and a bunch of flowers in his hand. As soon as he sees her, the man comes over to her. He is visibly moved.

Together with Wanda and her companions on Passeggiata Archeologica, Cabiria is eating some chocolates that the accountant gave her. She tells them about her date, that the two of them went to the Metropolitan Cinema to see *I gladiatori* (*The Gladiators*). She defines him as a "Southern Italian," very intelligent and very much in love. The conversation is interrupted by a police raid.

Cabiria has another date with Oscar at a tram stop. They go out on the Aventino road, where he tells her sad stories about his childhood in a small town in Puglia.

At home in bed, Cabiria smokes a cigarette and sings. When she leaves the house, she runs into Father Giovanni (Polidor), a monk who kindheartedly advises her to live in God's grace.

Under the rain out on Passeggiata Archeologica, Cabiria is so lost in her own thoughts that she doesn't even realize when clients are calling her.

On a road on the outskirts of the city, Cabiria is dressed up in a sailor suit like a little girl, walking along with Oscar, who asks her to marry him. Swept up by a giddy wave of happiness and disbelief, she doesn't even know what she is saying. She comes running up under Wanda's window and shouts that she is going to get married, to sell everything, she is going away. In her exuberance, the prostitute adds an emphatic "Tiè," an entirely Italian "Up yours!" (making the same crude

gesture as Sordi in *I Vitelloni*). Then she runs down to the convent to confess to Father Giovanni, but she can't find him anywhere.

Back in Cabiria's house, Wanda is helping her friend pack her bags. Outside, the family that is going to move into the cube of cement is waiting, their things piled on top of a cart. As Cabiria is leaving, she wants to say good-bye to everyone and no one. At the bus stop, Wanda tells her how worried she is: in reality, she has never seen this fiancé. But now it is too late, there is just enough time for a quick embrace and the bus takes Cabiria away.

On Lake Albano, from atop the terrace at a trattoria called Castel Gandolfo, Oscar and Cabiria have just finished eating. Somebody is playing the guitar and singing a song, "Lla-rì-lli-rà." Cabiria takes out a roll of banknotes,

"Yes, I saw the film the Americans made from Cabiria *while I was on the plane. What did I think? Humph. A film made from a musical made from a film . . . Mah!"*

which she proudly refers to as her "dowry": 350,000 lira from the sale of her house; 400,000 lira from her bank account. Oscar pays for dinner and invites her to watch the sunset over the lake. The couple kiss one another in the woods. Cabiria walks along behind Oscar, singing. She believes that they are headed for some hidden glade where they can make love. The dark silhouette of the accountant is captured onscreen from behind, etched out against the lake waters shimmering with the last rays of sunlight. Looking down the high bank, Cabiria tells him how somebody once pushed her into . . . A terrible thought crosses her mind. The two face one another on the edge of the abyss. Cabiria starts to scream: "What, are you going to try and kill me?" There is a brief struggle. Cabiria falls to the ground, crying desperately: "Kill me, just kill me. . . ." Oscar rips her purse out of her hands and runs away, just as Giorgio did at the beginning of the film. Cabiria remains on the ground, on her knees, reduced to nothing, all her hopes lost. Just like Zampanò, just like Augusto.

Night has come. Cabiria drags herself up, walks through the woods, and reaches the road. There are some young people there, some on foot, some on scooters, all headed toward the little town, singing and playing music. They dance around her, as if celebrating her. A girl says, "Buonasera." Life in all its absurdity starts up once again. Cabiria looks this way and that. She even looks into the camera, out at the audience, and manages a small smile.

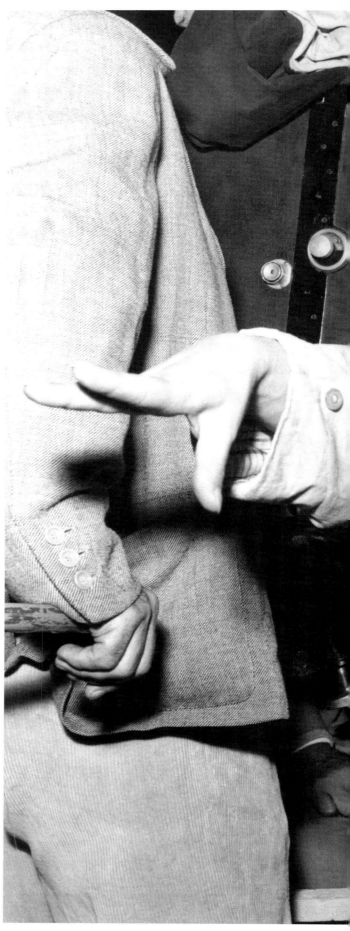

A CARDINAL AGAINST THE BIGOTS

March 1957. *Nights of Cabiria* was ready. It was even selected for the 10th Cannes Film Festival, to be held in May. But there was trouble on the horizon. The Italian Ministry, tipped off by the usual Fascist-style bigots, had no intention of granting an export visa to a work of art that denigrates the Capitol of Christianity. The Jesuit priest Angelo Arpa intervened, relying on the strong influence he had over the Cardinal of Genoa, Giuseppe Siri. Someone suggested presenting the film to the illustrious churchman, screening it secretly at night in a little back alley cinema. Arpa accompanied Siri to the screening, while Fellini and his inseparable companion Gigetto hid out not far away, waiting for the verdict. It was well after midnight by the time the clergymen left the cinema. Arpa nodded imperceptibly to Fellini, who rushed to hear for himself *ad audiendum verbum*. The response was positive: even though Siri was an unrepentant member of the ecclesiastical right wing, he fully approved of the movie. *Nights of Cabiria* moved him. He murmured a few words of empathy for the living conditions suffered by these defenseless sinners—conditions that would become that much worse less than two years later when the Italian government abolished bordellos, known as "closed houses." The following morning, De Laurentiis received an early phone call from someone in the Ministry, protesting the interference from one of the princes of the Catholic Church, but no one dared go against the will of one many considered to be in line as the next Pope. The film was free to travel to Cannes. Fellini came under heavy fire from Italy's left-wing newspapers for having accepted to submit his movie to the will of the Church. Fellini didn't know what to say: he had saved *Cabiria*, and that was all that was important. The movie opened at Cannes on May 10 and enjoyed a marvelous reception. De Laurentiis, Fellini, Masina, and others who collaborated on the production were all present. The jury, presided over by Jean Cocteau, awarded Masina the prize for Best Actress and paid homage to her husband's directing. The film was warmly received by critics and the public alike, debuting in Italy on May 26 and earning a total of 602 million lira. But its success didn't stop there: the film quickly traveled around the world, winning prizes and accolades wherever it was shown. On March 26, 1958, it won, before the eyes of the stunned and deeply moved Masina, the Academy Award for Best Foreign Film. It was the second success in a row, after *La Strada*. The film's fortunes continued through a Bob Fosse musical based on the *Cabiria* screenplay: *Sweet Charity*. The film was directed by Bob Fosse and starred Gwen Verdon. Ten years later, the musical was turned into a film by the same name. Bob Fosse directed once again, with Shirley MacLaine in the lead role.

Fellini was honored but hardly enthusiastic about the entire affair. He insisted that his name be kept out of both the musical and the subsequent movie. He would do the same for *Nine*, inspired by his own *8½*.

Opposite: *Poster for* Sweet Charity, *the Broadway show based on* Nights of Cabiria.

Below: *Giulietta Masina wins Best Actress at Cannes, and celebrates the Academy Award with Fred Astaire, in Hollywood.*

"I told my screenwriters: we have to make a statue, then break it and put the pieces back together. Or attempt to create a Picasso-esque deconstruction."

LA DOLCE VITA

THE POPE DIES AND VIA VENETO IS IN AN UPROAR

In the summer of 1958, just as Pope Pius XII's health began to worsen, all hell broke loose in Rome. On Via Vittorio Veneto, the electric nightlife that the Pope had always opposed took off. Seated at tables in open-air cafés, or simply walking along the sidewalk, VIPs wound up at the center of a merry-go-round of petulant, aggressive photographers who proved ready to do anything and everything in order to grab a scoop. Fellini, who was busy reworking the screenplay of *Moraldo in città* (*Moraldo in the City*) he had abandoned earlier for De Laurentiis, found a new source of inspiration in this picturesque phenomenon, an event that was widely covered by the weekly papers. He had an idea. Talking things over with Pinelli and Flaiano, Fellini suggested updating the character of the young city-dwelling vitellone, describing the situations around him in a deliberately fragmented series of episodes.

The result was a voluminous screenplay that alarmed the producer from the point of view of cost, and didn't really fully convince him, either. De Laurentiis in particular couldn't really digest the insane gesture of an intellectual in crisis murdering his little children before taking his own life. As far as he was concerned, the most concrete problem was the choice of writing Marcello Mastroianni (whom Fellini barely knew, but insisted on having play the part) into the script, while the budget and size of the project meant it was much more advisable to bring in an American film star. After a series of endless diatribes and having listened to the negative comments of a trio of expert consultants, De Laurentiis made the decision, which he would regret forever, to abandon the film when it was already well into the preparation phase. The subsequent waltz of potential producers brought in to pick up the project was more confused and disappointing than usual, and came to an end only when Peppino Amato managed to get Angelo Rizzoli involved. Rizzoli took an instant liking to Fellini, whom he nicknamed "caro Artista" ("dear Artist"), and decided to shoulder the risky undertaking more as a patron than for any financial advantages it might bring. This faith from a charismatic financier, the only man in cinema who was capable of investing his own money without turning to the banks for assistance, remained intact even during the drawn out and draining preparation directed by Clemente Fracassi. And Fellini didn't make things any easier, either. The filmmaker was assailed by doubts about which actors to involve in the project, who would be in part professionals and in part people taken from real life. He applied the same logic to his choice of locations, only in part natural and mostly imaginatively designed by Gherardi, including a reconstruction of the cupola of Saint Peter's and the sidewalks of Via Veneto out in front of the Café de Paris. After being postponed a number of times, the first filming took place on March 16 in Theater 14 at Cinecittà, with the voluptuous Anita Ekberg gamely tackling the winding staircase in Saint Peter's cupola, followed by a gasping Mastroianni. The presence of this statuesque Swedish actress earned the production great attention from the media, especially when she was filmed fully dressed in the Fontana di Trevi (a historic moment in cinema that has since become a classic emblem of the era and which Ettore Scola would evoke fifteen years later in the film *C'eravamo tanto amati*, or *We All Loved Each Other So Much*, involving both Fellini and Mastroianni). Work on the film moved forward from one scene to the next, with the situations, locations, and characters changing constantly as if it were a production of numerous different movies rather than a single opus. Filming didn't really finish until six months later, when in September, Fellini filmed the outside shots used in the finale in Passo Oscuro.

The first version of the movie was ready in November. It was just over three hours long, slightly longer than the final version would ultimately run, and Fellini organized a number of screenings at Cinecittà for his friends and those curious to see the movie. Those who saw it would continue to prefer this initial version with the original voices, director's interjections, and music in playback (subsequently substituted by the brilliant Rota, who often imitated the earlier models) to the shorter final version. Unfortunately, the reels of this original version have been lost.

Page 105: *Anita Ekberg in the fountain. The image is now iconic.*

Opposite: *Fellini with cameramen Ennio Guarnieri and Arturo Zavattini (behind).*

Below: *A drawing of Anita Ekberg by Fellini.*

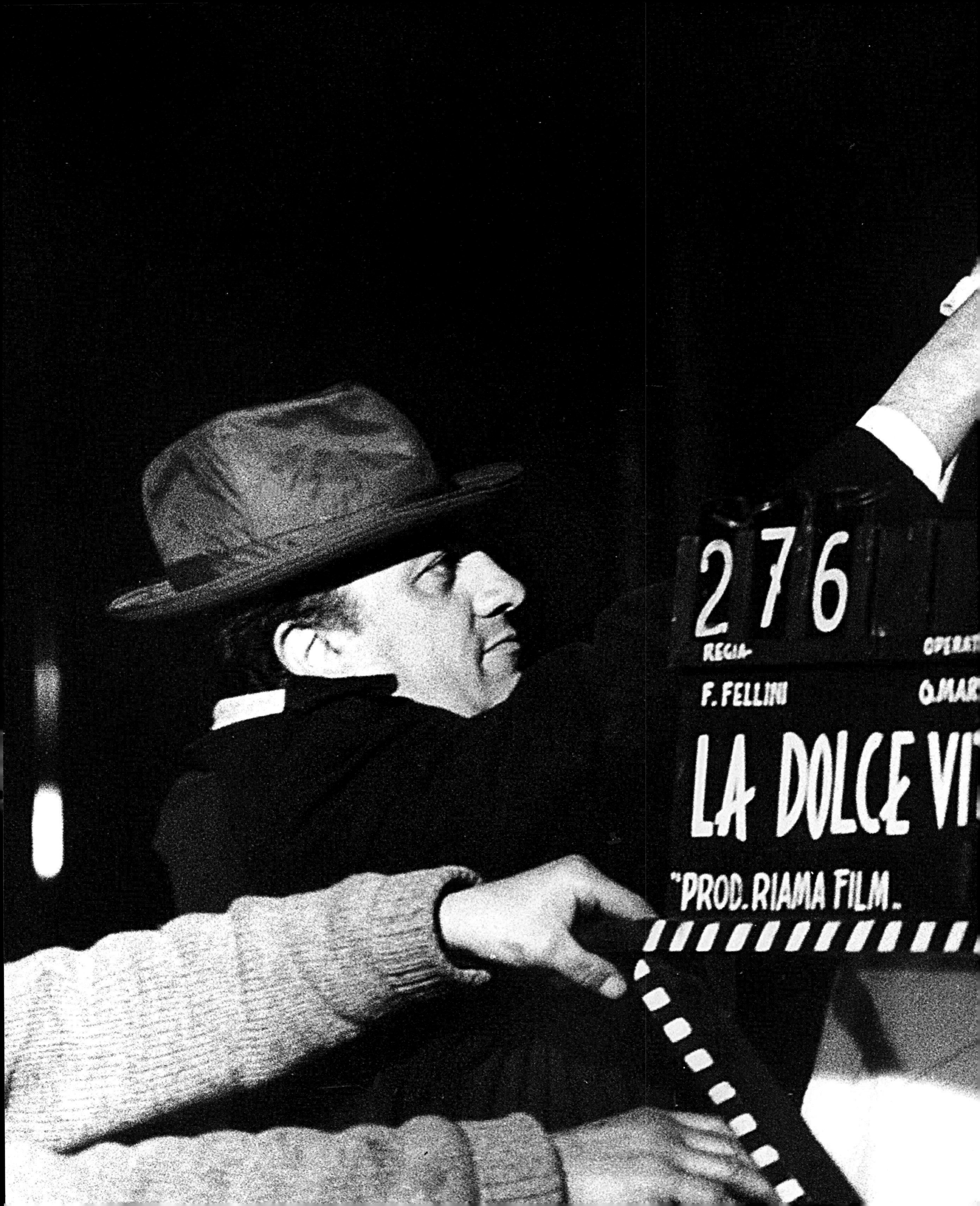
276
REGIA
F. FELLINI
LA DOLCE VI
"PROD. RIAMA FILM..

Left: *Federico Fellini, Anita Ekberg, and the little kitten.*

Above: *(from top to bottom) Anita Ekberg at Caracalla's; Winie Vagliani with a guitar, Anna Salvatore and Leonida Repaci in Steiner's house; commissioner Giulio Girola, Renée Longarini, and Marcello Mastroianni.*

109

Opposite: *The orgy set in Cinecittà: Marcello Mastroianni, Federico Fellini, Lucia Vasilicò, and director's assistant Gianfranco Mingozzi, who in 2009 filmed the documentary* Noi che abbiamo fatto la dolce (We Who Made La Dolce).

Above and left: *Valeria Ciangottini in the finale of the film, and in a drawing by Fellini that illustrates one of the filmmaker's dreams: Fellini and Clemente Fracassi escort Valeria into a bordello managed by Sophia Loren.*

A PICASSO-ESQUE FRESCO

Framed between a prologue (Christ flying over Rome) and an epilogue (the fish-monster) that are symbolically symmetrical and divided by an interlude that includes the apparition of the angelic Paolina, the principal episodes of *La Dolce Vita*, a cinematic fresco/mosaic, center around the journalist Marcello Rubini (Marcello Mastroianni). There are seven main episodes: Marcello's brief encounter with the heiress Maddalena; his wild night with the American diva; Marcello's relationship with Steiner, his intellectual friend (subdivided into three parts: the meeting, the invitation, and the slaughter); the false miracle; the father's visit; receiving the nobility; and the orgy. The story of Marcello's difficult relationship with his lover, Emma, runs through from one episode to the next. A brief interlude involving a furious fight with her is also part of the film.

The opening image is of an enormous white statue of Christ the Laborer that is being flown over Rome, from the ruins of the Felice aqueduct to modern-day building construction sites. A group of beauties bathing on a terrace look up and shout, "Look, it's Jesus!" From

Above: *Photographer Pierluigi Praturlon, on the left, and cameraman Otello Martelli.*

the cockpit of the helicopter, Marcello and a paparazzi photographer (Walter Santesso) signal with their hands to show they would like the girls' phone numbers.

A male dancer dressed up as an Asian idol is performing in a nightclub. Marcello and Paparazzo are there hunting for a scoop, but a man (Cesare Miceli Picardi) threatens to smash the journalist's face in for having insulted the lady he is with (Donatella Esparmer). Maddelena (Anouk Aimée, voiced over by Lilla Brignone) arrives. She is a young, fascinating heiress who

is hiding a nasty bruise under her dark sunglasses. The orchestra strikes up "Mama, She's Put Her Blame on Me," the bizarre characters in the nightclub start dancing and Marcello offers to accompany Maddalena.

Moving along Via Veneto, they face the usual problem of avoiding photographers in search of a story. Maddalena and Marcello escape in the heiress's large American car and drive off and park under the big wall in Piazza del Popolo. They talk about Rome, which he defines as "a sort of jungle it is easy to hide in." The heiress, on the other hand, would like to go live somewhere else, but she doesn't know where, or with whom. They meet a prostitute named Ninnì (Adriana Moneta) and offer to give her a lift home. When they are in the Cessati Spiriti neighborhood, Maddalena asks the prostitute to make her some coffee, but she draws back behind the partition in the flooded cantina where they've arrived and doesn't waste a minute in asking Marcello to go to bed with her. Marcello: "You want to make love here?" Maddalena: "No?" At dawn, the two lovers leave and are cordially waved off by Ninnì under the watchful eyes of her pimp, who sits astride a scooter.

Once he is back home, a space without furniture except for a bed, Marcello finds his girlfriend, Emma (Yvonne Furneaux, voiced over by Gabriella Genta), in a coma, an attempted suicide. All he can do is put her over his shoulders and drive madcap to the hospital. After the woman's stomach has been pumped, the doctors allow Marcello to visit her. She is exhausted, lying prone on the bed. He seems deeply moved by her situation, but then he asks one of the nuns if he can make a phone call. Marcello rings Maddalena, but she is asleep and doesn't answer.

At Ciampino Airport, amid a delirious crowd of photographers and a giant pizza, the American film star Sylvia (Anita Ekberg) has landed. A long line of cars forms behind her along Appia Antica, every once in a while blocked by a herd of sheep. At the Excelsior Hotel, during the actress's press conference, Marcello is on the telephone trying to placate Emma, who even manages to be jealous of the American film diva. Hired by the producer Totò Scalise (Carlo Di Maggio) for the advertising, Marcello reassures the man about the campaign. The actor Robert (Lex Barker) arrives drunk and ironic. He is Sylvia's companion, and is itching for a fight.

Strong as a horse, Sylvia runs straight up the seven hundred steps to the top of the cupola in Saint Peter's. Marcello catches up with her on the last little terrace, just in time to see the little priest's hat that completed the bizarre ecclesiastic outfit (similar to Augusto's costume

Right top: *Fellini and Valeria Ciangottini.*

Right bottom: *Fellini and Domino in the orgy scene.*

Below: *Fellini at Passo Oscuro with Otello Martelli (kneeling) in front of the fish-monster.*

in *The Swindle*) fly away. At the Caracalla nightclub, amid the authentic ruins of the Roman baths of the same name, Marcello dances to "Arrivederci, Roma," enveloped by Sylvia. One of the film star's colleagues, Frankie Stout (Alan Dijon), shows up shouting and yelling. He insists on changing the music, striking up a cha-cha-cha that culminates (once again!) in a military fanfare. Sylvia and Frankie engage in an acrobatic dance routine that becomes a bacchanalia when an Elvis Presley imitator (Adriano Celentano) bursts out in rock 'n' roll. The actress is the star of the moment, but when she gets back to her table, she finds a sarcastic and irritated Robert. After exchanging a few bitter words, Sylvia takes off, followed quickly by Marcello.

Riding along in the journalist's Triumph, Sylvia complains about Robert, but the two find it hard to hold a conversation because Marcello doesn't speak English. They stop for a while along the Appia, where the excited diva answers back to the dog's cries in the nearby villas. They don't know where to go. Marcello would like to take advantage of the situation, but he doesn't know where to take the woman. He even asks Maddalena to take them in—the heiress is spending the evening alongside her father, played by Giacomo Gabrielli. Wandering around the winding streets of ancient Rome, Sylvia finds a little kitten and insists that Marcello find the animal some milk, right away. When he gets back, she has waded into the monumental Fontana di Trevi, still in her

Opposite: *Drawings by Fellini: in one, he dreams of helicopters with film editor Leo Catozzo, and in another, he and his wife Giulietta Masina are hosted by Pablo Picasso.*

Below: *During a break, Fellini has breakfast with Nino Rota and Marianna Leibl, psychologist and psychic.*

dress, like some pagan goddess. Marcello doesn't waste a moment and wades in himself, but the enchantment doesn't last for long: the rushing, cascading waters slow to a stop, the illusion disappears, and another dawn has arrived. On Via Veneto, in front of the Excelsior Hotel, the paparazzi see the Triumph pull in and wake up Robert, who had fallen asleep in his car while waiting for Sylvia to return. Exasperated, the actor starts slapping Sylvia and punching Marcello. The assembled photographers are overjoyed and continue shooting, nonstop.

While he is working on a fashion shoot, Marcello sees Steiner (Alain Cuny, voiced over by Romolo Valli) from afar. More than a friend, Steiner is a sort of spiritual guide for Marcello. He catches up with the man inside a church. They confabulate with the same old affectionate intensity until finally Steiner, with the priest's permission (played by the director's assistant Gianfranco Mingozzi), plays a few jazz notes on the organ as a joke before breaking into a rendition of Bach's *Toccata and Fugue in D minor, BWV 565.*

In the original screenplay this scene was followed by an episode of the writer Luise (written in as Luise Rainer) that was never filmed. Marcello meets the writer on Maddalena's yacht during a lunch out on the water. The encounter is rendered funereal by a tragic accident that takes the life of a beautiful young girl, Sandra, who is burned alive in a gasoline bonfire. The story with the intellectual and neurotic Dolores continues in the writer's solitary tower by the seaside.

Dragging Emma along with them, Marcello and Paparazzo head out in the Triumph to a field outside Rome. There is a rumor that two children have seen the Madonna there. The episode is not unlike the Divine Love scene in *Nights of Cabiria*, only more ruthless and violent. The children are cryptic, the family is trying to take advantage of the situation, and the television crews are laboring to turn the false miracle into a genuine entertainment spectacle. Underneath bright spotlights near the tree where the "appearance" took place, a small gathering of miracle searchers has come together. All of a sudden, a thunderstorm breaks out. In the ensuing race to find cover amid the darkness, someone dies. Emma, somehow touched by the sacredness that exists in the event for all its apparent falseness, angrily takes things up with her lover. At dawn, a priest recites a prayer in Latin over the victim of this collective folly.

We catch back up with Marcello and Emma during an evening gathering in Steiner's beautiful home out in Rome's EUR neighborhood. They are welcomed by Steiner's wife (Renée Longarini). The group gathered

Right: *Marcello Mastroianni, Giorgio Fabbri, Maddalena Fabbri Fellini, Fred (Mario Borgognoni, former dancer and Mastroianni's secretary), Ida Barbiani, Fellini's mother, and Federico Fellini.*

there includes a number of people taken straight from real life, who more or less play themselves: the writer Leonida Repaci, the painters Anna Salvatore and Letizia Spadini, the Irish poet Desmond O'Grady, the poetess Iris Tree, and Winie Vagliani, who sings and plays "Ten Thousand Miles" on her guitar. In an atmosphere that is a mix of the sublime and ridiculous, Steiner has the group listen to the sounds of nature he enjoys recording. In Steiner's company, Marcello is keenly aware of having betrayed his own talents as a writer, as well as Steiner's faith in him as a friend. Struck by a still life by Morandi and a poem by Iris, the protagonist pronounces art "clear, useful, and something that will come in handy in the future." Steiner shows Marcello his children, who are already fast asleep, and shares disturbing thoughts with the journalist, saying in his high, abstract tone of voice: "Peace. That's what scares me. . . ."

In a little trattoria in Passo Oscuro, sitting alone at a table outside, Marcello tries to apply Steiner's advice while working on his typewriter, but he is distracted by the presence of a young waitress who looks like the angel Paolina from a fresco in his native Umbria.

Back on Via Veneto, two men are busy fighting. An even larger surprise awaits: the paparazzi tell Marcello that his father (Annibale Ninchi) has arrived at the Café de Paris. Smiling and cordial, the old man's eyes are aglow with the excitement and activity of the metropolis at nighttime. Everything is so different from the quiet gray evenings in his small hometown. The man has come to Rome to take care of some business at the Ministry, and has to leave the next day. He makes it clear he wouldn't mind visiting a nightclub called the "Kit-Kat." Marcello accompanies his father to this old-school locale, together with Paparazzo. In the nightclub, Fanny (Magali Noël), one of Marcello's dancer friends, comes and sits with them at their table. The father offers some champagne and strikes up a friendly banter with the girl, almost flirting. Fanny is a rather strange girl and is moved by the performance of an old clown (Polidor), who drags a host of small colored balloons behind him while playing the trumpet like a circus pied piper.

When they leave the nightclub, Fanny and Marcello's father take off in the girl's car. Marcello takes Paparazzo and another pair of dancing girls away in his Triumph. The women are Lucy (Lilly Granado) and Gloria (Gloria Jones), and together they waste some time before reaching their destination. At the door to Fanny's building, located in the Italia neighborhood, they find the girl, as white as a ghost: Marcello's father isn't feeling well. Upstairs the old Ganymede is sitting in a chair

Above and right: *Testing the extremely cold waters of the Fontana di Trevi.*

Page 120: *Anita Ekberg in the fountain during the photo shoot by Pierluigi Praturlon.*

Page 121: *Anita Ekberg in the film, with production director Alessandro von Normann.*

Above: *The reception in Via Veneto, rebuilt in Cinecittà. From the left: Marcello Mastroianni, Anouk Aimée, Luise Rainer (who was not in the film), Federico Fellini, Anita Ekberg, and Yvonne Furneaux.*

facing an open window, his shirt unbuttoned. It's nothing serious, but the incident has embarrassed him enormously. He wants to leave on the first train out of town. At dawn, a taxi arrives to carry him away.

Cars driving to Prince Mascalchi's (Vadim Wolkonsky) palazzo in Bassano di Sutri are heading out from Via Veneto. Marcello has slipped in next to a foreign blonde (Nico Otzak), the girlfriend of one of Mascalchi's boys, Giulio (film director Giulio Questi). The party is packed with people, elderly signors, gentlemen, beautiful women decked out in marvelous evening gowns. While dancing around the palazzo, Marcello runs into Maddalena. Taking advantage of an echo chamber, she asks him "Would you marry me?" from afar, while letting a random young man (Ferdinando Brofferio) embrace her at the same time. In a heady dash between the palazzo and the guesthouse, Marcello has a series of singular encounters fraught with curious dialogue. He even joins in a spiritual séance: in the end, inevitably, he winds up making love to a woman he has only just met (Audrey McDonald).

Dawn has come once again and the melancholy revelers, on their way through the park and heading back into the palazzo, cross paths with the elderly Mother Princess heading out to the little chapel for mass. Prince Mascalchi and his two children follow along behind her dutifully with bowed heads.

Marcello and Emma begin quarreling on a street in the EUR neighborhood. He forces her to get out of the car and races away, only to come back at dawn and pick her up. The phone rings while they are still in bed. Tragedy has struck the Steiner home. Marcello races to Steiner's house, where he quickly learns that his friend has shot his children and himself. The police are gathering evidence around Steiner's body, still seated in an armchair like a carved statue. The police commissioner (Giulio Girola) brings Marcello along with him to the bus stop where they are to meet Signora Steiner. She is on her way back home and doesn't know a thing. This horrible news is given to her amid the usual cruel throng of news-hungry photographers.

A group of people is gathered in a villa in Fregene, celebrating the separation of Nadia (Nadia Gray). Now she can finally get together with her lover (Mino Doro). A motley group of people are present: an American ballerina just back from Spoleto, a few actors (Umberto Orsini), the singer Laura (Laura Betti), a black male dancer, an elderly playboy (Mario Conocchia), cinema divas of the past (Enrico Glori, Oretta Fiume), a pair of transvestites, and a film star (Jacques Sernas) who

Left: *The real Pope, Urbano Fellini.*

Below: *The fictional Pope (Annibale Ninchi).*

Marcello works for as a press agent. The party has an excited feel: Nadia plays an album entitled *Patricia*, a mambo by Perez Prado, and performs a striptease. An ingenuous girl (Franca Pasut) gets drunk and publicly ridiculed and embarrassed (a reference to the "Montesi case" that shocked Italy a few years earlier), while arguments and fighting go on. The scene continues until Riccardo (Riccardo Garrone), the owner, arrives and cordially kicks everyone out.

At dawn, making its way out of a little pine forest and onto the beach, the little group of *dolce vita* revelers witness the miraculous (or diabolic?) scene of the fish-monster. On the other side of a canal, Paolina is calling to Marcello. She has recognized him and would like to tell him something. He doesn't understand, and makes a few resigned gestures, clowning around and following along after the group. Paolina smiles, absolving him.

SPIT AND APPLAUSE

The film's debut on February 3, 1960 at the Fiamma Theater in Rome was relatively calm, though interrupted by a few whistles. But the film had a much more tempestuous screening in Milan at the Capitol Theater, where it was shown on February 5. Fellini and Mastroianni were publicly insulted ("Communist!") and shouted at. One hothead in the audience even went so far as to spit on the filmmaker. Rizzoli, who had already picked up on the generally cold reactions among the friends he had invited to a private screening in his little palazzo on Via del Crocifisso, proceeded unafraid, ready to pay for the flop in person. Another private screening was organized by Father Arpa in the Jesuit's hall in the San Fedele Center. After giving the movie a favorable review, the priest was reprimanded and punished by his superiors. Overall, the Church immediately came out strongly against the film. Even Cardinal Siri, who had been instrumental in defending *Nights of Cabiria* and personally approved of the film, didn't feel comfortable going against his traditional rival, Giovanni Battista Montini, Archbishop of Milan and the future Pope Paul VI, who strongly opposed the movie. Montini first set up a meeting with Fellini, then refused to see the filmmaker. This all took place at the same time as a series of anonymous attacks were published in *L'Osservatore Romano*, starting with an article entitled "Schifosa vita" ("Disgusting Life"). The Italian Parliament even weighed in on the affair, most notably the

Opposite: Federico Fellini and Anita Ekberg aboard the special train headed for opening night in Milan in February, 1960.

Right: A clipping of one of the many attacks published in L'Osservatore romano, *and a holy warning against the film, put on display in Padua.*

Below: A crowd of people at the entrance to the movie theater, trying to get tickets for the film.

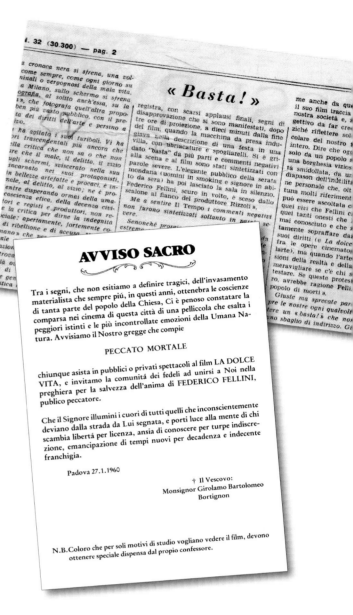

neo-Fascists, who strongly protested the presumed offenses the film flung at the country's beloved capitol, but the government surprised everyone by stifling their complaints. Controversy surrounding the film continued for weeks, boosting ticket sales all the way to the record amount of 2,220,716 lira. Although the world of cinema was generally against *La Dolce Vita* (though often out of spite and envy), numerous intellectuals championed the film, including forceful defenses from Alberto Moravia and Pier Paolo Pasolini. The film's success continued to grow internationally, earning it the Palme d'Or award at the 13th Cannes Film Festival, where the jury was presided over by Georges Simenon, who would remain a sincere friend and admirer of Fellini. On Academy Award night, the film disappointed, earning nothing more than an Oscar for Gherardi's costume work. But *La Dolce Vita* would earn accolades and awards just about everywhere else it was shown. One of the more unusual outcomes of the movie was that Ekberg and Barker both moved to Rome for the rest of their lives.

"It's a bit of foolishness, a story straight out of a children's magazine. But most of all, it's a way to avoid thinking of more serious matters."

THE TEMPTATIONS OF DOCTOR ANTONIO
AN EPISODE IN BOCCACCIO '70
LE TENTAZIONI DEL DOTTOR ANTONIO

INSIDE A MINI-EUR

After having worked through the aftermath of *La Dolce Vita*—a mostly celebratory collection of compliments and praise since the film garnered extraordinary positive consensus everywhere—Fellini began to mull over another project. Everyone was waiting with baited breath, especially the producer Rizzoli, who hoped to repeat the success at the box office. But the forty-year-old Fellini was a somewhat changed man. His inventive vein no longer had that same explosive exuberance it once had, as while he was making *La Strada*, and each new idea was immediately assailed by doubts. Furthermore, he suffered from the feeling that now, having finally achieved the height of popularity, he could not afford to make any mistakes. Fellini wanted to rediscover the thrill of entertaining the general public and thought he could do so by keeping *The Cure*, a film Chaplin shot for Mutual, as his creative guiding star. It was with Chaplin in mind that the filmmaker decided to spend time at Chianciano Terme, observing and taking endless notes. But in order to make people laugh, you have to want to laugh yourself, and while Fellini would never completely lose this desire, his comic verve had waned considerably. The moment he arrived on the set of *8½*, loyal to his original ideas, Fellini shocked everyone by attaching a little note to the side of the camera: "Remember that you are making a comedy." It was an entirely unexpected self-exhortation. Meanwhile, work on the film proceeded in fits and starts, and when thinking about it—in what would soon become an existential judgment—the filmmaker felt many more moments of sadness, perplexity, and discomfort than good humor. As he continued to discuss the undefined project with Pinelli and Flaiano, deliberately avoiding setting a precise date to start shooting, Fellini received a phone call from Tonino Cervi, the young producer and son of the famous Italian actor Gino Cervi, who was working on a film entitled *Boccaccio '70*. The project was similar to what Zavattini had done for *Love in the City*: gather together a group of filmmakers willing (as with *Il Decamerone* [*The Decameron*]) to entertain themselves by challenging the Italian censorship boards with stimulating subjects. Tonino Cervi had already gotten several important film directors to sign on to the project, including headline names such as Luchino Visconti, Mario Monicelli, and Vittorio De Sica. The opportunity to be the fourth name in this group came to Fellini in a moment in which he had just finished getting over the religious censorship and Fascist attacks that had been leveled at his films. The filmmaker was anxious to participate. All he required was a guarantee that he would not have to cross paths with Visconti, with whom his old Venetian diatribe still rankled. The entrepreneurial Cervi was quick to reassure Fellini that he wouldn't need to meet with the other filmmakers: each director would work on his own segment in complete autonomy and freedom. Once again, this failed to satisfy Zavattini, who continued to dream of unrealizable group barricades and protests.

Starting in September 1960, Fellini took full-time residence in his new downtown offices at Via della Croce 70. The offices took the company name "Federiz" (**Fed-e**rico – **Riz**zoli), and had been founded together with Fracassi and Rizzoli (often known as the *commenda*), mostly to help young people break into the industry—an activity that would never really take place. At Federiz, Fellini quickly began to sketch out a plot for Cervi's film.

Page 129: *Peppino's nightmare.*

Opposite: *Peppino De Filippo.*

Below: *Doctor Antonio Mazzuolo (Peppino De Filippo) awards the boy scouts.*

It was to be a funny portrait of an out-and-out moralist who becomes involved in an extraordinary adventure that Fellini wanted to write specifically for the Italian actor Romolo Valli. Valli was enthusiastic about the opportunity and began studying films and photographs of the enigmatic Italian leader Giulio Andreotti—the prestigious head of Italy's Christian Democratic political party, who defined himself "as the most upstanding hunchback in Italy." Valli's friend, director Giorgio De Lullo, would fill in onstage for the star actor toward the end of the theater season so that Valli would be free to participate in the movie.

Trouble arose the moment it came time to sign the contract: the actor asked for too much money, especially since he was generally considered a supporting actor, albeit an important one. The production staff decided to bide its time. After a round of back-and-forth discussions with the actor, which Fellini did not participate in directly, the filmmaker decided to take the bull by the horns and call in Peppino De Filippo to take Valli's place. Valli was insulted and the two camps accused each other of betrayal before a period of cold relations settled in. Fortunately, rapprochement was not far off. Even Rizzoli accused his "dear artist" of having betrayed the cause.

Rizzoli was jealous first and foremost because Sophia Loren's Pygmalion Carlo Ponti had approached Cervi and in exchange for ceding the diva's rights for the De Sica episode had earned a spot above the title of the production: "Carlo Ponti Presents." A compromise was found by reserving the distribution rights for Cineriz. The group was also joined by a pair of Parisian coproducers, Francinex and Gray Film.

During the summer of 1961, having called in Ekberg yet again, shooting for the episode took place against two different EUR backdrops: the real EUR and a miniature version built by the architect Piero Zuffi as part of his only collaborative work with Fellini. Trapped in the world of special effects, Ekberg made no attempt to hide her disappointment at having to embody a caricature from an advertising billboard rather than an actual character in the film, and this created a permanent atmosphere of unhappiness on the set. In August, the film was dubbed and mixed, more quickly than usual because its total running time was barely an hour. But all the filmmakers were running a bit over schedule. As was to be expected, when the first private screenings were held individually for the filmmakers, the rivalry among colleagues came through.

Left: *Romolo Valli in a drawing of one of Fellini's dreams.*

Below: *Romolo Valli and Fellini in the office. Valli was supposed to play Antonio.*

DRINK MORE MILK

The Temptations of Doctor Antonio (the title appears to be a parody of Gustave Flaubert's *The Temptation of Saint Anthony*) boasted the name of writer Goffredo Parise alongside the usual Pinelli, Flaiano, and Brunello Rondi. Fellini's episode is "Act Two" of *Boccaccio '70*. The titles are in gothic lettering, with Doctor Antonio Mazzuolo (Peppino De Filippo) staring out of his car window, half furious and half ridiculous, with bonfire flames superimposed on the image. An off-screen cupid (voiced over by Isa di Marzio) provides the narration, offering an idyllic description of the EUR neighborhood, an area on the outskirts of Rome where happiness appears to reign supreme. This was Fellini's first color film: a multihued carousel that included children, priests, models, a bicycle race, shots from a film by Ercole (Giuliano Gemma, voiced over by Alghiero Noschese) including the director in a wheelchair, water-skiing, and in paddle boats. "There's just one gentleman who's not happy with me," says cupid.

Dressed in a black suit, this supercilious and bespectacled gentleman by night surprises amorous couples ("Shame on you! You dirty devils! Go somewhere else and do your disgusting deeds!"), reproaching them in their cars and dragging the police out to the scene of their innocuous crimes. We see him at a variety theater performance, where he rushes onstage during the dancers' routine and brings down the curtain. During an open-air meal with a group of like-minded moralists (told in silent film style), Antonio runs to cover up a lady's neckline with his napkin. (Actually, this was a real episode that took place in Italy when a Christian Democratic parliament member, who would later rise all the way to President of the Italian Republic, fell victim to an especially zealous fit of moralizing.) Antonio alternates good deeds, such as collecting donations for prisoners during mass, with efforts like keeping a watch over pornographic magazines. Sometimes, the best he can do is to buy these magazines and rip them up, earning the approval of a newspaper director (a direct, vindictive caricature of the Vatican, which had led the crusade against *La Dolce Vita* with its "Disgusting Life" campaign).

While handing out awards to boy scouts (including burlesque medals for well-known names: Rodolfo Sonego, Otello Martelli, and others), Antonio is interrupted by a growling bulldozer. A pile of tubes is being set up while a band of worker-clowns (all played by variety theater actors: Alfredo Rizzo, Polidor, Dante Maggio, Giacomo Furia, and others) appears on the scene. The billboard for

Left: *The uncompromising moralist Antonio tries in vain to take down the giant billboard displaying a provocative Anita Ekberg.*

Below: *Another of Antonio's nocturnal nightmares.*

their show is still in pieces, resting there enigmatic and disturbing: a woman's feet, her legs, and more.

A bus deposits a group of musicians carrying tambourines and bongo drums in the piazza. They play music and dance to the soundtrack of *La Dolce Vita*. Now we see two fragments of the neon writing: "drink" and "milk." A loudspeaker is turned on and the leader of the band (Maggio) orders everyone: "Set up our sign." The song goes:

Bevete più latte	Drink more milk
il latte fa bene	milk's good for you
il latte conviene	milk's worthwhile
a tutte le età!	For people of all ages!
Bevete più latte	Drink more milk
prodotto italiano	an Italian product
rimedio sovrano	a sovereign remedy
di tutte le età!	for people of all ages!
Bevete più la…	Drink more m . . .
Bevete più la…	Drink more m . . .
Bevete più latte!	Drink more milk!

The musicians play a jazz tune along with the chorus, while the worker clowns carry Ekberg's face and neckline over until they've finally finished putting together an image of a woman laying down with a big glass of milk in one hand. Surrounded by a festive crowd, the clowns clean the billboard with a hose while Antonio protests the obscenity. Then he climbs up the stairs leading to a gathering of prims, where he presents the case: "I have five windows in my apartment, and my legs take up all five!" The manager (Antonio Acqua, the commissary in *The White Sheik*, voiced over by Alghiero Noschese) is perplexed by the definition of "tempting": "There's American tempting, French tempting, Turkish tempting. . . . " Antonio insists that the billboard is an offense to "the most sacred job of maternity: feeding milk to a baby."

Tormented night and day, Antonio writes letters in which he uses the invocation *Basta!* (*Enough!*, the title of an editorial in *L'Osservatore Romano* against *La Dolce Vita*). He tries to drag a bishop to the scene of the scandal, but only manages to get a pair of Church adjuncts involved. After the sun goes down, an underworld of vice and sin sets up shop around the billboard: whores, male prostitutes, *Cabiria*-style dancing. Antonio continues to curse the construction, keeping an eye on the situation from his window with a pair of binoculars. Even in the light of day, the site becomes a real carnival: puppeteers, a wandering photographer, carousels, children, and Fellini's omnipresent Bersaglieri soldiers. In order to bring the scandal to a head, the protagonist finally splashes ink across the front of the billboard and gets himself arrested. Only then is the giant Ekberg finally covered with sheets of paper.

The moralists are having a party in Antonio's house. Just as he is singing a Neapolitan song, he has his first hallucination: he sees the woman from the billboard lying on his dinner table. Amid thunder and lightning, the doctor hears his words against pornography. Suddenly he realizes that outside the heavy rains are pulling the paper covers off the billboard. Then it seems that the giant Ekberg is making faces at him.

The poor man is so overcome with emotion that he pulls his raincoat over his pajamas, grabs his umbrella, and runs outside to get a better look. Standing underneath the billboard, he has no more doubts: the woman is making faces and suddenly she starts to talk. Out on the grass, a glass of milk as tall as a man appears. The billboard is blank and the woman is no longer there. Antonio winds up between the feet of a giantess. The gigantic Anita Ekberg runs around, stretching out on the grass and calling to Antonio just as she did to Marcello in *La Dolce Vita*. She makes fun of him, dragging him out and around the EUR neighborhood, lifting him up to her breast. Even as he continues to protest, the champion of upstanding morals starts to feel his defenses wearing thin. He snuggles up to her enormous, soft neckline ("Oh, this is so comfortable!") only to rebel once again ("No, I don't want to, you temptress!"). In order to win a kiss from Antonio, Ekberg shrinks down to his size. Antonio, by now a slave to love, offers to make an honest woman out of her. Ekberg grows back to giant size and threatens to do a striptease right then and there. The doctor takes off his clothes in order to cover the camera lens, warning the audience directly: "Don't watch! Leave the cinema!" Finally he imagines himself as a sort of medieval knight-in-armor and tosses his spear right into Ekberg's chest. The woman is struck through the heart and closes her eyes and dies.

There is a funeral procession. All the characters are there, chanting rhythmically for Antonio: "Hey, hey, hooray for Mazzuolo!" They circle around him. Antonio shouts desperately: "She's mine! She's mine! I don't want you to take her away!" At dawn, they find Antonio clinging to the billboard. The firemen have to intervene to get him down. A doctor (the director Gianfranco Mingozzi) climbs up to give Antonio an injection so that he'll relax and they can take him down. The poor man is taken away on a stretcher as the "Drink More Milk" chorus starts up again. The little cupid from the beginning of the film sits on top of the ambulance that is taking Antonio to the insane asylum, laughing and sticking out a pink tongue.

THIS TIME, NO BOOING

As was customary for the time, the gala evening for *Boccaccio '70* was preceded by a private party and screening. On February 22, 1962 at the Capitol in Milan, the same cinema where two years earlier *La Dolce Vita* had been so stridently booed, the movie made its debut. But this time things went much more smoothly, although the screening was not met with particular enthusiasm from the audience. The viewers seemed to prefer Visconti's episode (*Il lavoro*, or *The Job*, with Romy Schneider), perhaps in part thanks to the film director's Milanese origins. Critics seemed to agree, favoring a rather lighthearted De Sica (*La riffa*, or *The Raffle*, with Sophia Loren) and Monicelli's *Renzo e Luciana* (*Renzo and Luciana*). Some criticized Fellini's episode, noting that once its brilliant premise was out of the way, the rest was unconvincing and not entertaining enough. The film did well at the national box office, earning 1,120,419.000 lira. On May 7, the movie inaugurated a series of films not up for awards at the 15th Cannes Film Festival. The inauguration almost fell through because when an attempt was made to omit Monicelli's episode (for banal reasons linked to the film's overall running time), the filmmaker went to his lawyers. But everything worked out in the end and the evening went off without a hitch. Once again, the response to the movie was a lukewarm, general acceptance.

Above: *Ennio Flaiano and Federico Fellini.*

Right: *Fellini and Piero Zuffi.*

Above: *Fellini, film producer Tonino Cervi, and Mario Monicelli.*

"8½ is an attempt, not a complete, finished result. For now, I believe it points the way to a solution: to become a complete friend to oneself—no hesitation, no false modesty, no fear, and without too much hope."

8 ¹/₂

I AM GUIDO

There is more than one person who claims to have been present at the moment when Fellini changed gears during the preparation of *8 ½*. The prize at stake, through a range of more or less manipulated memories, is the pride of having been a close friend of Fellini, the Maestro, during a period destined to become a classic moment in the history of cinema. I don't want to brag (or do I?), but I clearly remember the day in which, after having picked up Fellini at his house, I was walking down Via Archimede together with him toward Piazza Euclide. I can even vaguely recall the date, because this took place not long after Antonioni's *La notte* (*The Night*) was released, in January 1961, perhaps halfway through that same year. For Fellini, who was thinking about his next film, the fact that Antonioni had entrusted Mastroianni with the tormented character of a novelist was something upsetting. For his next film, still far from earning its final title of *8 ½*, Fellini was considering a character grappling with writer's block. Or would it be a "forty-year-old's block"? I think it must have been a little of both.

"What should I do? Turn Marcello Mastroianni into a writer again?" Fellini kept asking. "And what about the crisis? What's this character's crisis? The inability to identify something you have imagined, to be unable to write it down, to keep having the feeling—true, incredibly true, I assure you—that you can't do it any more . . . Isn't that what I'm experiencing right now?" Moving from one thought to the next, Fellini reached his main point: "I'm reflecting my own crisis in that of the character; and a writer's crisis is no different than that of a film director's. It's still a crisis." He paused, then: "At heart, and let's be completely honest, I am Marcello. I've said it a thousand times, but not with the same conviction with which I'm saying it now. What if it really is me? What if he represents me when faced with the relentless nightmare of a signed contract, a film that has to be made, risking showing up at the starting line empty-handed and with nothing more than an overwhelming desire to run away?" At that moment, neither he nor I knew that was precisely what would happen

just a few years later, when Fellini ran away from De Laurentiis amid clinical pretexts and real illnesses, abandoning the set at Dinocittà for *Il viaggio di G. Mastorna* (*The Voyage of G. Mastorna*). "There is such a thing as director's block, just watch me and you'll see. . . ."

At that moment a taxi drove by and Fellini shouted out to it. As he was getting in he said: "Please excuse me, I'm going to see Flaiano. I want to talk to him right away, see what he thinks . . . What do you think?" But he didn't stay long enough to hear my answer; by the time I opened my mouth he had already taken off and the film in its final, definitive version had taken off with him. That's how I remember the scene, exactly as I'm writing it here for you.

One cannot underestimate the importance that the psychoanalysis Fellini had begun in the meantime played in this matter. He had started therapy on advice from a colleague—Vittorio de Seta—with Ernst Bernhard, who had studied directly under Carl Gustav Jung. During the tri-weekly appointments he held in his studio at Via Gregoriana 12, apartment 15 (the same apartment currently inhabited by Dante Ferretti and Francesca Lo Schiavo), Fellini gleaned a more concrete perspective of his interior life, began writing down and illustrating his dreams, and experienced a constant flow of ideas that helped him focus on the themes, feelings, and situations of his films.

Once he had chosen the new path for his movie, things got underway very quickly. From time to time, problems suggest solutions that prove to be fortuitous opportunities. Fellini's relationship with his cameraman, Martelli, grew problematic, so the director was forced to find a new one. But the job search and interviews had to take place in such a way that *sor Otello*, as Martelli was known, wouldn't

Page 139: *Marcello Mastroianni in his harem. In the background holding a bottle is assistant director Guidarino Guidi.*

Opposite: *Marcello Mastroianni.*

Below: *Saraghina in a drawing by Federico Fellini.*

Above: *A sequence from the scene with Guido at the boarding school.*

suspect anything. So I suggested Gianni Di Venanzo to Fellini. I had a great appreciation for the work he did in the spring of 1961 in Sicily, filming for Rosi's *Salvatore Giuliano*. For his part, Fellini had tried to get Di Venanzo to work with him on *Matrimonial Agency*, but the two hadn't had an opportunity to get to know one another during such a short period of time.

I called Di Venanzo immediately, and he was very interested in the opportunity. I made arrangements to go and pick him up in Fellini's car, meeting him in Piazza dei Cinquecento, the very location Fellini used as the final shot for the episode in *Love in the City*. We went and had something to eat in Fiumicino, and seated in front of a plate of spaghetti and mussels, Fellini and Di Venanzo started chatting together while I watched excitedly in silence. This encounter eventually led to what may well be the most beautiful film in black and white shot by Fellini. It was an art in which Di Venanzo was an undisputed master. That glorious moment, which celebrates the theatrical qualities of light, marked a turning point in Fellini's career. From that moment on, everything Fellini shot would be in color. Color was even destined to infringe upon the filmmaker's future relationship with the cameraman, as we will see later. When Martelli found out what was going on behind his back he was deeply hurt, and he warned Fellini: "Be careful, Federico, because I'm a vindictive person. . . ." Fellini responded: "What are you going to do, steal the wheels off my car?" Thus, to the sound of bitter laughter, ended ten years of fraternal collaboration. But as anyone who has worked in the movie business knows, that's how it goes: you bond with people for periods of time. There is no such thing as an eternal bond on a movie set.

Having set aside the initial title—*La bella confusione* (*The Beautiful Confusion*)—which had been Flaiano's idea, based on a questionable accounting of his films and because he liked the cabalistic quality of the gothic lettering Gherardi had created, Fellini opted for *8½*. Shooting got underway on May 9, 1962 and finished barely six months later, on October 14. The outdoor shots were taken in real or adapted locations in Tivoli, Filacciano, Viterbo, Ostia, and Fiumicino. But much more important filming was done against constructed backdrops, which the filmmaker had taken a particular liking to in the wake of his experiences with *La Dolce Vita*, in full agreement with his art director. Mastroianni was a blissful man among countless women, from his wife Aimée to his lover Sandra Milo, not to mention the harem that he dreams up at a certain point during a famous sequence in the film. Mastroianni threw himself into the role with giddy enthusiasm that lasted from the first scene to the final shot.

EVERYBODY ON THE CATWALK

An oneiric neorealist, Fellini begins *8 1/2* by narrating a dream: imprisoned in traffic, the film's protagonist, Guido Anselmi (Marcello Mastroianni), escapes out the car window and flies high up into the sky. Is he free? No, he still has one foot tied to a cable of a member of the production staff working on the beach down below. That is until the person we will come to know as the actress Claudia's agent (Mino Doro) issues a peremptory order: "Bring him down for good," and Guido is pulled back down to earth. He wakes up in his room at a hotel and spa where he has taken refuge under the pretext of sickness, either real or make-believe, that has enabled him to delay filming for another two weeks. A doctor (the musician Roberto Nicolosi) takes his blood pressure, asks him how old he is (forty-six according to the script, but forty-three in actual fact: Fellini's age at that precise moment, four years older than Mastroianni). "What interesting things are you working on right now?" asks another doc-

"I reflect my crisis in the character's crisis. At heart, if truth be told, Marcello is me. Every once in a while I feel like I just can't take it anymore."

tor. "Another hopeless film?" The film critic Daumier (the French author Jean Rougeul, voiced over by Alberto Bonucci) comes in wearing a bathrobe. Rougeul was selected after many screen tests, including some by Giulio Cesare Castello and Brunello Rondi. Daumier is supposed to revise the script but he doesn't seem satisfied. The doctor prescribes the usual remedies: spa waters, mudpacks, and baths.

To the sounds of "Ride of the Valkyries," played by a typical little hotel orchestra, hordes of socialites head up the hill toward the springs. To Guido, the beautiful girl who offers him a glass seems just like Claudia (Claudia Cardinale). She will appear often to him later on, as Fellini wrote in a note to Rondi: "Apparitions are an offering of authenticity that the protagonist no longer knows how to accept." Daumier notes, among other reservations: "The symbol of Claudia simply confirms that cinema is irrevocably behind the other arts." The protagonist's friend, the producer Mario Mezzabotta (Mario Pisu), together with his lover Gloria (Barbara

Steel), welcome Guido, calling him "old Snaporaz!" (This will later be Mastroianni's last name in *City of Women*). Mezzabotta is in the middle of divorcing his wife and is totally infatuated with Gloria, who is beautiful, sophisticated, but a real pain in the neck.

Guido goes to pick up his own lover, Signora Carla, at the train station. "The relationship that binds him to this easygoing, big-bottomed woman," reads a note from Fellini, "is based on a sort of opaque physical pleasure, like suckling up to a stupid, nourishing nanny and then falling asleep, satiated and drained." (But the character, played by Milo, comes across more capricious and silly than the one Fellini had imagined based on one of his own sources of inspiration.) His lover is disappointed to discover she has been put up in the train station hotel. While they are eating, Carla tells Guido how good her husband has been while he sings a little, distracted.

On the bed, Guido puts a heavy layer of makeup on the woman and gets her to play other erotic and somewhat morbid games. After making love and while she is reading some comics, Guido falls asleep and dreams of his mother (Giuditta Rissone, De Sica's first wife), dressed in black and standing in an enormous white cemetery. His father (Annibale Ninchi, the same as in *La Dolce Vita*) is there as well, complaining that his tomb is too small. The film producer Pace (Guido Alberti, the "patron" of Italy's Strega Prize, voiced over by Carlo Croccolo) arrives, accompanied by the director of production Conocchia (Mario Conocchia, voiced over by Mario Carotenuto, a playful caricature of Gigetto Giacosi). "How's my boy doing?" asks Guido's old man. Not too well, it seems. Dressed in a school uniform, Guido helps his father climb down into his grave. His mother grabs at him with violent affection, kissing him on the mouth and turning into his wife, Luisa (Anouk Aimée, voiced over by Fulvia Mammi).

On the way back to the hotel and spa, Guido runs into the Cardinal (an eighty-six-year-old retiree and nonactor Tito Masini) in the elevator: "What a wonderful, mystical figure," comments the production inspector Cesarino (Cesarino Miceli Picardi, voiced over by Enzo Liberti). Claudia's agent is there, asking for some commitment on the schedule. Conocchia is there, too, asking for explanations for the scene with the spaceship, as well as the French actress (Madeleine LeBeau, Bogart's ex-lover in *Casablanca* and the future second wife of Pinelli, voiced over by Deddi Savagnone), who wants to talk about her role just as Luise Rainer had wanted before. Guido is struck by an extremely beautiful and mysterious matron (Caterina Boratto).

Cesarino tries to get him to choose the actor who will play the Cardinal from among three old men. Pace comes down the stairs together with his friend (Annie Gorassini) and the director welcomes him by prostrating himself before the producer. He receives a little wristwatch as a gift and happily shows it to everyone.

At an open-air nightclub the orchestra is playing Lehar's "Dance of the Dragonflies." Mezzabotta is dancing—a little too youthfully—with Gloria. Guido has attached a fake Pinocchio's nose to his own face and Conocchia is whispering gossip in Pace's ear. Carla is all alone to one side: Mezzabotta whispers to Guido that his new love, despite the difference in their age, is making him happy. A telepathy performance is underway starring Maya (Mary Indovino) and Maurice (the Scottish comedy writer Jan Dallas, voiced over by Gianrico Tedeschi). Gloria proves once again that she is somewhat of an idiot, in a hysterical scene where she is afraid of Maurice. The magician and Guido speak affectionately with one another, in the way of old accomplices (although in the original script, Guido didn't know Maya and Maurice, and invited them to dinner only to be disappointed by the experience). The telepathist reads Guido's thoughts, revealing a strange phrase that Maya writes down in the background on a blackboard: "asa nisi masa" (which contains the word *anima*, Italian for "soul").

This serves as an imaginative path back to the farmyard of his youth, where peasant workers gave Guido and the other children a bath in the wine tubs. Then, wrapped in a sheet, Guido was led to the bedroom, inebriated from his contact with that perfumed flesh, and a little girl presents him with the riddle: "asa nisi masa."

Below: *Mario Conocchia and Guido Alberti.*

Later on in the atrium of the hotel, there is a feeling of oppression in the air. The extremely beautiful signora is in the middle of a passionate phone call, the French actress is in the midst of a crisis, and Mezzabotta is banging away foolishly on the piano to entertain Gloria. Luisa calls from Rome and Guido asks her: "Why don't you come and visit me?" Before going to bed, the director makes a brief stop in the production room, where he finds everyone at work. However, just like in his dreams, Cesarino is in his underwear and has two girls in his bed. Conocchia shows up in a bathrobe and takes Guido out into the hallway, then makes a scene. He breaks into a self-pitying tone in order to try and convince the director to tell him something about the film, concluding in a mellifluous and threatening tone of voice: "Be careful, because you're not who you once were either!" Guido is struck by what he says: "What if this turned out to be the definitive breakdown?" Back in his own room, he imagines he sees Claudia dressed up as a maid, making his bed. But the telephone rings and his fantasy is interrupted: Guido has to run and see Carla right away. His lover is holed up in the train station hotel with an extremely high fever. Yet another complication.

At the park around the spa, the film director has his long-awaited encounter with the Cardinal. While he tries to talk to the man about his movie, the elderly Cardinal listens to an albatross that calls out oracular phrases for the clergyman's ear. Guido is distracted and starts watching a woman walking down a hill, revealing her legs: he has been familiar with this overlapping of sex and religion since he was a young boy (Marco Gemini). Cutting classes together with a group of rascals, he used to go stare at Saraghina (the American Edra Gale and former singer) alongside the bunker on the beach where she lived. The incarnation of primitive sex, at once horrendous and enthralling, Saraghina drags the young Guido into a sort of dance. When the priests

finally come running and catch up with him, the young scalawag is taken back to school, upbraided before his mother's weeping eyes, crowned with a dunce's cap, and forced to kneel on grain. But the worst moment is yet to come: the confession. Is he remorseful? Not even a little bit. As soon as Guido has another chance he runs back to spy on Saraghina, who turns around to look at him and smiles. At dinner Daumier pounces on Saraghina as a subject: "What does she mean? She is a character out of your childhood memories."

Amid steam and sweat reminiscent of Dante's *Inferno*, the naked people wrapped in their towels and descending to the mudroom foreshadow the Trimalcione swimming pool scene we will see later in *Satyricon*. Conocchia shows up, excited, carrying Guido's clothing. He has to run and see the Cardinal right away; the clergyman is waiting for him. The Cardinal gives Guido five minutes of his time while he rests after having been in the thermal baths. Rather than talk about the film, Guido suddenly feels driven to talk to the Cardinal about himself: "I'm not happy." The Cardinal responds (or doesn't respond?), reciting phrases in Latin.

Out on the main road, among the streetlamps and well-lit cafés, Luisa suddenly appears to the sound of "The Sheik of Araby." A note by Fellini reads: "Their relationship is agonizing and, in its own way, extremely tender. Both of them believe that serenity lies in escaping from the other, but no sooner are they apart then each feels the need to seek out the other and be together. They talk about getting separated but without any real conviction, like two cellmates talk about a prison breakout that they are the first to believe is entirely impossible." (There is a clear reference to Fellini's marriage to Masina, but also to Mastorianni's marriage to Flora Carabella, which was never undone despite the actor's ceaseless sentimental meanderings). Guido watches his wife for a while as he remains out of sight. Their meeting is affectionate, but by the time we see

them again—dancing together at a nightclub—the spell has broken. Something has made Luisa anxious and upset and their friend Rossella (Rossella Falk) scolds Guido.

The entire group moves along, following the producer, to visit the spaceship that has been built for the production. In the film, the ship is supposed to allow the survivors of World War III to escape into outer space (or so everyone says). Small groups climb up the ramp of the tower under the bright spotlights. Luisa is still in a bad mood and refuses to be comforted by kind words from Enrico, a young admirer. Guido lets off some steam with Rossella. He has two problems: the movie and Luisa. "My head is full of confusion right now, and I've got this tower to deal with right here . . . I don't have anything to say but I want to say something all the same." He asks Rossella to try and communicate with the spirits on his behalf, which she does from time to time. Their answer is: you have to hurry up. In the intimacy of their own room, conversation between the

Preceding pages: *Snapshots of life in the harem.*

Above: *Claudia Cardinale plays the extremely beautiful Claudia.*

two spouses turns cross and unpleasant. "What do you want from me?" protests Guido. "What do you want?"

Sitting at an outdoor café with Luisa and Rossella, Guido sees Carla arrive, all dressed up, and sit down by herself at another table. The appearance of Guido's lover exasperates Luisa, but Guido insists he is innocent: "I swear I just saw her now for the first time . . . What's wrong? Who cares if that poor wretch wants to sit down over there?" Now Luisa is sure: "That's what drives me crazy, that you talk as if you were telling the truth. . . ." Guido has no options left but to dream of the impossible: Carla starts to sing, Luisa runs up to compliment her, and the two women become friends.

At this point, what Fellini refers to in his personal notes as "the now inevitable scenes of the home/harem with all his women, including his wife," appears. All the

women in the movie (as well as a few we have not seen before) are gathered together in a large room in a house in the country. Guido returns to distribute gifts, kisses, and sweet words among them. The women undress him and give him a bath in the wine basin like when he was a little boy. Then they dry him off and cover him with caresses.

But there is a problem. Jacqueline (Yvonne Casadei, whose stage name was Jacqueline Bombon) refuses to go "upstairs" because she considers herself too old. The ladies consider this rule unfair and there is a feminine revolution to protest it. The women rise up to the sounds of Wagner's "Ride of the Valkyries," and Guido has to lash them in order to get things under control. It is a sort of game that ends on a rather bitter note with Jacqueline's last performance in Padilla's *Ça c'est Paris.* Then everyone sits down to dinner while Luisa continues to take on domestic responsibilities. Even within the harem their relationship seems to embody a different emotion, and Guido is struck by memories from their wedding.

Pushed to the limit and stirred up by Conocchia, the producer insists that the film director choose the actors he will use in the film. He has brought clips of the audition and screens them in the local movie theater. Daumier is willing to perform as his usual, hypercritical self, but Guido (even though he is daydreaming), has him hung up on the spot by the production thugs. Various auditions by a number of different would-be actresses for the roles of Carla, Saraghina, and the wife all roll by. For Guido and Luisa, these tryouts, interwoven with personal and authentic references, are like the theater performance Hamlet organized for the Danish royalty. At a certain point, Luisa cannot take it anymore and leaves the theater. Guido follows her out and she nails him to the wall with a definitive: "Go to hell!"

Claudia appears, sparkling with youth and enthusiasm, and the film director takes off with her in his car, doubly happy because this way he has also managed to escape making a final decision. Once again, we hear the persuasive notes of "The Sheik of Araby." Guido and the actress stop for a while in an abbey cloister. He talks to her, trying to explain his crisis, his inability, his desire to start everything all over again from scratch.

The time has come: caught between two thugs from the production staff like Josef K. at the end of Kafka's *The Trial*, Guido is literally carried to the room where the press conference is being held for the start of filming in the shadow of the spaceship. The journalists are restless, aggressive, and resentful. Guido doesn't answer and the producer growls at him: "Say something, anything!" The director hides underneath the table. He feels that the only escape left is suicide.

"Take it all down, nobody's going to make the movie any more," shouts someone by the half-dismantled tower. Chatting together, Daumier compliments Guido for having given up on the project, which he considers a step along the path to a healthy "education in silence." As Guido is about to leave with the critic, Maurice the telepathist comes dashing up: "Everything's ready," he announces happily. It's true: the characters from the film are all on their way back, dressed in white, headed toward the tower. No one is stopping them anymore. In fact, the spotlights are already being turned on and Guido cannot stop himself from taking over. Mega-phone in hand, he orders everyone to climb the stairs that lead up into the spaceship, and sets them off in a circus parade (the only person exempted is the Cardinal, in view of his tender old age). Holding one another by the hand to form an extremely long line, the characters start to skip a ring-around-the-rosy to the sounds of a fanfare played by three clowns (Polidor is there, too) and directed by Guido as a child, wearing a white school uniform. Guido takes Luisa by the hand and heads off with her to take her place in the midst of all the hullabaloo.

It is nighttime. There is a small fanfare of people in the spotlight, then only the little boy is left, playing the final notes of the marching tune on his flute. Then he also disappears into the darkness.

Above: (clockwise from left) Characters in the film begin to descend; Guido's mother (Giuditta Rissone); Jan Dallas and Marcello Mastroianni; a clown.

8 ½   **149**

FROM ONE TRIMPH TO THE NEXT

The film debuted on February 14, 1963, earning 755,971,000 lira at the box office. The coproducers were once again Francinex in Paris. It was presented (though not entered for an award) at the Cannes Film Festival in May. However, it won the grand prize at the Moscow Film Festival on July 18, to the displeasure of conformists, the enthusiasm of young people, and the bewilderment of famous astronaut Yuri Gagarin, who commented: "This film is more mysterious than the cosmos." Wherever *8½* was shown, it was a success, even though among the audience, there were those who couldn't seem to distinguish between dreams and reality, so much so that the distribution company created copies of the film for outlying towns and the provinces in which the dream sequences were sepia-tinted. But in the wake of this exhilarating success, a tragic event struck Fellini deeply a few years later: the boy who had played him in the film died.

One particularly curious and extremely fortuitous development was a Broadway musical adaptation of the film, which Fellini and the screenwriters agreed to as long as their names were not associated with the production in any way. There were numerous changes, starting with the title, which became *Nine*. The adaptation was written by Mario Fratti, with Arthur Kopit, words and music by Maury Yeston, and the production was directed by Tommy Tune. The whole experience of film director "Guido Contini" takes place in an allusive, abstract, 1960s Venice, where the protagonist and his younger self are surrounded by sixteen women. The star of the show's first run was Raul Julia, and it played for 729 nights at the 46th Street Theater. In addition to various versions of the show that toured the world, the musical was revived in 2003, with Antonio Banderas starring in a production at the Eugene O'Neill Theater for more than 283 shows. In 2009, Rob Marshall eventually turned the show into another movie (the same thing that happened with *Nights of Cabiria*), with a cast that included male characters and set in a different location.

Left: *Federico Fellini and Angelo Rizzoli at the Academy Awards.*

Above: *Federico Fellini holding his Oscar, with Annabella and Sidney Poitier.*

"A week before starting the film, I dreamed that someone was scooping out my right eye with a spoon. It didn't hurt. I was surprised. Maybe that dream meant that I didn't need my right eye—the eye of reality—to make this film, but just my left eye, the eye of imagination."

JULIET OF THE SPIRITS

GIULIETTA DEGLI SPIRITI

THE FILM OF SEPARATIONS

For fifty years, Fellini's marriage to Masina was the most solid relationship in Italian cinema but at the same time the one that people gossiped about the most. These things rarely got out into the press, with the exception on the eve of *The Swindle*'s debut, when there was brief talk in Venice of "lady swapping" between the Fellinis and Richard Basehart and his wife Valentina Cortese. Some people claimed that marital relations between the newlyweds came to a halt after the death of their only son and her long illness following the dramatic event. Others, mostly women jealous of Masina's good fortune, insisted that she wasn't woman enough for Fellini or able to deal with his imaginative and fantastical side. But these rumors were categorically contradicted by the filmmaker's almost morbid attachment to his wife, which manifested itself in continuous phone calls—sometimes as many as ten per day—in which he would ask where she was, where she had been, whom she had met, what she was planning to make for dinner, and so on. On the other hand, Masina was equally fond of her husband, so much so that she gradually turned into his best public defender. While always ready to challenge him and argue in private, publicly Masina remained, always and under all circumstances, her husband's official advocate. Anyone who went against him had to be prepared to deal with her.

It is important to add that Masina had always appeared unwilling to tackle the characters that her filmmaker husband had created for her. Disappointed when she was not given the role of the newlywed bride in *The White Sheik*, and equally so when there was no role for her in *I Vitelloni*, she only accepted to dress in rags and play the fool Gelsomina out of obedience. Not unlike most actresses, and still young enough to cut a pretty figure, Masina thought her character in *The Swindle* was rather miserable (and she had a point); and even *Nights of Cabiria*, which her vital, invincible nature led her to sympathize with, was more appropriate for dramatization than for the grotesque. Going back to work with

her husband after a seven-year interval, during which she had experienced a turning point in her life (Masina was over forty), she finally entertained the hope that she might play a woman she resembled. Masina was even willing to sacrifice her own personal discretion: in fact, she accepted to interpret a questionable chapter from her own personal life—a wife who pays a detective to investigate her husband's clandestine love affairs. In short, Masina offered herself over completely to the project. But despite this, their reasons for disagreement remained, and even grew worse.

Masina wanted the film to concentrate on her quarrel with her husband, played by Mario Pisu. She did not appreciate—and would never appreciate—the esoteric, phantasmagoric, and sexy surroundings that Fellini invented for the main character. Furthermore, she felt that Gherardi had outfitted her character in an inappropriate manner. He even went too far as to force her to wear a large, crushed hat to make her look like a mushroom that emphasized her short height. She didn't even like how Di Venanzo shot her from close up. A rumor began to spread among the troupe about a night meeting called by Martelli in order to shoot some of the scenes again. By then, Masina no longer trusted Fracassi either, ever since she had heard some of his private contacts with Katherine Hepburn's agent in an attempt to substitute her as the protagonist.

Page 153: *Fred Williams and Giulietta Masina.*

Opposite: *Alba Cancellieri, Sandra Milo, and Lou Gilbert.*

Below: *Sandra Milo as Suzy in a drawing by Fellini.*

14-9-65.

Left: *Giulietta Masina and Sandra Milo.*

Below: *Giulietta lets herself be seduced by Suzy's (Sandra Milo) esoteric and falsely captivating world.*

Opposite: *Federico Fellini and Giulietta Masina in the pinewoods outside Fregene.*

Shooting began on July 27, 1964 amid this rather unpleasant atmosphere. The first scene was filmed on the steps at the hotel and spa in San Pellegrino, with the scene between Masina and Cortese on their pilgrimage to see the holy man Bishma. Shooting was long and tormented and would last until January 31 of the following year. Over the course of those six months, it seemed that every single relationship Fellini had held dear up until that moment was destined for destruction, starting with his collaboration with Di Venanzo. Things went awry right from day one: Fellini and Di Venanzo both vented their anger with friends who arrived on the set, apparently for the same reasons. They claimed that "that other guy" was good in black and white, but still didn't know what to do with color. Fellini's fraternal relationship with Fracassi was also on the rocks, which

resulted in a daily deterioration in the relationships around the Fellini-Rizzoli axis, a bond that had previously appeared solid enough to weather any storm. *Juliet of the Spirits* marked the end of their collaboration as well. In any case, Fellini had secretly reconnected with De Laurentiis as early as February 1964. Fellini fought with the screenwriters as well. He quarreled with Flaiano for silly reasons, some of them personal, and grew distant from Pinelli, who wouldn't return to work on another Fellini movie until twenty years later.

Filming took place at the Safa Palatino, where a little beach house was re-created that was an accurate reproduction of Fellini's family place in the pine forest outside Fregane. A number of scenes were shot on Fellini's favorite beaches on the Tyrrhenian Sea, which played a part in various films starting with *The White Sheik*.

SIEGE OF
THE BARBARIANS

The camera frames a villa that seems to come straight out of a drawing by Antonio Rubino. Signora Giulietta (Giulietta Masina) lives here and we see her interacting with the two maids, Teresina (Milena Vukotic, voiced over by Anna Rosa Garatti) and Elisabetta (Elisabetta Gray, voiced over by Lily Tirinnanzi), trying on one wig after another for the candlelit dinner she has planned as a surprise for her husband to celebrate their fifteenth wedding anniversary. But Giorgio, a brilliant PR executive, shows up with a group of friends, including Val (Valentina Cortese), the lawyer (Mario Conocchia), the sculptor (Silvana Jachino), and the Genius (Eugenio Mastropietro, voiced over by Silvio Spaccesi), whom he presents as "simply the greatest diviner in the world." Once she has gotten over her disappointment, Giulietta allows the Genius to perform experiments on her with his pendulum, earning applause from Giorgio's friends as the group celebrates her wedding dance with her husband.

The small group of guests have gathered together in the darkness around a séance board, where almost immediately the diviner invokes a ghost by the name of Iris, who has a message to send: "Love for everyone." In a flash, Giulietta gets the impression that she can see

"I said what I could about women, but they didn't get it."

Iris (Sandra Milo). An evil spirit, Olaf, interferes with the séance, insulting the ladies. At the same time, the phone rings. It's the same call they have been receiving more and more often: someone listens to hear who answers the phone then immediately hangs up. Speaking through the medium, Olaf forcefully reproaches Giulietta: "Who do you think you are? You're nobody, nobody at all. You're of no importance whatsoever." Overcome with emotion, the protagonist faints. The Genius responds: "But this lady is extremely gifted."

The next morning, Giulietta wakes up to the sound of Giorgio's car driving off. She thinks she sees a monster appear down in the garden, but it is just the gardener doing his work. But when she goes near the séance board, she hears it knocking around like it did during the séance.

Out on the beach, where Giulietta has gone together with her sister Adele's twin daughters, her friend

Doctor Raffaele (Felice Fulchignoni, voiced over by Renato Cominetti) advises her not to participate in any more paranormal experiments. Giulietta describes the fairy-tale visions she had when she was a little girl, but the doctor insists: "A scientific mind cannot help but be offended listening to such naive words." And yet, when she closes her eyes, Giulietta still feels she can see Iris. In the meantime, a real Iris arrives—the beautiful Suzy who lives in an adjacent villa, a house enveloped by scandal and mystery. She appears together with a large court of Asian servants, an image that is reminiscent of the shots taken on the beach in *The White Sheik*. During a moment of drowsiness, Giulietta dreams of an old man wearing a homburg hat and red dressing gown (Alberto Plebani, voiced over by Ennio Balbo; Plebani would reappear later as a private detective.). The old man emerges from the water dragging a large boatman's hemp rope and takes advantage of the fact that the woman is standing there in order to pass it to her. Despite the fact that she would rather not get involved, Giulietta drags a number of things up on the shore: a raft with several dried out, stiff horses then a rudimental sailing vessel that we find to be filled up with savage, obscene characters. It's a veritable barbaric invasion; others show up in a second vessel or emerge from the waves.

Fortunately, Giulietta wakes up. Suzy has sent over a basket of fruit as a gift and waves to her from afar before running down into the sea.

Going back to her house through the little pinewoods, Giulietta meets her sisters, Adele (Luisa Della Noce) and Sylva (Sylva Koscina), together with their mother (Caterina Boratto), who despite her age is still a beautiful woman. The sophisticated figures of these three women depress Giulietta and she struggles to ignore their provocative remarks about her husband as they accuse him of various rash acts. When the little group finally separates, her mother issues Giulietta a severe order: "You have to take better care of yourself!"

That evening, while Giulietta is watching television with the maid, Giorgio returns home. Giulietta wants to tell him about the dream she had on the beach, but he is tired and just wants to go to bed and sleep. While he is asleep in their big bed, Giorgio says a name, twice: Gabriella.

The following morning at breakfast, Giulietta struggles to hide her anxiety while she asks Giorgio who "Gabriella" is. Her husband avoids the question. Giulietta is threading peppers onto a string when Val shows up to invite her to a meeting with Bishma:

"The man/woman who embodies the secret of the two sexes."

Walking up the dark stairs of a grand hotel (filmed in St. Vincent), Giulietta has an almost surreal vision of a wedding feast. But Val calls out to her from the terrace to introduce her to Bishma. Bishma (Valeska Geert, voiced over by Alghiero Noschese) proves to be an ambiguous little person, somewhat of a caricature, and practically in catalepsy. Two Indians—a man and a ballerina—act as Bishma's assistant, entertaining an almost entirely female audience. They let everyone listen to their master's recorded voice as Bishma invites them to look at a simple apple with new eyes and so on.

Giulietta has a private encounter with Bishma, during which she confides that she is afraid Giorgio has a lover. The guru expresses himself with enigmas, while his assistants mime his every word. But suddenly Bishma explodes in an obscene, incomprehensible manner, causing Giulietta to have alarming visions in which Iris turns into the sinful image of Fanny the dancer. Once it is time to leave, a more reassuring message arrives announcing something beautiful and new for the evening,

connected with something called the "oblivion drink."

Behind the wheel of her car, Giulietta is driving through the night, telling her friends about an episode during which her grandfather ran off in a fit of passion when she was a young girl. The event had a deep effect on her. She had been with her grandfather (Lou Gilbert, voiced over by Romolo Valli) at the circus, when suddenly he began to flirt with the star of the troupe: "A beautiful woman makes me feel more religious." Later on Giulietta imagined that the mature Professor Defilippis and the dancer flew away on the old circus airplane, followed by the whole family and the headmaster (Friedrich von Ledebur, voiced over by Roberto Bertea), who was furious.

On her way home, Giulietta encounters Josè (José Luis de Vilallonga, voiced over by Riccardo Cucciolla) in the garden. José is a Spanish nobleman and a friend of Giorgio's. He is preparing the "oblivion drink" useful for predicting the future, in other words "sangria" (Although Fellini hardly ever drank, he had a fun time making a batch of this Spanish beverage for paparazzi during a break while filming *La Dolce Vita*). The Spaniard

Preceding pages: Suzy on the swing.

Above: *Giulietta Masina dancing with José Luis de Vilallonga on the lawn of the little villa in Fregene— a perfect copy of the one she owned in real life.*

continues his monologue during dinner. He is so fascinating that he almost seems unreal. José tells of his friendship with bullfighters, using Giulietta's red scarf to imitate their movements. Giorgio improvises a parody of the bull, frightening his wife, who retreats into the arms of their guest. When they are left alone, José recites verses by Garcia Lorca to her. Giorgio takes the telescope his friend has given him as a gift out into the garden and uses it to spy on the window in the neighboring house, watching Suzy. They talk about the bawdy parties that take place in the neighbor's house, suspicious festivals that the other neighbors have complained about and that have drawn the police on more than one occasion.

When they go to bed, Giulietta wants to talk to Giorgio, but he is sticking earplugs in his ears. While they read before falling asleep, the woman listens to José's quiet footsteps on the floor upstairs. Waking up in the middle of the night, she realizes that Giorgio is making a phone call. Her question—"Who were you calling?"—goes unanswered.

Adele believes that Giulietta has a right to know everything and drags her down to the "Lynx Eye" detective agency, despite Giulietta's reluctance. Dressed as a priest for professional reasons, the director of the agency (Alberto Plebani), together with his suspicious looking colleague (Federico Valli, voiced over by Nino Dal Fabbro), outlines a plan for following Giorgio. "Are you sure you want to know?" he asks. Giulietta remembers the headmaster's moralistic words and replies "Yes."

The Spaniard is in the garden, playing the soundtrack to the film on his guitar. But Giulietta doesn't feel up to dealing with him and goes for a walk in the pine forest.

Below: *Giulietta Masina as a little fairy in a drawing by Fellini.*

She visits the sculptor, who is with her powerfully muscular models. Convinced that she needs to give the Creator back his physical dimension, the artist claims that "God is the most beautiful body in existence." Giulietta, on the other hand, remembers that when she was a little girl, she imagined that God hid behind a large door in the ceiling of the sisters' little theater. She made a deal with a friend of hers, Laura, to tell her what God was like. She approaches the door when, while playing the part of a martyred saint, she is bound to a grate and hoisted up high into the air. But her grandfather interrupts the show, protesting: "What are you trying to make of these poor innocent souls, crazy girls?" He stands behind the hoist himself, brings the girl down, unties her, and takes her away amid the usual complaints and insults from the headmaster.

Giulietta discovers Suzy's cat in her garden and takes it back to its rightful owner. It is an excuse to get a better look at the house of sin. There is a Charleston playing as she peers in, half curious and half afraid: it is a sort of enchanted palace full of strange people. A monk (Carlo Pisacane, voiced over by Alghiero Noschese) is gathering alms. Suzy's grandmother is babbling in bad Italian. Between one phone call and the next, Suzy gives her neighbor a friendly welcome, offering her a glass of champagne and drawing a few muscle-bound men, who are there to work on the house, in as well. During her guided tour, Giulietta meets a girl named Ariette (Dany Parîs, alias Eliana Merolle), who is always attempting to commit suicide and is reminded of a schoolmate who threw herself in a canal. Looking out a window, Giulietta sees the property around her own house. It is as if she were looking at it through the eyes of someone else. She is amused by the vulgar furnishings: the mirror over the bed, a slide that leads directly down into the pool, from which Suzy emerges, completely naked, inviting her guest to do the same but to no avail.

Now that they have become friends, Suzy and Giulietta pedal on their bicycles across the little pine forest to the notes of an equestrian circus tune. Suzy puts Giulietta in an elevator made from a wicker basket that leads into a sort of tree house, where she draws in two young men who are passing by. Invited to join in their group frolicking, Giulietta runs away instead.

While Giulietta is reading a story to her nieces, a phone call comes from the Lynx agency: the result of the investigation on Giorgio is ready. At the agency headquarters, the investigators provide proof of her husband's infidelity. Offering the usual hypocritical commentary, the investigators show her a film and a series of photographs of Giorgio together with a woman who hides behind the wide brim of her hat. They have identified her as Gabriella, a fashion model, and give Giulietta her address. Giulietta watches the film in silence, even when she listens to a conversation between Giorgio and his lover that they have recorded. Advising her not to take things too hard, the director presents Giulietta with the bill.

There is a party at Suzy's villa. Giulietta appears wearing a flashy red dress. She claims that she really wants to have fun, but she is more repulsed than attracted by the *dolce vita* style characters and entertainment she finds there. The party is dominated by Mody, Suzy's boyfriend (Raffaele Guida, voiced over by Enzo Liberti), a Middle Eastern patriarch who concentrates on playing cards, indifferent to what is going on around him. Amid morbid and esoteric games, the women have organized a sexy catwalk down the stairway like the ones held in Italy's legalized bordellos. Giulietta wills herself to join in. She is struck by the image of a new "White Sheik," the extremely handsome son of Suzy's boyfriend. After a voyeuristic raid with electric flashlights to try and surprise couples who are hiding from view, Suzy brings Giulietta into the alcove, where women prepare her for a love encounter. She is destined for the young sheik and is more than a little tempted to give herself over to him: but suddenly an image of the martyred saint appears in the mirror over the bed. A voice shouts out: "Giulietta, what are you doing?" and the woman runs away. We see her leaving at dawn amid the statues in the garden.

At a garden party in Fregene, the horde of friends has taken back the garden . Everyone is there, even Signora Muller (voiced over by Benita Martini), an American psychotherapist who has introduced a game of psychodrama. Giulietta is running late, trapped between the bedroom and the bathroom, assaulted by apparitions that later, as the crisis grows worse, turn into a real invasion: the barbarians of the subconscious are putting the villa to siege! Wide-eyed, bewildered, and distracted, the protagonist joins the party. Here and there in the garden, she catches glimpses of a disturbing group of spirits: nuns in a line running around; Iris; the threatening headmaster; the martyred saint; and the detectives. The situation grows worse when she takes part in the psychodrama: even the characters from everyday life seem to have become detached from reality. José says, a little more reassuringly: "I wouldn't know what advice to give her. I just want her to be

happy." Giorgio slips away without anybody noticing; the lawyer wants Giulietta to sue Giorgio for adultery and to betray her husband immediately by going to bed with him. As the group is breaking up, the psychotherapist goes for a walk with Giulietta and tries to open her eyes to the truth: the pain over her imminent breakup with Giorgio is not real; by now the wife actually wants, albeit subconsciously, her husband to leave.

Giulietta shows up at Gabriella's house for the central scene, but the only person she finds is an old governess who is getting her lady's suitcases ready. Gabriella is set to take off with her boyfriend. The telephone rings. It is Gabriella. She is willing to talk with her rival, but

Above top: *Fellini in a basket among the trees.*

Above below: *Fellini works through a scene with Sandra Milo.*

doesn't give Giulietta much satisfaction: this is the way things are and there is not much to say about it.

When Giulietta gets back home, Giorgio is packing his suitcases. He doesn't say so openly, but he has decided to leave her. While her husband eats alone, Giulietta watches a dance act on the television. At the end of the performance, an old clown gives her an ironic, compassionate look from the television screen. Giorgio pronounces a few unsolicited excuses, advice from the doctor, and jumbled plans. When he finally leaves, Giulietta has to face an empty, desolate house.

It is time for the grand invasion. Spirits mixed together with images of real people come flooding in from all corners: from policemen to the governess, from the psychologist to the Genius, from the nuns to the headmaster, from the Spaniard to the Sheik. We see a funeral hearse carrying Laura away, followed by a horde of different figures—warriors, Nazis, nuns, Roman soldiers, revelers from Suzy's parties. The most threat-ening apparition seems to be her Mamma. Giulietta is about to fall asleep when she wants to open that famous door in the ceiling that now appears in her bedroom. Her mother forbids it, but Giulietta finds the strength to respond: "You don't scare me anymore." With these magical words, the door springs open and Giulietta climbs into the storage space where she finds herself as a little girl, tied up on a grate and surrounded by red paper flames. Defeated like a wicked old witch, the mother retreats, growing older and uglier. The grandfather and the ballerina show up on the little cir-cus airplane again to take care of the child. Meanwhile, the spirits have packed up their carnival and are pulling back. There is a great mess and a sense of defeat, as they make their way to the ships they came in on and head out to sea.

Giulietta goes into the sunlight and starts walking along a path in the little pine forest, while a friendly voice says: "Listen carefully, I can help you. . . ."

DOUBT

Several painful events took place between the time the film was completed and its release. On February 3, 1965, Di Venanzo died suddenly. In addition to the sadness caused by his untimely death, Fellini felt guilty for having had such a heated argument with him during the final phase of their collaboration. On June 27, Bernhard, the analyst who had been Fellini's faithful guide for four years, died, leaving the filmmaker alone, upset, and emotionally shell-shocked.

In August a quarrel with Luigi Chiarini, the director of the Venice Film Festival, began. Chiarini was furious that Fellini had unexpectedly abandoned the festival, after having promised to debut *Juliet of the Spirits* there. The two made ferocious accusations at one another in the newspapers, but no one was able to ascertain what had really happened between them. It was not clear whether the failed screening was really due to technical delays in the film itself or to the filmmaker's reluctance to return to Venice after the scathing reviews he had received for *The Swindle* ten years earlier. In lieu of what was supposed to be its glorious festival debut, the film was released on September 30, with mixed reviews. Its overall box office earnings would top 770,340,000 lira. The first edition of the film was 3,593 meters long. In France, the film was 129 minutes long, 145 in Great Britain, and 148 in the United States, where *Juliet of the Spirits* debuted in New York on January 4, receiving the same mixed reviews.

*"I think I read the short story
by Edgar Allan Poe, but only
after having finished the film.
I thought it was wonderful."*

TOBY DAMMIT
AN EPISODE IN SPIRITS OF THE DEAD

THE DEVIL IS A LITTLE GIRL

In the aftermath of what had been an overall unsatisfactory experience with *Juliet of the Spirits*, Fellini's private life became afflicted with a series of painful events that would last for a few years. It began with Masina: even though she defended "her" film, she remained unsatisfied with it and began quarrelling with Rizzoli, Fracassi, Flaiano, Pinelli, and Di Venanzo. The honeymoon was over with Gherardi as well: Fellini's art director was accused of doing things a little too much his own way, undercutting the director and so on. Fellini's relationship with De Laurentiis also soured: Fellini agreed unenthusiastically to shoot *G. Mastorna's Voyage* using the screenplay he had put together with Dino Buzzati. Construction had already started at Dinocittà (a large piazza with the overarching Cologne cathedral and fake airplane with which the protagonist would land in the hereafter) when Fellini brought the crisis of *8½* to the extreme, withdrawing from his responsibilities with a sudden, embarrassing letter of resignation presented to De Laurentiis. If that weren't bad enough, Fellini also suffered from poor health and was admitted at the Salvator Mundi clinic on April 10, 1967. The diagnosis was pleurisy, but the doctors suspected something worse. Everyone spent a few days in deep concern for the filmmaker's health, including De Laurentiis who, despite the legal action he had taken (even including an order to seize Fellini's property), continued to care about him. Fortunately Fellini's health improved, and during his convalescence, another Neapolitan appeared, the producer Alberto Grimaldi. Fresh from the enormous success of his two films with Sergio Leone, Grimaldi was determined to bring Fellini back onto a film set. He was willing to make *Mastorna,* so much so that he bought the rights from De Laurentiis, paying off the considerable debts that De Laurentiis had incurred and placating his ire. However, conversations on the subject yielded little success, despite the fact that preparation for the film moved haltingly forward, with research conducted in Bulgaria and Romania in an attempt to find external locations at bargain prices. But ultimately, the choice of switching projects prevailed. It was championed by Fellini himself, who had become convinced that the film Buzzati had baptized "La dolce death" couldn't help but bring him misfortune. And in fact, despite having put together an excellent screenplay, Fellini would continue to talk about the movie, imagine it, and plan for it without ever actually sitting down and making it.

This stagnant situation was resolved by an unexpected proposal from a Parisian producer, Raymond Eger, who was planning to shoot a film titled *Histoires extraordinaires* (*Extraordinary Stories*), based on the short stories of Edgar Allan Poe. Eger owned Les Films Marceu and had dreamed up the idea while reading a book by the American author during time in a clinic, recovering from a heart attack. He had already attempted to get something done in the United States, but without success, and had decided to make a go of it alone. After inquiring with a number of star directors, he had finally reached several less ambitious agreements with Roger Vadim, who would make *Metzengenstein* with Jane Fonda, and Louis Malle, who would film *William Wilson* in Bergamo with Brigitte Bardot and Alain Delon. At that point the producer, who needed Fellini as a way to

Page 167: *Terence Stamp with the veteran theater prompter Luigi Battaglia, whom the Italian writer Luigi Pirandello included in his* I gigantic della montagna *(The Giants of the Mountain), and Paul Cooper.*

Opposite top: *A guest at the awards celebration.*

Opposite bottom: *Toby Dammit (Terence Stamp) welcomed at the arrival of Father Spagna (Salvo Randone).*

Below: *A drawing of Toby Dammit by Federico Fellini.*

Above: *Three drawings by Federico Fellini: The Cockpit of the Airplane, The Broken Bridge, and The Road.*

Below: *Federico Fellini and Alberto Grimaldi.*

elevate the ambitions of his undertaking, avoided pushing any one title on the Italian filmmaker. Even though he wanted to see Poe's *The Tell-Tale Heart* included in the film, he gave Fellini the freedom to choose. Unfortunately there was no better way to plunge Fellini into doubt, which had become the director's daily bread. Fellini was a rather unwilling reader, in part as a way to keep interference out of his own work, and turned the necessary literary research over to his faithful collaborator, Liliana Betti. Betti quickly set about reading and summarizing all of Poe's stories. For a little while, Fellini toyed with the idea of teaming up with Sordi and shooting *The Cask of Amontillado* in Naples. But images of the collapsed Ariccia Bridge led him to favor *Never Bet the Devil Your Head* instead.

In his office on Via della Fortuna 27 (an address the superstitious filmmaker considered to be a positive sign), Fellini sketched out the story and updated the tale with his new collaborator, Bernardino Zapponi. He thought up the story of an English film star who travels to Rome to shoot "the first Catholic Western" and survives right until the final consequences of his alcoholic delirium. The character was undoubtedly inspired in some ways by his experience with Broderick Crawford years before. The part was offered to Peter O'Toole, who initially declared he was flattered by Fellini's interest and was ready to sign, but later on, after having read the script, believed he had glimpsed some glaring allusions to his own private behavior and phoned Fellini from London, insulting the filmmaker roundly. O'Toole's invective was paid back. Rarely in the history of cinema has an erstwhile agreement ended with such a brutal phone conversation.

There was a moment of crisis, as other hastily selected candidates proved impossible to hire, including Marlon Brando and James Fox. Finally an agreement was reached with Terence Stamp, an entirely respectable name for the billboard. Fellini had never seen any of Stamp's films, and Stamp was welcomed by the filmmaker with the usual mistrust Fellini reserved for actors who were in some way forced on him by circumstances. But Stamp immediately proved considerate and friendly, and before long Fellini had nicknamed him

"Terenzino Francobollo," an Italian term of endearment that played on the literal translation of Stamp's last name. Painters with incredible imagination such as Renzo Vespignani and Fabrizio Clerici sketched out potential set designs, but the final plans were not established until Piero Tosi stepped in to take care of both design and the costumes. In the meantime, Fellini had decided that Poe's limping, black-suited devil would be a sinister child in the film, shot playing with a ball, and gave the job to a twenty-two-year-old Russian.

An authentic maestro, Giuseppe Rotunno arrived to operate the cameras. Peppino, as Rotunno was affectionately nicknamed, would remain Fellini's magical eye for the following three films, up until *And the Ship Sails On* and Fellini's customary (although in this particular case,

much later than usual) tumultuous breakup. Overall, filming lasted twenty-six days, beginning in October 1967. It started in the airport, where Toby Dammit was welcomed by a film-loving priest named Father Spagna and moved on to Hadrian's villa, where the imaginary and grotesque "Lupa d'oro," or "Golden Wolf" awards were held. In an attempt to escape this party, the English film star heads recklessly down the hairpin curves of the roads around the Castelli Romani until. . . .

Above: *Federico Fellini and Bernardo Zapponi.*

Below: *Fabrizio Clerici's vision of the collapsed bridge.*

Non scommettere la testa col diavolo Dammit. Di F. Fellini.

A CRAZY MAN'S STORY

Toby Dammit begins, like the unrealized film *Mastorna*, with an airplane landing. In this case there is no deadly accident suggested, but the protagonist's voice declares from offstage: "It was the first time I came to Rome, and I had the feeling that this trip . . . had some extreme importance for me." He hopes that the captain will turn the plane around, but "the invisible lines of the airport had already imprisoned the airplane, drawing it irresistibly down to the ground." The famous actor Toby Dammit is welcomed by a horde of paparazzi, just as Sylvia was in *La Dolce Vita*, but given the situation, there is no trace of festive charlatanism. Against the spectral backdrop of Fiumicino Airport at sunset, the crude white light of camera flashes and the way Toby violently chases the photographers is somewhat shocking. Under the combined effects of drugs and alcohol, the actor defends himself from an enemy only he can see.

Father Spagna (Salvo Randone, voiced over by Giuseppe Rinaldi), the priest who represents the producers of the "first Catholic Western," is there to meet him. (Spagna is an elegantly ironic send-up of Fellini's friend Father Arpa, who had produced Rossellini's *Era notte a Roma*, or *Escape by Night*: a generous undertaking characterized by a certain impertinence that got him briefly thrown in jail.) Toby's only concern is the Ferrari they promised him in his contract. Father Spagna nods kindheartedly while the actor takes in a host of chaotic visions of Rome from the car window: the individuals wandering its streets, the Colosseum, the traffic jams, an accident. A gypsy comes up to the car, intent on telling his fortune, but after one glance at Toby's hand, she refuses to talk. Toby sees an image of the blonde girl (Marina Yaru) in nineteenth-century dress, ready to throw him a ball: it is a vision not unlike those in *Juliet of the Spirits* that the actor had already experienced at the top of the escalator in the airport and would have countless times again as the movie unfolds.

In a TV studio, the actor unwillingly submits to an interview, answering the silly questions in an arrogant, sarcastic manner: "Did you have an unhappy childhood?" "Oh no! My mother was extremely happy when she was beating me." He claims he does not believe in God at all, but does in the Devil. And the Devil does not look the way most people think of him. The Devil is a little girl.

In an open-air nightclub that seems like an expressionist version of Caracalla's, surrounded by grotesque and spectral guests, Toby is involved in an absurd award ceremony not unlike the one planned for *Mastorna*. A "Golden Wolf" is given to an old blind comedian who is wearing dark sunglasses and uses a cane (this is Polidor, in an obvious reference to Totò). When it is Toby's turn to take the stage, everyone applauds him, asking him to give a little performance. He launches into a speech, interjecting his words with lines from Shakespeare's *Macbeth* that perfectly sum up his own situation: "Life is a tale told by a fool / full of sound and fury / signifying nothing." At a certain point he runs away, just like Ekberg did from Caracalla's, though this time, driven by a self-destructive impulse.

Outside there is the flaming red Ferrari that has become his. The actor starts racing through the Roman night, leaves the city, and heads into the labyrinth of the Castelli Romani, small towns bordering the city. The silhouettes of painted cooks inviting him to dine at restaurants in the area appear in front of him like sinister signs. Driving like a madman, he crashes against a wooden fence, nearly sweeps away a flock of sheep and a crew of workers laboring at night. We reach the crumbled bridge, preceded by various street signs indicating that this is no longer a through-road. Like a date with destiny, the child-devil reappears in his headlights: she throws the ball, inviting him to play, and Toby races off at top speed to try and jump over to the other side of the bridge. He barely makes it, but there is a cable suspended halfway in the air, now covered with blood. The ball bounces along until it reaches Toby Dammit's severed head. We see the little girl's face and then dawn arrives.

Below: Toby Dammit as Edgar Allan Poe in a drawing by Fellini.

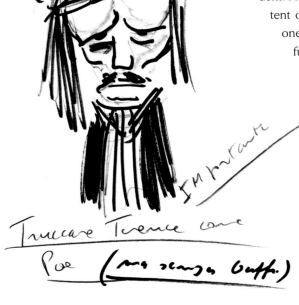

AT CANNES, FELLINI IS FOLLOWED BY A DELUGE

The French title was *Histoires extraordinaires*, produced by Cocinor and Film Marceau, Paris, PEA (Produzioni Europee Associate). The other episodes included Vadim's *Metzegerstein* and Malle's *William Wilson*. The film debuted at the Cannes Film Festival on May 17, 1968. That year was marked by cultural rebellion across Europe, and the film was the last movie screened before the more political cineastes had the festival suspended. Critics responded well to the movie, which was subsequently released in Italy, debuting on July 24. It earned a total of 512,729,000 lira at the box office. Stamp would work with other Italian film directors, including Pasolini (*Teorema*, or *Theorem*) and Nelo Risi (*Una stagione all'inferno*, or *A Season in Hell*, in which he played the poet Arthur Rimbaud). After that, Stamp experienced a spiritual crisis that led him to trek around Asia, but his work with Fellini had left its mark on him, so much so that not long before this volume was published, Stamp tried to acquire the rights to *Mastorna* in order to make the character his own in an Australian production.

"When you work for television, your imaginary audience grows thinner, becoming a single person: the one standing in front of the TV. Therefore you feel more available, open, intimate."

FELLINI: A DIRECTOR'S NOTEBOOK

BLOCK-NOTES DI UN REGISTA

ON THE RUNDOWN FIELDS OF DINOCITTÀ

As happened from time to time for Fellini, the enterprising producer Peter Goldfarb contacted him out of the blue. Goldfarb had produced *Sperimental Hour* for American television and wanted at all costs to do something, even just a fifty-minute piece, with the great filmmaker. He was dying to discover Fellini's secrets, rummage through his drawers, understand his method. Relieved at the opportunity to take a break from preparing *Satyricon*, which in the meantime Fellini had agreed to make for Grimaldi, the filmmaker entertained himself by inventing relatively impossible programs, such as interviewing Mao (a challenge that an important member of Italy's Communist party would attempt to help him meet, though to no avail) or make his way behind the closed doors of an unspecified Tibetan convent. Writing to "Pietro Colodoro" (the instant Italianization of Goldfarb's name concocted by Fellini for his new American friend), the filmmaker wondered: "Have you ever seen the auditions I shoot while I'm preparing to make a film? A lot of the time, they are more entertaining, moving, or disturbing than the film itself." He could also meditate on a visual guilt trip: the buildings created for *Mastorna* slowly rotting away on the field at Dinocittà, the rampant weeds, vagrant gypsies, and lawlessness.

Filmed in September 1968, *A Director's Notebook* acted as a sort of intermission between Fellini's regrets over the film he had not made and the problems of the film he was supposed to make. It was a freewheeling sketchbook, rich with impressions, anticipations, and fantasy. In it, Fellini felt freer than ever to open up, hide, or meander. If *8½* was a long, simulated confession, *A Director's Notebook* was a short but honest outpouring of the soul.

Page 177: *Federico Fellini with the cello from the film* Il viaggio di G. Mastorna *(The Voyage of G. Mastorna).*

Opposite: *Marcello Mastroianni before the cathedral in Cologne, Germany.*

Left: *Federico Fellini and Marcello Mastroianni at an audition for* Mastorna.

MASTORNA BLUES

A *Director's Notebook* opens on the rundown field in Dinocittà, where the fake Cologne cathedral and framework of the airplane stand. A wild horse is grazing on the grass (and according to some who decipher Fellini's symbols, the horse represents the filmmaker's mother). The narration in first person is read in rather buffoonish English by Fellini himself. A band of hippies has set up shop amidst the ruins, and we understand immediately that this little film is setting out in part to parody the Andy Warhol Factory style in fashion at the time. Or perhaps, at certain points, to embody that style? Fellini claims he doesn't know anything about it and that he doesn't watch other people's movies, but evidently he doesn't entirely ignore them, either. His chat with the hippies is good-natured and entertaining. One of them reads a poem entitled "Mastorna Blues."

A fake thunderstorm breaks out, the airplane is struck by wind and snow, and the cellist Giuseppe Mastorna (seen from behind) wanders through the ruins and crosses Piazza del Duomo, just like the black-clothed director in *8 ½*.

In Cinecittà, accompanied by Marina Ceratto (voiced over by Melina Martello), the beautiful daughter of Caterina Boratto and the stagehand/clown Gasparino, Fellini visits a sort of museum of horrors, the warehouse where all the material collected for the film has been piled up. Then the filmmaker announces that he has changed plans. He has decided to make "another voyage, a voyage through time." Suddenly we are in the Colosseum, right in the middle of a nerve-racking to-and-fro of gays, prostitutes, pimps, transvestites, and others. Giulietta Masina presents a mysterious benefactor, calling him the "bag man," and a shortened episode from *Nights of Cabiria* is inserted into the film.

We see the Roman Forum in a silent movie, humorous fragments of Latin life: historical archeology according to the archeology of cinema. We see the audience in a typical 1920s movie theater, the Fulgor, all shouting and whistling, with a small boy dressed up as a marionette and sitting on his father's knee. The scene is bound to be from Fellini's preparations for *Satyricon*.

Fellini is out for a drive with Bernardino Zapponi, Marina, and the magician Genius, who will be playing the freed slave on Trimalcione's chaise lounge: they are headed out to "listen to the dead" underground along the Appia Antica. It is a grotesque ritual with some rather disturbing moments that actually took place.

There is a ride on the subway with a professor, anticipating an analogous episode in *Fellini's Rome*: through the little windows, during a trial run, we can see them move ancient Romans from one station to the next like underground characters. The professor is extremely alarmed.

Amid the disorder of the notes, this scene is followed by a countryside version of the "Rape of the Sabine Women," once again on the Appia Antica, with truck drivers (transformed into Roman soldiers) clutching prostitutes and dragging them into the neighboring fields.

Now we are in the villa in Porta San Sebastiano, on the Appia Antica, that Marcello Mastroianni bought halfway through the 1960s. (Someone had convinced him, though only temporarily, that a film star had to have a sumptuous private residence. Mastroianni is there, surrounded by women, with sideburns and a flashy wardrobe. He has just finished working on a musical comedy entitled *Ciao, Rudy*. His pandering waiter is the usual Cesarino Miceli Picardi: Mastroianni happily welcomes Fellini, gives interviews, takes pictures, and gives himself over to the applause from tourists who arrive on a bus that pulls up right in front of his house.

More auditions for *Mastorna*: Mastroianni, with a little moustache, pretends to play the cello as the camera moves around him. The director and Mastroianni exchange a few rather tense comments about whether or not the actor will be able to portray the difficult character.

Shadows at dawn around a slaughterhouse, where Fellini has arrived with his film crew to look for "an atmosphere dark with blood; a slice of ferocious Rome . . . Cruelty that has survived intact for two thousand years." The slaughter of a bunch of pigs is interrupted from time to time with marble busts of the ancient Romans housed in Rome's Museo Capitolino. Next it is time to choose the minor actors for *Satyricon*, a selection of exaggerated and monstrous individuals. In a rather morbid twist, the beautiful matron Caterina Boratto is placed before a gladiator battle.

In Fellini's offices at Cinecittà, candidates for a role in the film are filing through. The filmmaker comments on the incredible characters: "All this may seem very cynical, even cruel . . . But it's not . . . I am extremely fond of these bizarre characters who have always followed me, who follow me from one film to the next . . . They are all a little bit crazy, I know . . . They say they need me, but the truth is that I need them just as much. . . ." The line of candidates continues to move by, including a tryout tape from American Martin Potter for the part of Encolpio, and the whole thing draws to a close, to the notes of the marching tune from *8 ½*.

Opposite top: A drawing of *Giulietta Masina* and *Federico Fellini (in bed)*, *with* Mastorna *on television.*

Opposite bottom: *Marcello-Mastorna.*

MASTORNA!!!!!

Sogno del
9. Sett.

WHAT FINE WORDS ON TV

Fellini: A Director's Notebook (the work's original title) was Fellini's first film (estimated length: between 52 and 54 minutes) not to be released in the theaters, but on American television. It was broadcast on April 11, 1969 (other sources cite March 15 as the broadcast date) on the NBC network. It was subtitled *Experiment in Television* and drew a relatively small but expert audience as well as positive reviews. During its first phase, the film was supported by the Burlington Industry (who produced chemical products), though they seem to have withdrawn their support afterward. The short film was also broadcast on Italian television.

"Before filming Satyricon I interviewed university professors, experts on ancient art, priests, magicians, astrologists, experts on the occult . . . The things they told me, the things I saw, were more fascinating than the film."

FELLINI SATYRICON

IS THIS HOW THINGS WERE IN ANCIENT ROMA?

Almost fifty years old, Fellini seemed to be a changed man. His recent illness would leave permanent psychological repercussions. The filmmaker began to see himself as having aged prematurely. For the first time in his life, he felt overwhelmed with a sort of pessimism that erased any and all traces of serenity from his life. Fortunately in the future, he would have more positive times when his traditional good humor returned, but *Satyricon* totally lacked the irony present in *The White Sheik*, the verve of *I Vitelloni*, the forceful vitality of *Nights of Cabiria*, the spontaneity of *La Dolce Vita*, the self-analytical curiosity of *8 ½*, and the female presence of *Juliet of the Spirits*. All these were replaced by a bitter retreat into contemplating history, whether real or imagined, within a context of powerlessness, morbidity, desperation, and even hate, expressed through his talent that had become increasingly refined, surprising, and penetrating. Yet it all risked being ruined by Fellini's negative, gloomy mood.

The idea of referring back to the writings of the mysterious Petronio (no one has ever established whether or not he really was the Petronius Arbiter, driven to suicide by the Roman Emperor Nero) had remote beginnings. Already as early as *Marc'Aurelio* there were plans with Marchesi to adapt it to a variety show for Fabrizi. Nothing came of it, but the title remained among those that Fellini would pull out during his recurrent periods of uncertainty concerning the next project to undertake. This is precisely what happened when, at Grimaldi's urging, the filmmaker had to finally admit that it was useless to keep stubbornly clinging on to the *Mastorna* project. Once he had determined that the film about a cellist's fatal travels in the afterlife was becoming impossible, Fellini bought time and calmed the producer, who anxiously insisted: "Well? What now?" Fellini responded: "What if we made *Satyricon*?" In other words, he said the first title that came to mind without having reread the text (and perhaps without having ever read it, period), and what is worse, without having even the faintest idea that Grimaldi would get excited about the

project, make calls left and right, and find everyone else was enthusiastic about it, too. The idea to shoot the film came about when Fellini had practically decided to take another stab at *Mastorna*.

Anything but convinced, and yet increasingly interested with every passing day, Fellini, assisted by Zapponi, began to do the research he needed in order to make the film. He went to visit various experts and professors, including the illustrious Ettore Paratore (who intimidated Fellini), and ultimately found a more approachable expert in Latin who was then teaching at a university in Pisa. Luca Canali was extremely helpful in freeing Fellini from the major structural problems inherent in a text that had been passed down to posterity only in bits and pieces. Thus the filmmaker embarked upon a punctilious crash course in the history of Roman society during the first century CE. Furthermore, in various writings on the subject, Canali had established the *Satyricon* as one of the grand predecessors of Picaresque literature.

In any case, the undertaking did not move forward in a philological manner, but required inventing (Fellini dictum) "a science fiction film from the past." In order for it to be credible, Fellini was tempted to have the characters speak in Latin, and he even recorded several dialogues translated by Canali and kept them as background sounds. In the meantime, he studied the history, customs, and art of the period. Fellini began to elaborate set designs on which he would put his signature for the first time ever, although he then entrusted them to a creative and exuberant art director, Danilo Donati, who had a wealth of experience.

The script for the film was faithful to the text, with the exception of some cuts and a few interpolations. The main variant was to have most of the story unfold in Rome, while in the book the reader is taken away to

Page 183: A view of Suburra.

Opposite: Martin Potter and Hylette Adolphe.

Below: "Il Moro" in his restaurant, near Fontana di Trevi.

the Empire's distant provinces, from Marseille to Magna Graecia. When it came to the actors, at first Fellini considered bringing together a group of important participants (only a pair of loyal French actors from *La Dolce Vita*—Magali Noël and Alain Cuny—would eventually be included in the film, as well as the fashion model Capucine and Lucia Bosè). But later on, he decided to look for less expensive solutions, considering that the elaboration of the film (entrusted to the rigorous talents of Provenzale, the same man Fellini had famously fought with over *The White Sheik*) threatened to run over deadline, and in fact eventually lasted seven months, from November 1968 through May of the following year. Unfortunately the two young British actors hired to play the lead roles, Hiram Keller (fresh from a musical version of *Hair*) and Martin Potter, failed to glean any great career boost from the film despite their considerable efforts onscreen for Fellini. Randone, then considered the best actor of Italian theater, did not have to work too hard because his character was subsequently voiced over. When the time came to choose the actor for Trimalcione, Fellini briefly took into consideration his old friend/enemy Fabrizi, despite the man's now gargantuan corpus. When he got official word he was under consideration for the role, Fabrizi was ready to cook spaghetti on set to celebrate what would have been a historical reconciliation, but instead was infuriated to learn that his place had been usurped by the venerated landlord of a famous Roman restaurant.

Ugo Tognazzi, who had been selected and then rejected as Mastorna, got his revenge by playing Trimalcione in a competing version of *Satyricon* produced by Alfredo Bini and directed by Gian Luigi Polidoro, put together at full speed just like when *It's A Dog's Life* was made to compete with *Variety Lights*. It also had the same good fortune for its release, hitting theaters in April 1969, when Fellini was still shooting his version, although with much less satisfying results. Given a lukewarm welcome that included a few positive reviews from film critics, this doppelganger version of *Satyricon* was quickly taken out of circulation, cut down by a malevolent censorship for presumed obscenities.

During the filming—which took place in Cinecittà and Maccarese, from the beach outside Focene to Ponza Island—an event was destined to remain among Fellini's more painful and unforgettable memories: he was visited on the set by his colleague Roman Polanski and Polanski's young, radiant wife, Sharon Tate, who was murdered less than a year later by a group of insane fanatics in Polanksi's villa in Hollywood.

*Trifena (Capucine) and
Encolpio, and other scenes
from the film.*

I VITELLONI AND ONE HUNDRED YEARS AFTER CHRIST

The young Encolpio (Martin Potter, voiced over by Pino Colizzi) is desperate. We find him talking to himself in front of a wall, lamenting the fact that his companion Ascilto (Hiram Keller, voiced over by Antonio Casagrande) has stolen his young lover Gitone (Max Born). Wandering around the baths at closing time, Encolpio calls out to Ascilto, who in the meantime tells us just how much he has enjoyed the young boy. When they meet, Encolpio and Ascilto wrestle until Ascilto, losing the battle, confesses that he has sold Gitone to an actor.

A bawdy show of Vernacchio (Fanfulla, voiced over by Carlo Croccolo) takes place inside a miserable shack. It is a tawdry farce based on the theater company leader's talents as an extraordinary farter. (This episode was invented and does not exist in the original text.) Amid foul jokes and scurrility, a scoundrel's hand is chopped off. But a caricaturized Caesar (Alvaro Vitali) intervenes, performs a miracle, and the hand grows back. When Gitone descends from the ceiling, dressed as Eros, Encolpio climbs up onstage and demands the effeminate young man be returned to him. A fight ensues but is stopped before it gets out of hand by a magistrate in the crowd who threatens Vernacchio while Encolpio and Gitone make their exit.

Out in Suburra (a district of ill-repute in ancient Rome) at nighttime, the brothels and dens of vice along the true "joyless road" overflow with human monstrosities. Encolpio and Gitone make their way to their little room in a big hostel called "Insula Felicles" and spend the night there in each other's embrace. Once Ascilto arrives, the disagreement continues, and the two young men decide to separate for good. But Gitone chooses

"I thought I'd make a science fiction film from the past. Is that possible?"

to stay with Ascilto. Left alone, Encolpio is desperate. But his personal crisis is made a little less tragic when an earthquake strikes, bringing down the building and others around it in a sort of grotesque version of *The Last Days of Pompeii*.

Encolpio meets the elderly poet Eumolpo (Salvo Randone, voiced over by Renato Turi) in an art museum. Eumolpo is scandalized by the gold fever, claiming that it has been the death of art. The poet accompanies the student to dinner at the house of a nouveau riche parvenu, Caio Pompeo Trimalcione, aka "Il Moro," (Mario Romagnoli, voiced over by Corrado Gaipa). The numerous dinner guests are bathing in a spectral swimming pool, surrounded by lit candles. The host wanders past, fawned upon by his servants. Trimalcione fancies himself a member of the literati and is quick to give Eumolpo a warm welcome: "There is true friendship between poets like you and I".

A vast triclinium—a couch extending around three sides of a table used by the ancient Romans for reclining at meals—dominated by a sort of veranda separates the guests according to importance. Bawdy laughter, music, and dishes accompany the meal. Stretched out on beds, the more important guests suck down sauces from the central dish through long reeds. Once he has paid homage to the three patron saints of the home, "Big Deal, Big Laughs, and Big Bucks," Trimalcione boasts about his personal wealth through a river of idiocies and vulgar wisecracks with his wife Fortunata (Magali Noël) at his side. At a certain point, the two exchange insults. The beautiful Trifena (Capucine, voiced over by Benita Martini) stares intently at Encolpio, who is busy listening to Eumolpo's ironic commentary.

The meal is full of surprises: a pig dressed up with sausages and a performance by four Greek singers called "operists." After the performance is over, Eumolpo tries to recite an ode of his own (in Latin), only to be roundly booed and bombarded with leftover food. The host's poetry, however, is met with resounding success. Eumolpo kisses his hand and proclaims him the "new Horatio." Spurred on by her husband, Fortunata starts performing a silly sensual dance reminiscent of Nadia Gray's in *La Dolce Vita*. Trimalcione mixes absentminded talk of business with a sodomist's game, upsetting Fortunata even as she lets herself become entangled in seedy embraces with her friend Scintilla (Danika La Loggia). In a rising tide of self-exaltation, Trimalcione tells his own personal tale of successful freedman and launches into another poetry recitation. But this time Eumolpo can't bring himself to let Trimalcione get away with it, and accuses his host of having plagiarized Lucretius. The poet is shoved into the kitchen and beaten until he is bloody.

Capricious and moody, Trimalcione brings the entire crowd to his tomb, where his own funeral is celebrated in a buffoonish parody. Another freedman (Genius), who had been shouting at Encolpio earlier, takes advantage of the situation to tell the tale of Efeso's matron. (In the original text, this tale is narrated by Eumolpo on the ship, *Lica*.)

The tale takes shape onscreen as well. Charged with guarding the body of a man who has been hanged for thievery, a soldier finds himself attracted to the thief's weeping widow, who is clinging to her husband's corpse. It is not hard to convince her to accept his comforting, but in the meantime someone steals the body. When he discovers he has failed his duty, the soldier wants to take his own life. But the woman insists that he take back her husband's body as a gift: "I would rather hang up a dead body than lose a life."

Encolpio recovers the beaten and bloodied Eumolpo and accompanies him through the streets of Rome, holding the poor poet up in his arms. The poet foretells his own imminent death, leaving nothing more than his poetry behind. He launches into a burlesque recitation of his will. The two fall asleep together on the street as dawn rises.

Encolpio wakes up by the seaside, only to find Gitone and Ascilto unexpectedly in chains. He, too, has been ensnared in a roundup, dragged aboard the ship of the terrible Lica of Taranto (Alain Cuny). Unlike the original text, this is no simple merchant, but a proconsul of vice who sails the seas together with his wife Trifena in search of new foul and vile entertainments to offer Caesar on his island palace. The prisoners are crowded together in the boat's hold and subjected to various sadistic practices. A fan of wrestling, Lica challenges Encolpio to a fight. Wrestling the young man to the ground, Lica falls in love with him while Gitone sings an ironic love song.

Up on deck, everyone is getting ready for a wedding: under Trifena's complacent gaze, Lica appears dressed up as a bride and marries Encolpio. The seamen capture an enormous fish, just like in the final scenes of *La Dolce Vita*, but their fortunes are changing.

The imperial ship comes under attack by smaller enemy ships (almost a scenic foreshadowing of *And the Ship Sails On*) and a fleet of military vessels: Caesar winds up in the water and drowns. The attackers bear down on Lica's vessel as well, and the newlywed captain is decapitated in the blink of an eye (in the original text, he drowns along with his ship and the shipwrecked survivors find his body). The new emperor, a general on a white horse, marches in Rome at the head of a column of hired thugs and prisoners, surrounded by crucifixes and tortured victims.

A husband and wife, members of the nobility who have remained loyal to Caesar (Lucia Bosè and Joseph Wheeler) calmly face suicide after having freed their slaves and sent their children away. Like the earlier sea-side coup d'état, this scene doesn't exist in the original text and can be considered homage to the suicide of the book's presumed author, Gaius Petronius Arbiter.

Wandering around at night, Encolpio and Ascilto find the suicide victims' bodies, only to have their attention drawn away almost immediately by a visit to the villa where they find a little black slave (Hylette Adolphe), who after running away ultimately agrees for the three of them to make love together. At dawn, the suicide victims' bodies are burnt on a pyre, surrounded by the victorious soldiers.

Below: *Lucia Bosè and Joseph Wheeler, the noble suicide victims.*

The film's protagonists have yet another encounter along their travels: the procession with a woman nymphomaniac, who Ascilto fails to help despite his best efforts, headed for a famous oracle.

The oracle is a young, milky-skinned, and fragile hermaphrodite (Pasquale Baldassare) who welcomes in all sorts of wicked persons and unhappy souls: a kind of historical review of the "Divine Love" sequence in *Nights of Cabiria*. Encolpio and Ascilto have ganged up with a robber (Gordon Mitchell) and the three kidnap the hermaphrodite at night, but the oracle dies in their arms not far from the sanctuary. During the ensuing fight, as accusations fly back and forth, Ascilto murders the robber.

Now Encolpio finds himself thrown down the hill at the center of a Roman arena. He has to pick up his weapons, go into the labyrinth, and battle the Minotaur.

Above: *Mario Romagnoli and Magali Noël.*

longings of Arianna. Egged on by the spectators, Encolpio tries but finds he cannot do the job. (This episode echoes Encolpio's sad love affairs with the enchantress of Crotone in the original text.) Fortunately, the logic of dreams intervenes, presenting us with Ascilto, who is announcing the arrival of the poet Eumolpo on a litter, surrounded by slaves. The poet escorts Encolpio to a specialized bordello, the Garden of Delights, where the young man is presented as a friend "whose scepter doesn't work, whose club is cracked, whose sword is broken." While Ascilto rejoices, surrounded by women, the harem sets about using every means possible to resuscitate Encolpio's virility: bare-bottomed whipping, belly dancing, flutes and tambourines. Eumolpo takes off, making a date with his friend for the following day aboard a ship about to set sail for Africa: "We still have another trip to take . . . New discoveries to make. . . ."

The boss of the Garden tells the story of the enchantress Enotea (Donyale Luna, voiced over by Rita Savagnone), and like the tale of Efeso's matron, this story takes shape onscreen as well. As a prank, the black Enotea locks a wizard, who had asked for her hand in marriage, up in a basket suspended midair. But the wizard takes vengeance on her, stealing fire from everyone in the land. Then he tells the inhabitants to look for their lost fire between Enotea's legs, who is forced to settle back, open her legs, and light all the people's torches in a tribal ceremony.

In order to heal Encolpio's woes, Ascilto accompanies him to Enotea. The two cross wild, swampy lands. The enchantress appears before the student—old, fat, and ugly. Her breasts are enormous. She draws Encolpio in for a healing embrace (a pantographic version of the incestuous-maternal kiss in *8 1/2*, as well as a foreshadowing of the scene at the tobacconist's in *Amarcord*, played by the same Maria Antonietta Beluzzi).

As the two friends leave the enchantress's abode, Ascilto dies unexpectedly from the blow he had taken while fighting with a boatman. Eumolpo has passed away as well, leaving behind a strange will and testament: those who want to get their hands on his inheritance have to eat his body. Out on the beach, while the beneficiaries, ready to turn into cannibals, unwind the bandages from the poet's corpse and prepare to tear away at his flesh with their teeth, Encolpio decides to leave with the ship. Thus he becomes, like everything else, part of a Pompeian wall fresco, chipped and flaked and only partially comprehensible

If he can kill the beast, he will enjoy Arianna (Elisa Mainardi). We find ourselves in one of "Mongo's Tournaments," just like in a Flash Gordon comic book. The Minotaur (Luigi Montefiori) is a giant with a bull's head, armed with a murderous bludgeon. Knocked to the ground, Encolpio begs for mercy: "I'm a student, not a gladiator." At this point, the Minotaur takes off his bull's mask, laughs, and embraces his adversary. The audience laughs scornfully and in the seats above, the public prosecutor informs Encolpio that this burlesque performance marks the beginning of the Rice God festival. But the poor young man has to publicly satisfy the lusty

HIPPIES LIKE IT

Satyricon was first screened on September 4, 1969 at the 30th Venice Film Festival. The film was not entered in the competition. Fellini hadn't been to Venice for over fourteen years, having sworn at the disgraceful ceremony for *The Swindle* that he would never set foot at the festival again. He was welcomed with full honors and even attended a crowded and controversial press conference during which the filmmaker refused to back down in the face of a large group of protestors, responding to their taunts in kind. The screening of the film was packed, so much so that a second showing was organized after midnight, for which the tickets disappeared almost immediately and were in turn sold at outrageous prices by scalpers. Reactions from the public and critics alike were entirely respectful, though the warmth with which Venice had welcomed *I Vitelloni* was lacking, as well as the sort of clamorous debate that *La Strada* had provoked when it had been shown there. The movie hit theaters across Italy at the same time as it was being shown in Venice, earning a total of 1,543,229,000 lira at the box office. It performed well outside Italy as well, including a memorable nighttime screening before an audience of hippies at Madison Square Garden in New York City. During his promotional tour in the United States, Fellini appeared on a number of different television shows, including an interview with David Frost, the journalist who would later become an internationally recognized star for his damning interview sessions with President Richard Nixon.

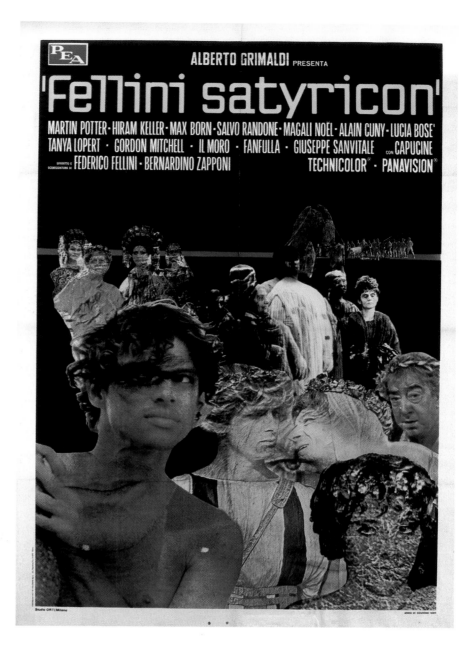

Far left: *Federico Fellini, Giulietta Masina, and actors from* Satyricon *in Venice in 1969.*

Left: *Federico Fellini at the Venice Film Festival.*

"I am convinced that all men belong to one of two categories: either White Clowns or Circus Clowns. What type am I? A Circus Clown, I believe. But nevertheless, sometimes I behave like a White Clown. Perhaps I'm simply Monsieur Loyal, the director of the circus."

THE CLOWNS
I CLOWNS

HEADED TOWARD THE SUNSET

During the filming of *Satyricon*, the filmmaker had been in contact with yet another promising young producer, once again an American. His name was Martin Poll (whom Fellini promptly nicknamed "Martino Pollo," or "Martin Chicken") and he wanted to bring together Ingmar Bergman and Fellini to make separate episodes in an engaging project entitled *Love Duet*. The two masters held a press conference in Rome in January 1969 and the project seemed guaranteed, but their individual efforts were not destined to appear in theaters together: the Swedish filmmaker made a film of his own, *Beröringen* (1971), or *The Touch*, while Fellini shot *City of Women*, ten years later in 1980. Once *Satyricon* was completed and Fellini finished accompanying the film on its world tour, the filmmaker found himself with no plans or projects in the works. He had been counting on Poll's promises, and now that those had fallen through, he was tired and unwilling to jump right into another major film project. With the pleasant experiences he had had making *A Director's Notebook*, Fellini decided to go back to television.

RAI (Radiotelevisione Italiana, Italy's national public television network) offered him the chance to film a version of Pinocchio in episodes, but the project died in the making and the miniseries (which would be the last project of its kind by Gherardi) wound up being shot by Luigi Comencini. Despite this, Fellini remained attached to the idea of doing his own version of Collodi's famous story, and brought it back onto the table in the wake of *The Voice of the Moon*, undoubtedly catching sight of actor Roberto Benigni's more Pinocchio-esque qualities. With executive producers such as Elio Scardamaglia and Ugo Guerra behind him, Fellini sat down with Zapponi and decided to shoot a sort of film-investigation dedicated to clowns: their origins, the golden age, and the modern decline. It would become another voyage through the mind, through memory, based on Fellini's emotional experiences as a child when he first saw circus clowns, and traveling back in time to echo an entire lost world of laughter, foolishness, and sequins.

When he came across a rare copy of the book *Entrées clownesques* (an anthology of famous clown acts) at an antiques dealer, Fellini believed he had all he needed and became excited at the thought of picking back up his old habits through the fantastical, imaginative cinematography that he admired most: Danny Kaye, Mae West, Groucho Marx. Of course, as always happens, once things got underway he would have to settle for less extraordinary choices. It proved impossible, for example, to involve the founding father of cinematographic comedy, the sublime Charlie Chaplin, by now too old and sick to work in the movies (Fellini had hoped he would read the clown's will and testament). Between one inquiry and the next, the screenplay began to take shape and preparation for the film moved ahead rather quickly, so much so that shooting began on color film and in 35 millimeter as early as March 23, with various locations in Anzio, Ostia, Cinecittà, and Paris.

The shooting in Paris—accurately depicted in the film but destined to reveal that the modern clown panorama had drastically impoverished even in the capital of circus delights—proved to be the most engaging. Of the city's two most famous and important circuses, the Médrano had been turned into a beer hall and the Cirque d'Hiver was only open three days a week. Although Fellini extended filming beyond his deadline, the editing was done at a breakneck pace and the film was ready that summer.

Page 193: *A white clown.*

Opposite: *Two clowns playing the trumpet.*

Below: *The legendary Enrico Sprocani, also known as "Rhum."*

THE MISSING BUFFOON

A child wakes up in the middle of the night, hearing strange sounds. He goes to the window and sees people raising a big tent in the piazza down below. Even prisoners are watching the events from behind the bars of a nearby jail. That morning, the boy asks a girl who is ironing in the kitchen: "What is happening?" Her answer is a blend of enchantment and fear: "It's the circus. If you don't behave, I'll let those gypsies take you away!"

Dressed up like a sailor, the child sets out to explore the circus: he sees clown costumes hanging out to dry, an elephant, and signs. The atmosphere in the large, empty arena under the big tent is magical. The animal tamer (Valdemaro) appears and starts to train a few horses. Toward evening, the countless circus lights shine. The whole circus cast—from the fire-eater to the showman, from the clowns to all the helpers—begin to attract an audience.

The show starts with a group of athletes wrestling over a cannon cart. A dwarf mimics them. A gaucho throws a bunch of knives around a beautiful woman. While a cage is being set up, the clowns provide comic relief, performing a series of skits, including pretending to roast the dwarf on a spit so that they can eat him. Lions jump through circles of fire. To the sounds of Wagner's "Ride of the Valkyries," the Herculean Woman bests the Greek wrestler Aramis then accepts a challenge from a pretend audience member, Miss Tarzan. The fakir Burmah is locked up in a glass box, where he is to remain for the next forty days, buried underneath the dirt in the ring. The siren Nettunia, who eats live fish, comes out, as well as a pair of Siamese twins. The clowns return for another wild performance to the music of Julius Fucík's "Entrance of the Gladiators," interspersed with part of the soundtracks from *La Strada* and *8 1/2*. Each clown has his own personal act: a series of grimaces, kicks in the derriere, hammer blows to the head, accidents and explosions. These grotesque and alarming characters frighten the little boy, who starts crying and wants to go home. His mother slaps him and drags him out.

The boy is back in his own room. Offscreen, Fellini narrates from his own memories: "That evening things ended quickly. The clowns didn't make me laugh. Actually, they scared me. . . ." They reminded him of "other strange, disturbing figures" who lived in and around his hometown. People like Giovannone the crazy man, who showered the local women with lewd and obscene remarks. There was the dwarf nun, who divided her time between the convent and the insane asylum (this character would reappear in *Amarcord*). There were drunks at the local tavern, and every once in a while the wife of one of them would appear and carry her husband off in a wheelbarrow. There were the Fascists: the Wounded Man from the Great War, the audacious Zig Zag, and Signora Ines, who knew Mussolini's speeches by heart. There were the horse and carriage drivers at the train station, who were always arguing. There was Cotechino, the head of the station, who was always greeted with raspberries from the boys on the train whenever he blew the whistle for the train to depart, until he finally hired a threatening-looking Fascist party official and the jeers were transformed into Roman salutes. There was Giudizio, the crazy fellow who made an appearance in *I Vitelloni* and who audiences would see once again in *Amarcord*. He could always be found near the billiard table, like that evening (music: "Fascination") when a blonde wearing an ermine coat crossed the bar with her German boyfriend, bewitching every man present. Giudizio said: "If that blonde gives me five *baiocchi* (traditional copper coins minted by the Papal States), I'll bend her over and I'll. . . ." Giudizio ultimately gave in to craziness, Fellini continues to tell us from offscreen, one day after watching a war film. He then went out and reenacted the war scenes on the street in front of the Caffè Commercio, making everyone laugh and feel a little uncomfortable.

Back in the production office, the entire troupe is standing around the director: his secretary Maya (Maya Morin); the soundman Alvaro (Alvaro Vitali), accompanied as always by his mother (Lina Alberti); the stagehand Gasparino; and the English cameraman Roy. The first segment of this fake documentary is the circus run by Liana, Rinaldo, and Nando Orfei. First they take in a bit of the show, then come presentations, kisses, and

Below: A scene from the film.

Opposite: Drawings of the white clown, Matilde, and Cotechino by Fellini.

salutations. The performance involves two clowns, Amleto and Ginetto, who are spitting water in each other's faces. Just as the elephants are making their way under the big top, Fellini spies Anita Ekberg alongside the cages filled with ferocious animals. A merry group meeting follows in Liana's caravan, with members of the film crew and circus people all gathered together: cakes and cookies for everyone. Squarzone, the circus's oldest clown, stops by to wish everyone a good evening and tells them to enjoy their meal.

Back in the empty circus, the animal tamer Migliori is shouting orders in German at the tigers: "The only human language that animals understand," as Maya informs us. A gentleman who is there explains that the name *Augusto* used to refer to clowns who distract and entertain the audience while the cages are being set up comes from a famous funny, late nineteenth-century servant. But the creator of modern day circus clowns was the Englishman Jimmy Guyon, who wound up drinking himself all the way to the hospital. He escaped from the hospital one evening—and we see him—in order to go to the circus. There are musical clowns (Geo) Foottit and Chocolat (the Cuban Rafaël Padilla), who perform to the tune of "Io cerco la Titina" ("I'm Looking for Titina"). Watching their act, which involves each of them stealing the chair out from under the other, makes Jimmy split his sides with laughter. Once the show is over, the circus hands dig out the corpse.

"We've come to Paris, the city that turned the circus into a true art. . . ." Once again, the voice is Fellini's, with "Io cerco la Titina" playing in the background. We see several images from the Ville Lumière, then an encounter with the old "white clowns" at the Café Curieux des Halles: they are Nino, Alex, Ludo, Louis Maïsse, the dwarf Robero, Pipo (who, poor soul, would actually pass away the following day). Stumbling over a read-through of her notes, Maya explains that "by 'white clown' we actually mean a clown with a white cone-shaped hat." Tristan Rémy, a historian and circus expert who specializes in clowns, shows up and starts fighting right away with Antonet, the famous white clown and ex-partner of Grock (whose real name was Umberto Giullaume, brother of the actor Polidor). Fellini's voice summarizes the heated argument they are having in French: Tristan claims that Antonet did not fall down and do physical gags, and especially that he was not funny. He limited himself to transforming the white clown into the arrogant director Monsieur Loyal, the ringmaster or head of the circus, mistreating his partner, Beby (real name: Aristodemo Frediani). And here's Antonet and Beby's gag: preparing

an omelet in an audience member's hat, with the egg splattering on the *Augusto*'s face.

Who created the clowns' costumes? Their wives, everyone says. But Tristan claims that they are the work of great tailors. And it is not hard to imagine a fashion show (foreshadowing the ecclesiastic runway show in *Fellini's Rome*) in which Antonet, Beby, and the other clowns present their new costumes on the catwalk, accompanied by the music of "Toreador, en garde" from Georges Bizet's *Carmen*, insulting one another and fighting.

The discussion in the Halles is degenerating, too, and Tristan asks Fellini why he wants to make this movie: "All the real clowns are dead. The circus has no more meaning for modern society."

Next comes a trip to the Cirque d'Hiver, the last Parisian circus in existence: it is only open three days a week and is run by Monsieur Joseph Buglione, who doesn't have any time to give an interview. We catch a glimpse of him while he is watching the tryout performance of a pair of young, refined, and surreal clowns: Jean-Baptiste Thierrèe and Victoria, who is Charlie Chaplin's daughter.

The troupe crosses Paris by taxi in order to reach the clinic where the former circus rider Jean Houcke lives. He is ninety-two years old, the oldest ringmaster in the world. But the elderly gentleman, bewildered at the visit and attended by a pair of garrulous nurses, can provide them with nothing more than a tune sung in bad Italian.

Now it is time for another circus legend, the Spaniard Charlie Rivel. In an apartment full of bull relics, the clown reminisces on his success as a circus clown, saying that he would love to teach someone his art. Finally he picks up his guitar and plays a flamenco that moves Gasparino.

On a nighttime expedition, everybody crammed together into a runabout, the group heads out to see an old film by the Fratellini brothers in the home of Pierre Etaix, an actor and director who married Annie, the daughter of Victor Fratellini, who was in turn the son of Paul, one of the members of the famous trio (together with his brothers François and Albert Fratellini). Although they grapple with the projector, neither Pierre nor Victor manage to get the film up on the screen. Fellini looks at the

Above: *Several clowns in a scene from the film.*

Above: *The producer Elio Scardamaglia and Fellini.*

photographs, leafs through an album full of drawings, and does not seem surprised that the film is inaccessible. While somebody plays the notes on a piano to a piece by Schubert, it seems better to simply imagine the Fratellini brothers: when they perform "The Musicians" on the terrace of an orphanage; in a field hospital during the 1915–1918 war; in a big room in an insane asylum, where they fly suspended on cables and wearing angel's wings.

The other half of the Parisian jaunt is to the home of the clown Loriot, alias George Bazot. Now eighty-five, George is still healthy and clearheaded and even spends a few evenings out on the town. He reminisces over his more important colleagues, especially Rhum (whose real name was Enrico Sprocani, an Italian from Trieste). When it is time to say good-bye he raises his glass along with his guests for a toast in memory of his dead wife, Lady (who was also an actress for Méliès).

Back in a taxi, Fellini asks the driver in vain if he has ever heard of "Rhum." Of course the answer is no, and he never goes to see the circus, either. At Bario's house, alias Manrico Meschi from Livorno, the clown, at first, does not allow the Italians to enter, out of fear he will be too moved by the experience. Signor Bario shows Fellini the usual photograph album, confiding in him just how much he misses the circus. Now Bario and Dario (his brother) make an entrance. The white clown gives Bario the love word that will let him win the heart of a feminine-looking mannequin, whose head he knocks off with a slap. The headless mannequin follows Bario around, frightening him half to death.

The real Bario, an elderly gentleman dressed with a jacket and beret, comes down to meet the troupe. He misses the circus a great deal, too: he spends humdrum days with his wife and canary. Once they have left Bario's little villa, Fellini and Tristan see him spy on them from behind a window. Back in the car, they start to talk about Rhum, a brilliant clown: he wore very little makeup and was a *clown pour intellectuels.* He drank to forget the disappointments he had in his love life.

In the hallways of the French television building, several rather rude film editors send Fellini to a colleague who welcomes him saying: "C'est vous Monsieur Bellini?" He has permission to see a segment in slow motion: Pipo (Gustave-Joseph Sosman) and Rhum in a scene that

passes by so quickly that it is impossible to assign any meaning to it. The director's voice comments: "I felt slightly uncomfortable, as if I had somehow failed at something. I felt like I had taken a trip that didn't lead anywhere. Maybe Tristan Rémy was right; maybe the clown is definitively dead."

The clown Fischietto Fischiagrilli has died. His colleagues mourn him, crying out loud to one another amid gags and water games. The ringmaster (Carlo Rizzo) asks for them to have some respect for the widow, a clown dressed up as a woman. A little old man with a beard that stretches all the way down to the ground cries over the coffin, calling for his daddy. The Notary Public (Tino Scotti) reads an odd will and testament. There is a group photograph with the dead clown. The magnesium for the flash doesn't work, and we discover the troupe, along with Fellini, rather annoyed by the setback. The technicians (Gasparino, Nino Terzo, Dante Maggio, and Galliano Sbarra) try to fix things. A few carpenter clowns show up with tools, hammers, and nails and set to work. A journalist asks the filmmaker what the message of the film is, but a pail thrown on the fly comes down over Fellini's head and another pail falls on the interviewer's head. The furious uproar out in the ring can go on unabated. A large funeral hearse comes in, drawn by six fake horses. The White Clown (Fanfulla) recites a funeral dirge that begins: "Ladies and Gentlemen, a painful bit of news is flying around town. . . ." He doesn't lament the dead circus clown in the least; in fact he claims he has put up with him for far too long. While the cabman hassles with an undisciplined horse, the others lay the corpse in the coffin and line up behind the funeral hearse. The crowd moves forward, first slowly and then faster and faster. Their absurd carousel finishes in a phantasmagoric fireworks display. A bunch of firefighter clowns arrive (music: "Stars and Stripes Forever") and entertain themselves by showering everybody with their hose. Thousands of ticker tapes drop down over everyone, there is a great deal of dancing, and Fischietto comes rising up out of the chaos, suspended on a circus cable.

The party is over. Fumagalli, an old clown who has gone to one side in order to take a break from the chaos, asks Fellini if he can go home. But first he tells us about a performance of his with his partner Fru Fru. The ringmaster said Fru Fru was dead and he would get the idea to look for him with a trumpet. On opposite sides of the circus, the two clowns, Fumagalli and Fru Fru, call out to each other with trumpet blasts (music: the Swedish song "Ebb Tide"). They walk down into the ring, meet one another at the center, and, while the spotlight stays on them, exit playing music. Darkness.

CHRISTMAS IN BLACK AND WHITE, SAINT STEPHEN'S IN COLOR

Though greeted warmly in general, the release of *The Clowns* was disappointing. It began at the 31st Venice Film Festival on Sunday, August 30, 1970, where RAI television organized a gala ceremony at Palazzo Labia to celebrate its central role in Italian film production. At that time, television and cinema were still considered (and considered themselves a little bit, too) opposing entities. Fellini tried to keep himself out of the controversy as much as possible, and although some attacked his role in the production, the filmmaker had no intention of becoming the poster boy for a new kind of movie production. His discomfort became tangible around Christmas, when RAI (still broadcast in black and white) decided to run *The Clowns* on Christmas evening. The broadcast earned little market share and even less at the box office when it was shown (this time in color) in theaters around Italy. Despite having been conceived and set up under the best possible pretenses, the entire affair was mismanaged in the final stages and left a feeling of disappointment in its wake.

An attempt to re-release the film a few years later together with *Toby Dammit* in a production entitled *2 Fellini 2* (in which Fellini had himself voiced over in *The Clowns* by famous Italian actor Gigi Proietti for no apparent reason) fared no better.

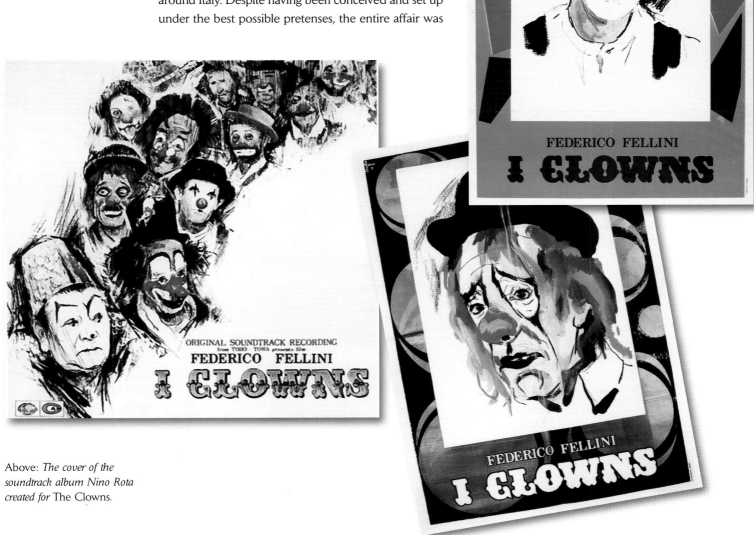

Above: *The cover of the soundtrack album Nino Rota created for* The Clowns.

"The first inspiration for making Roma *was the curiosity to know, along with a number of other things, where the Ponentino (a light Western summer wind) comes from. Where does the famous breeze go, how do people who feel it across their skin react?"*

FELLINI'S ROMA

FELLINI ROMA

AN ADOPTED HOME

Shot like a film project but in the spirit of a television documentary, during *The Clowns*, Fellini learned to appreciate the advantages of a discontinuous, interrupted narration. He liked substituting premeditation with extemporaneous invention, replacing even his simplest plot constructions with a first-person narration that no longer needed to hide behind anyone or anything. At the same time, by evoking the masters of an entertainment art that was on the road to extinction, the filmmaker had garnered his first taste of personal and collective nostalgic recollection. This Rimini-born Roman now felt the pulse of a doubly sentimental voyage, a reflection formed around the two cities that had shaped his identity. He would begin in Italy's capital, his adopted home and a town that he quickly came to consider impossible to give up: a city Fellini fell in love with even before he moved there (it was where his mother Ida was born and where her tumultuous love affair with his father, Urbano, began). For Fellini, Rome began as a mirage, and he was finally able to conquer it as a young man in search of a new existential perspective. Rome, on the eve of World War II, still presented itself as a viable mecca for pilgrims from the countryside, a city that could conquer men's hearts before the men themselves could even attempt to conquer the city.

With Zapponi still faithfully by his side, Fellini imagined a gallery of images alternating between the past and the present, with shots of the city's transformed urban landscape blending with images of what was now its distant past. He was not in the least bit tempted to transform the operation into a traditional film project; instead of a central plot, there would be nothing more than documents, testimonies, fragments. Complications arose from the fact that Fellini's presumed "television" style was not simply to film things the way they appear as in a documentary, but to create attractive, phantasmagoric copies of them. (It would be important to closely examine the variableness of "television style," given that it is considered a negative appellation for many, if not most, but was entirely positive for the filmmaker.) This implied

commitment, construction, and expenses that ran the dangerous risk of ballooning out of proportion as they sought to keep up with his ambition to create an infinite spectacle capable of continuing ad libitum. Given this premise, it is not hard to imagine the entirely understandable anxieties of those responsible for organizing and financing the overwhelming enterprise.

Not by chance, *Fellini's Roma* changed producers more than once. At first it was overseen by Scardamaglia, the same producer who had handled *The Clowns* and who was initially enthusiastic about the project's first scenes—the so-called ecclesiastic fashion show—but became alarmed immediately afterward when he saw the abyss that was opening up in front of him. Scardamaglia was replaced by Turi Vasile (through Ultra Film), who aside from the uncertainties linked to the production was pulled to a sudden and unexpected halt when his majority partner went bankrupt. Thus in March 1971, production came to a stop and remained so for about six months until in October, when it finally resumed. Filming ended in February 1972 under the aegis of Italnoleggio. Overall, the movie had taken slightly less than a year to make. The project was brought to a close by an order from above, where people continued (and not without reason) to fear the worst, making Fellini relatively unhappy. The director felt he had more to say, other stories to tell, leaving behind a string of producers, all exhausted by the arduous process and equally unsatisfied with the results.

Page 203: The street singer on the reconstruction of Via Albalonga.

Opposite: Scenes from the variety show.

Below: A drawing of the brothel by Fellini.

THE WAY WE WERE, THE WAY WE WILL WIND UP

The film opens with flute music that suggests the ancient and mysterious attractions of Rome. A prologue in Fellini's hometown. The first image we see is of a scythe carried over one shoulder by a farmer who is bicycling through the fog. Offscreen, the narrator begins by drawing our attention to a road sign with "Roma 340 km" written on it.

The headmaster solemnly invites a group of schoolkids out on a field trip to follow him across the Rubicon, copying Caesar's famous declaration: "To Rome!"

Snow is falling on the statue of Julius Caesar located in a piazza in the small town where we hear a rambling speech by Giudizio, the local crazy man:

Giulio Cesare romano	Julius Caesar the Roman
Fa il saluto con la mano	Salutes with one hand

Once again we see Caesar, this time in a theater. The curtain comes down on the scene of his murder in the Roman Senate. The old, hollow-eyed actor comes out on stage to acknowledge the applause. We see the same actor at a bar, admired by some vitelloni, or local boys.

At school. Didactic delirium from teachers dealing with Roman history. Images of the beautiful sights of Rome are projected in the cafeteria. The Monument to Vittorio Emanuele II earns applause from the students, but they are far more moved by the unexpected image of a naked woman's enormous behind that has somehow made its way among the teacher's slides. The headmaster cuts the uproar short by having them all sing Rome's anthem.

At home the women drive the anticlerical father crazy by interrupting lunch in order to kneel during the sound of ringing bells being broadcast over the radio directly from the Vatican in Saint Peter's Square.

The whole family goes to the movie theater where a silent movie set in ancient Rome is being shown: there is a cruel emperor, a battle between gladiators, and fighting in the theater where people are trying to get an empty seat. The flute music rises up again. Now the movie reportage *Luce* appears onscreen, with special Fascist soldiers jumping through a ring of fire and Fascist youths marching proudly. The pharmacist's wife is among those in the audience. She is known as the "local Messalina." Adults and kids vie for her fiery glances. And they catch glimpses of what everyone says about her: she makes love in a car and outside there is a long line of men waiting for their turn with her. People talk about the scandal in a local café.

At the station, the train headed for Rome stops for only two minutes. This is the scene of the young Fellini's arrival (ten years later) in the chaos of Stazione Termini during the period immediately following World War II. (The actor onscreen is Peter Gonzales, from Texas.)

Hanging onto the handle of a tram, the young country bumpkin sees Rome for the first time: the Esedra fountain, the steps leading up to Santa Maria Maggiore, jets of water, and church bells. The tram reaches the San Giovanni neighborhood, where the Palletta family lives. The young traveler is going to stay here in one of the family's furnished rooms. Via Albalonga is alive with the loud voices of theatrical characters; a girl beats a rug hanging out of a nearby window while singing "Luna marinara" ("Sailor's Moon"). The elevator is broken and he has to walk all the way to the fourth floor. Out in the courtyard, the voices of people calling out to one another blend with the sounds of a radio turned on full blast. When the young man goes into the apartment, followed by a little boy wearing a colonial helmet, the radio plays "Macariolita" (this is the song of *Il pirata sono io*, or *I Am the Pirate*, perhaps the very first film Fellini ever wrote a script for). His first views are like Attalo's vignettes in *Marc'Aurelio*: hallways packed with furniture, the saucy maid, children going to the bathroom, a young man in his underpants with a hairnet, and elderly people. A voice speaks: *Torna, piccina mia, Chitarra romana, Fiorin fiorello.* . . . The guests include a gentleman dressed in white, a minor film actor who worked with Righelli and in Camerini's *Batticuore* (*Heartbeat*). A bald, thickset man is imitating Mussolini, the voice starts in with "La strada nel bosco" ("A Road in the Woods"). The extremely fat landlady is lying stretched out in her bed and warns the young man not to bring home any women: "Don't you blaspheme in this house." The boy runs away and lies down next to his mother, curling up in a fetal position.

That evening there is a big meal out in the open, amid the wheels of a derailed tramcar. The accordion tune from the song "Quando suona Veronica" ("When Veronica Plays") can be heard. The young man is the object of attention at more than one table, immediately welcomed in as one of the tribe. The pasta-ordering ritual is underway: people impart laborious requests and the food is tasty. A woman explains the proper way to eat snails. A fight takes place, later followed by reconciliation, between a man at one of the tables and a beautiful woman who remains stubbornly up on the balcony. The men are all wearing tank tops, and the women, sleeveless clothes. An old street performer and singer, her straw hat tattered and worn à la Nino Taranto, sings "Ciccio Formaggio" ("Cheesy Darling"). Another roadside singer, accompanied by a blind guitarist,

Opposite: *A scene from the film.*

Opposite inset: *Federico Fellini on the film set. The filmmaker is preparing for the scene at the open-air trattoria prior to the war.*

Opposite: *Federico Fellini
and Anna Magnani
on the set.*

Above: *A drawing by Fellini.*

sings "Gita ai castelli" ("Trip to the Castelli"). Both attracted and repulsed by what he sees, the young man feels won over by the vitality of the scene even as he is frightened by the people's aggressiveness.

At night, illuminated by floodlights, workers labor to repair the tram lines. The halo from this extremely strong, bluish light gives the shops, palm trees, and surreal buildings on Via Albalonga an apocalyptic feel. A herd of sheep wanders through and the dogs all start barking. Among the ruins along Appia Antica, a majestic, incredible prostitute gets out of a car. She is immense and maternal and casts a proud gaze at the surroundings. (She is truly a symbol of Rome and will wind up on the billboards advertising the movie. Originally, Fellini intended for her to recite Belli's sonnet *Il padre delli santi*, or the *Father of the Saints*, but the physical presence of the woman chosen to play the part—an office clerk named Anna Maria Pescatori, whom Fellini discovered by chance on a street somewhere—seemed more than eloquent to get the job done.)

"What about today's Rome?" With a simple audible hook, the speaker introduces us into the segment on the "Raccordo anulare," Rome's ring road. We see Fellini prepare for the sequence, climbing into the sedan that will drive alongside the crane truck carrying the film camera. There is interminable chaos on the ring of asphalt that surrounds Rome. It is raining outside and we catch glimpses of prostitutes and transvestites along the side of the road. Amid the chaos of honking cars bumper to bumper under the rain, we see a bit of everything: a white horse, a man with a wheelbarrow, a rickshaw, a bus with the banner "Forza Napoli" ("Go Napoli!" a banner expressing fan support for the Naples soccer team) filled with fans throwing firecrackers. The cars wallow in the rainwater, the noise gets louder, and the exhaust smoke grows thicker. Someone shoots flares off from the camera truck so that they can film the nearby Roman ruins in the darkness. A police siren comes wailing through, pushing the traffic to either side: there has been an accident. The cars are caught in a surreal traffic jam, the vehicles packed with all sorts of people sneering, mimicking, making obscene gestures. Amid a storm of honking, a protest march comes through carrying banners and signs. This is what has caused

the traffic jam. We hear the chorus of a protest slogan popular at the time:

Vigliacchi, borghesi   Cowards, Bourgeoisie
ancora pochi mesi   you've only got a few months left

And the enormous traffic mess arrives at the Colosseum, surrounding it.

One splendid sunny morning in Piazza di Siena, Fellini films a bus that has just arrived, filled with foreign tourists who are immediately sized up by local scoundrels. The lawyer Conocchia (an amateur actor who has already appeared in a couple of Fellini's movies) deplores the hastiness with which just about everyone faces life in the city nowadays and says that all the Romans have disappeared from Rome. Fellini talks to a group of young people in what is another situation typical of life in Italy following the 1968 protests across Europe. The film crew is busy eating. A voice confesses: "I'd like to tell you about what the little Barafonda Theater was like thirty years ago . . . Its incredible audiences. . . ." This is a variety show from the summer of 1943, which we see through the eyes of the young man, accompanied now by an old intellectual (perhaps the famous Gattone present in the screenplay for *Moraldo in città*, or *Moraldo Goes to the City*). On stage a group of dancers are performing to Ravel's *Bolero*. The audience is commenting out loud on the performance, arguing with one another, devouring snacks. A beautiful girl performs a belly dance. There is a little ballet set to "La carovana del Tigrai" ("The Tigrai Carovan," a famous song from Italy's Fascist period). A mediocre variety performer is booed off the stage. Three comedians in a row (Galliano Sbarra, Alfredo Adami, and Mario Del Vago) come in through the audience carrying lit candles, but their songs are interrupted by sonorous cheers. A child urinates between the chairs and two boys throw a wet rag into the face of a sleeping bald man (Veriano Ginesi) who is the usual target of practical jokes. Under the curtain backdrop bearing the acronym EIAR, a boorish host presents an imitation of the popular show *L'ora del dilettante* (*The Amateur's Hour*). Alvaro (Alvaro Vitali) performs a dance à la Fred Astaire. Somebody throws a dead cat from the audience, but he sends it right back where it came from and courageously launches into the final. A young singer (Loredana Martinez) performs "Tu mi hai pres oil cuor" ("You've Stolen My Heart") from the operetta *Il paese del sorriso* (*The Land of Smiles*). Somebody in the audience is arrested. The Fisa Trio, a spin-off of a famous trio starring the Lescano sisters, launches into a blend of famous Italian songs from the past: *O bella piccinina, Serenata del somarello, Fili d'oro,*

> "I'd like to tell the story of the little Barafonda Theater the way it was thirty years ago . . . the entertaining show that was its audience."

La famiglia canterina, La bella romanina ("O my Beautiful Little Darling," "The Donkey's Serenade," "Gold Threads," "The Singing Family," "The Beautiful Little Roman Girl").

During the performance, the leader of the theater company arrives onstage to read the latest news bulletin, announcing that the Allies have landed in Sicily (June 10, 1943). His report ends with the usual salutes to Il Duce (Mussolini) and to Italy, but the Fisa Trio immediately resumes singing "Maramao perché sei morto" ("Why Have You Died, Maramao?"), welcomed with happy mewling from the audience, who finally joins in with the singers on the chorus. The grand finale is "La canzone dei sommergibili" ("The Submarine Song"), performed while a lit beach scene is projected onto the dancers. An air raid siren interrupts the performance and everyone runs out.

In the bomb shelter, people calmly wait for the raid to end. There is a brief argument between a Fascist and someone accused of being a rumormonger. Our young man has made friends with a foreign dancer, resting his head on her shoulder as she sings Brahms's lullaby in German.

At dawn, after the alarm has ended, the couple exit the bunker. We hear powerful explosions—it is a bomb raid—and people come out running and screaming.

The film crew visits the construction site for Rome's subway. An engineer shows them a mammoth's tusk they found while building the Piazza Re di Roma station. As they are going down toward the tunnel, the engineer informs them that as far as public transportation goes, Rome is at least a century behind schedule, in part because construction is constantly being interrupted by archeological discoveries. Aboard the little underground train, the visitors cross through Dantesque scenes and mysterious settings full of smoke and water. They reach the center of the construction, where they see the "mole," in other words the enormous drill that cuts through the earth beneath the city. The instrument panel displays the existence of a large empty space: the workers very carefully cut through the diaphragm, penetrating it and entering a space decorated with incredibly beautiful paintings from the Roman period. But just as soon as the light strikes them, the paintings dissolve in a few minutes. The construction site secretary is desperate: "Look, what a disaster! What are we going to do! We have to do something!" But there is nothing that can be done: as soon as they are discovered, the frescoes are lost forever.

Back in the sunlight, amid the chiming of church bells, we see hippies stretched out on Roman monuments, practicing free love. And in a contrast, reminders of Italy's formerly legalized whorehouses. The alleyways of the ancient city are crowded with soldiers free on leave. A door paint-ed red, a peevish doorkeeper, a series of tiled hallways. Inside there is a long line of men, while the women can be glimpsed in the background as they go up and down the stairs amid shouts from their maîtresse. The prostitute rodeo, where the women are dressed in the most outrageous fashions, in an orgy of winking, catcalls, and obscene gestures. Insults, snickering, promises of seduction: there is one prostitute who jumps up and down like a crazy woman, another who sticks out her tongue, an impertinent lady. We see every imaginable example from the human bestiary, all set within an atmosphere of reciprocal aggressiveness between women-merchandise and men-clients. When the lady orders someone to turn off the lights, chasing everyone out for the ritual changing of the guard, the women enjoy a few minutes of relaxation, massaging sore feet and thighs. One girl sings "Macariolita."

Now we are at a luxury bordello, where our young protagonist has arrived, accompanied by a friend. There is another prostitute rodeo underway here as well, but this

Above: *The procession of ecclesiastical outfits.*

Above: *Romans out in front of the Arch of Titus.*

Death, decorated with skeletons. Finally, everyone jumps to their feet when, gesticulating from his chair and surrounded by shining lights, the Pope appears (played by Guglielmo Guasta, the veteran humorist from "Travaso").

"One, two, three!" shouts Fellini. There are dozens of lights out on Ponte Garibaldi as well, set up for the Festa de Noantri celebrations in Rome's Trastevere neighborhood. Accompanied by the song "La società dei magnaccioni" ("The Society of Big Eaters"), we head down into local alleyways and winding streets. We find Fellini surrounded by Romans and tourists in an increasingly larger crowd. Hippies sitting around Santa Maria in Trastevere fountain are singing together, but the police chase them off with sudden and unexpected violence. At this point Marcello Mastroianni and Alberto Sordi appear in the film, but in the final version the scene was cut. In it Sordi pushes aside a one-eyed man, shouting at him: "Move it, blind man! Let me look. . . ." Then he says to Fellini: "Yeah, I know you're shooting a movie about Rome . . . Hey, listen this time I'm going to get your papers taken away!"

Another scene with American writer Gore Vidal made the cut. We see Vidal seated at a table at a Roman trattoria together with John Francis Lane. He and others claim they have chosen Rome as the place where they are going to wait for the world to come to an end. In Piazza De Renzi, a boxing ring has been set up to host a prize fight.

Images of the neighborhood, half empty now that the party is over. The flute music returns. Near Palazzo Altieri, we see Anna Magnani heading back to her house, alone. We hear Fellini offscreen. He would like to ask her a few questions, but she only smiles at him and shuts the big door to her building in his face. "I don't trust you!" says Anna, her face as splendid and radiant as ever. That line concludes the film and her career as well. The famous Italian actress died two years later, on September 26, 1973.

On Ponte Garibaldi, with the party lights still turned on, about fifty motorcyclists come rumbling up out of the Trastevere neighborhood. Their helmets and scarves make them impossible to identify, as they plummet down into Rome like new age barbarians. They drive through Rome at high speed, almost as if they wish to disfigure the city's ancient monuments one by one. They ride around the statue of Marcus Aurelius in the Campidoglio. There's no music, just the sound of their engines. There is no merriment, just the insolent vitality of a thing that imposes its presence simply by existing. After saluting/insulting the Colosseum, the gang disappears into the darkness of Via Cristoforo Colombo, headed toward the sea. The sound of their rumbling motors dissipates and the image fades to black.

one is more stately: the clientele has been preselected. The young man is thunderstruck by the appearance of Dolores, a beautiful prostitute. He wants to ask her to stay with him, but there is an officer in front of him. The curtains are ordered shut and the ladies move into separate rooms to give themselves over to a few important clients.

The young man goes back to the luxury bordello one afternoon and goes up into a room with Dolores. After making love, he asks the woman to tell him a story. He keeps telling her that she is beautiful and asks her to go on a date with him out in the city.

People are feverishly getting ready for a big reception to be held in a noble family's palazzo. The old princess (Pia de Doses) welcomes a cardinal (Mario Giovannioli), while everything is ready for the ecclesiastical fashion show. Her illustrious guest sits down in a sort of small throne, surrounded by prelates and nobility in full style of *La Dolce Vita* (and we hear the same music once again). Up on the catwalk, accompanied by an electric harmonium played by two nuns, an unbelievable collection of sacred garments, clothing, and frocks appear. There is a black silk model for nuns and novitiates. There is a *tourtorelles immaculées,* in other words nuns wearing large, white-winged hats. There are other models for older nuns or missionaries. Then two little red priests come in on roller skates, two priests on bicycles, three clergymen with a censer, and a group of well-dressed cardinals just glittering with rich cloth, lamé, and neon lights. There is even a glowing costume without a priest inside. Another group of bishops come in at the head of an allegorical cart carrying the Triumph of

"ROMA LADRONA" IS BORN

Fellini's *Roma* was first screened on March 8, 1972. It garnered relatively modest box office earnings: 882,230,000 lira. The general public's apparent lack of interest in the movie may have had to do with the fact that the word "Rome" alone was enough to arouse hatred, especially in the northern part of Italy, where the pseudo-secessionist movement known as the Lega Nord (Northern League) was being developed. Lega Nord supporters would make "Roma Ladrona!" ("Rome the Thief!") their motto. The various reviews of the film tended to celebrate some segments and ignore others, without ever grasping the full breadth of what Fellini had attempted to do. On May 14, the film was presented at the 36th Cannes Film Festival, where it earned a lukewarm welcome, but over time film critics, artists, and intellectuals began to express a deep admiration for the work that was destined to endure.

"What do you mean, a film about memory, adolescence, and Rimini?! I made the whole thing up from scratch!"

AMARCORD

GOING BACK HOME WITHOUT GOING TO RIMINI

Titta Benzi, a lawyer from Rimini who was a childhood friend of Fellini's and would remain his friend throughout his life, considered *Amarcord* a group snapshot of Fellini's family, with his own father, Ferruccio, at its center. Ferruccio was the man who Benzi himself—encouraged in vain by Fellini—was supposed to play in the film. He did not feel up to the responsibility. The lawyer's reaction was the same expressed by all of Rimini, as people crowded into the local theater to watch the film and enthusiastically set about trying to identify people who had lived in real life and situations that had really taken place. This was precisely the reaction that Fellini feared the most and did everything he could to avoid: starting with the decision not to shoot even so much as an arm's length of film on the Adriatic coastline (this was particularly true for *Amarcord*, but for the rest of his films as well), but rather to reconstruct the entire setting. He began with a neighborhood designed and built in Cinecittà by Donati. This construction included a number of real elements from Rimini, but for the rest was simply invented ad hoc.

Fellini wrote the screenplay together with the poet Tonino Guerra, who was born in Sant'Arcangelo, a town just a few miles away from Rimini. Therefore, their script naturally intertwined shared memories. Even the bizarre title—*Amarcord*—was the result of a postprandial conversation at a restaurant that led the two to combine into one word a typical Romangnolo (native of Italy's Romagna region) expression: *A m'arcord*, in other words, *Io mi ricordo*, or "I remember."

Fellini, always careful not to reveal trade secrets to journalists, announced that he was preparing a science-fiction film entitled *L'uomo invaso* (*The Invaded Man*). When people discovered that the actual title was *Amarcord*, Fellini changed the graphics of the film to read "Hamarcord" and presented it in press conferences as "the adventures of a Swedish scientist." Thus, between one gag and the next, work on the film moved forward joyfully and the result was considered entirely promising. For the first and only time in Fellini's career, the movie was produced by Franco Cristaldi's Vides. When Benzi refused to play the father in the movie, the filmmaker chose an unknown actor, Armando Brancia, for the role. His wife was the grand Neapolitan actress Pupella Maggio, and the young Titta was played by Bruno Zanin. Sandra Milo was set to play Gradisca, but she withdrew from the production at the last moment and had to be substituted by Magali Noël. Filming took place during the summer of 1973.

THE SMALL TOWN TAKES CENTER STAGE

Above: *Franco Cristaldi.*

Above: *Federico Fellini and Tonino Guerra.*

Right: *Federico Fellini and Sergio Leone on the set.*

Opposite: *Drawings of the entrance to the Grand Hotel, the Hotel, and Madonna by Fellini.*

Action in *Amarcord* lasts exactly one year, from one spring to the next. But what year is it, in which era? Ever reluctant to supply precise details, Fellini distributed contradictory information left and right. It might be 1933, the year of the seventh Mille Miglia car race, as well as the inaugural transatlantic voyage of *SS Rex*, both cited in the film. But it could also be 1935, when the war in Ethiopia led Italians to sing "Faccetta nera" ("Black Face") for the first time; or 1937, when Ginger and Fred were dancing and entertaining audiences everywhere (we can see a billboard advertisement with Ginger Rogers and Fred Astaire on it). Essentially, the film is set somewhere between 1933 and 1937, the heart of the 1930s.

In March, the small town is being rained on by *manine*, small cottony seeds. Following them, we discover the home of the boy Titta Biondi (Bruno Zanin, voiced over by Piero Tiberi), the temple, the local piazza. Looking directly into the camera, the local village idiot Giudizio (Aristide Caporale), who we have already seen in *I Vitelloni* and *The Clowns*, describes the whirling white wisps along the coast, the town's Grand Hotel, and the dock, where we meet the Lawyer (Luigi Rossi) on a bicycle.

Clients are talking together at the barbershop as the sun begins to set. The sister of the hairdresser Ninola, also known as Gradisca (Magali Noël, voiced over by Adriana Asti), the town beauty, has come to pick her up. The date is March 19 and everyone is excited about the upcoming festival in honor of Saint John. The barber gives everyone a foretaste of a piece he is going to be playing on his clarinet that evening in the piazza, and Gradisca sways her hips, exciting everyone in the shop. When it is dark outside, the crowds descend on the piazza carrying boxes, crates, old furniture, and firewood for the *fogarazza*, a traditional bonfire lit during spring festivities. Among the crowd are Titta's parents, Miranda (Pupella Maggio, voiced over by Ave Ninchi) and Aurelio (Armando Brancia, voiced over by Corrado Gaipa). The boys throw firecrackers, and Volpina (Josiane Tanzilli), the local nymphomaniac, is on the edge of the crowd. Giudizio is acting crazy atop the heap of stuff. To the delight of the men assembled there, Gradisca and her two sisters arrive. Titta makes his father angry when he throws a chair that is still in good condition onto the heap of wood for the bonfire. Titta's uncle is there, too: Lello, also known as Pataca (Nando Orfei). He and his vitelloni friends entertain themselves by tossing rotten fruit at Giudizio. Then come the ritual invocations that inaugurate the bonfire.

Con sto fuoco, vecchietta mia
> With this fire, my dear old lady
l'inverno e il gelo ti porti via
> take winter and its chill along with you

The town crier/clown invites Gradisca to set fire to the heap of abandoned things. The local boys have taken away Giudizio's ladder and the poor man is frightened half to death that he won't be able to get down again. Standing before the flames, people are moved by the ritual: the headmaster Zeus (Franco Magno, voiced over by Mario Feliciani) sticks his head out of a window alongside the math teacher (Dina Adorni, voiced over by Isa Bellini). An elderly man (Ferruccio Brembilla) appears at another window and fires pistol shots up into the night sky.

In the courtyard of a wealthy home, a private *fogarazza* is burning brightly for the Count of Lovignano (Antonio Faà di Bruno) and his family. In the empty piazza, the local boys make fun of Volpina, while Pataca horses around by jumping over what is left of the bonfire, earning Titta's father's disapproval. Aurelio upbraids the boy, threatening: "I'll stick you in a school for naughty boys if you don't watch out!" A lone idiot on a motorcycle comes roaring into the piazza and drives straight through the bonfire embers. Late that night, after the festival is over, the Lawyer jots down a rapid historical overview for the audience, starting with prehistoric finds from the area and continuing through 268 CE, when Rimini became a Roman colony and the starting point of the famous Via Emilia. But his presentation is interrupted by loud cheers from hidden pranksters (Fellini personally recorded this): "This, too, is

Preceding pages: *Gradisca and Titta; inset: Magali Noël and Fellini during rehearsal.*

part of the mocking personality of the local population, a group of people with mixed Roman and Celtic blood in their veins, producing a character at once exuberant, generous, loyal, and tenacious . . . ." But the raspberries keep him from continuing.

Students make noise running down the stairs while the headmaster scolds them. They head out into the courtyard and line up for a picture, constantly joking and making fun of each other. Beneath photographs of Vittorio Emanuele III, the Pope, and Mussolini, the physics teacher is busy showing students a rudimentary pendulum and the whole class does a tick-tock, shaking their heads.

The history teacher is giving Titta an oral test. The boy gets the dates wrong and acts the fool. During a thunderstorm, the Italian teacher (Mario Silvestri) reads Alfieri out loud. The philosophy teacher (Mauro Misul) patriotically celebrates Italy's reconciliation of Church and State. The local priest, Father Balosa (Gianfilippo Carcano), holds forth on the wonder of the Trinity without realizing that his class is in turmoil. The art teacher (Fides Stagni) announces that she will be giving a lesson on Giotto, but the schoolkids act up and interrupt her. Infuriated by this lack of discipline, Zeus kicks a student out of the class.

While the math teacher gives an oral quiz, a few rascals are peeing down a long tube of paper that reaches the feet of the student being tested. Even the Greek teacher, as enthusiastic as possible about his own subject, manages to get something out of his charges. Kids are smoking in the bathroom, outside we hear a girl's voice singing "Stormy

Below: *Gradisca and her sisters (Marina Trovalusci and Fiorella Magalotti).*

Opposite: *A scene from Gradisca's wedding.*

Right and opposite: *The family around the dinner table: the uncle (Nando Orfei), the mother (Pupella Maggio), the father (Armando Brancia), the grandfather (Giuseppe Ianigro), Titta (Bruno Zanin), and Olivia (Stefano Proietti).*

Weather." Titta sighs: "Who knows who will be out on the dock this morning. . . ."

The motorcycle driver is out on the dock. Meanwhile, Volpina is walking along the beach and the workers in a nearby building yard call out to her. Their boss, Aurelio, steps in immediately and sends her off. The bricklayer, Calcinaccio, recites a poem of his entitled *I mattoni* (*The Bricks*):

Mio nonno fava I mattoni	My grandfather laid bricks
mio padre fava I mattoni	my father laid bricks
fazzo i mattoni anche me	I too lay bricks
ma la casa mia dov'e?	but where's a house I can call my own?

It is time to sit down at the table in Titta's house. His grandfather (Peppino Janigro), parents, little brother, and vitellone uncle are all there. They are making faces. Everybody's nervous. Miranda tends to spoil Pataca, the grandfather tries to feel up the maid, and Aurelio sighs amid conversations started here and there. A visitor comes to see him, making the situation worse. The man is Signor Biondi. Last night at the movie theater, Titta peed on his hat from up in the balcony. A general fight ensues, during which Titta's mother and father shout hysterically at one another, while threats, dishes, and glasses fly around.

Out walking in the evening, Gradisca asks the owner of the Fulgor movie theater (Mario Liberati) when he will be showing *The Valley of Love*, starring Gary Cooper (even though we can see a billboard poster for the film, the movie does not exist; the image of Cooper was taken from *Beau Geste*, a 1939 film that was not shown in Italy until after World War II). One of the local boys shouts something off-color at the beautiful girl and she immediately responds in kind. One vitellone holds up a telegram from a Swedish lover who wants him to move up north. Accompanied by the notes of "La cucaracha," the new "talent" for the local bordello comes through, admired and commented upon by everyone present.

It is nighttime. The town's main street is empty except for the motorcycle racing past. Colonia's (Fredo Pistoni) street-cleaning truck drives through as well; this scene originally introduced another that was later cut, and which can only be viewed in Fellini's television special, *Fellini nel cestino* (*A Basketful of Fellini*). The street cleaner Colonia climbs down into a cesspool to recover a diamond ring the Countess of Lovignano has lost. According to Fellini, the scene was cut upon request from the Americans, who didn't have local cesspools and feared U.S. audiences wouldn't understand what was going on.

It is raining on the victory monument. The statue is a female figure with an enormous behind that Titta admires deeply. The boy says good-bye to his mother, who tells him to make a good confession. When Father Balosa asks him: "Do you commit impure acts? Do you touch your-

self?" Titta's offscreen voice evokes exciting images: the corpulent tobacco shop owner in her store, the math teacher, the derrieres of the farmer women on their bicycles at the blessing of the animals, Volpina asking him to inflate one of her bicycle tires, Gradisca alone in the Fulgor, watching a Gary Cooper film and smoking a cigarette. After making a big fuss about getting close to her, Titta puts his hand on her thigh and she turns and asks him calmly: "What do you want?"

It is pointless to tell Father Balosa these things, so Titta's confession is short, his absolution quick, and penitence minimal. Next, another boy from the local gang—Candela—comes in to tell the priest about that time in the garage when four of them masturbated together in a Balilla automobile, conjuring images of women in the movies and in real life.

It is April 21, the anniversary of the founding of Rome. A parade of children wearing Fascist uniforms, Fascist Youths, young Italians, and even a few Garibaldi supporters march around the train station. (Here it is possible to make out the typically Fascist architecture of the entryway to Cinecittà, seen from inside the structure.) A federal official (Antonio Spaccatini, voiced over by Oreste Lionello) arrives in a cloud of smoke and surrounded by prominent local authorities. He has brought "salutations from Imperial Rome" and urges everyone to run along with him. Gradisca is in the middle of the enthusiastic crowd, chanting slogans for

Il Duce. The sounds of the soldier's fanfares accompany this Fascist fervor all the way to the large stairwell of the main headquarters, where everyone cheers "For us!" at the federal official's urgings. He concludes: "Of all the seas, the Adriatic Sea has always been the most Fascist."

Miranda has locked the gate to their house in order to prevent Aurelio, a well-known opponent of the regime, from getting himself into trouble. For good measure, she takes away his anarchist's black ribbon as well.

School kids are gathered to march and perform exercises in the local piazza. The Fascist Youths perform, followed by the young Italian girls. An enormous flower tribute to Mussolini is raised up while the band plays the Roman anthem and a federal official orders a salute to Il Duce. A boy named Ciccio dreams that this flowery copy of Mussolini magically opens its mouth and speaks in order to celebrate his marriage to the young Italian he loves.

At night in the center of town, the festive atmosphere continues. People are eating out in the open air and a few are even dancing among the tables. The Fascist Youths

are singing "Faccetta nera." There are a lot of tipsy people stumbling around.

Down at the Café Commercio, the Fascists are toasting to the federal official. Pataca, dressed in a Fascist uniform, uses a pool stick to perform a rifle salute before the official. "That's tough to get right," says the official, and he would like to show Pataca the right way to do it when suddenly the lights go out. Darkness. Chaos in the café. The sounds of someone playing the violin drift in from above: the tune is the "Internazionale" ("International"). In the darkness, the exasperated Fascists order everyone to go back home and try to figure out where the music is coming from. Then they start shooting like crazy at the bell tower. Frightened half to death, Pataca has lost all his cockiness. Finally, struck by a pistol shot from a Fascist's revolver, an old gramophone falls down off the bell tower and smashes onto the ground. The Fascists react to the surprise by breaking into song: "All'armi, siam fascisti" ("Get Your Weapons, We're Fascists").

Back at the Fascist headquarters, Aurelio is dragged before a group of more violent Fascists. He is accused of having said: "If Mussolini keeps this up, I can't say. . . ." Suspected of having been involved in the gramophone incident as well, Aurelio is forced to drink several glasses of castor oil while his persecutors snicker around him.

As the clock strikes two in the morning, Miranda is still waiting for her husband in front of their house. She sees him come staggering home, clutching his stomach. She washes Aurelio in a washtub. Woken up by surprise, Titta complains about the foul smell and laughs. Aurelio threatens Pataca and accuses him of spying, but the young vitellone pretends he is still asleep.

The Grand Hotel on a sunny day. The Lawyer confesses that he calls the building "the Old Lady," telling us how, behind those very walls, Ninola first earned the nickname "Gradisca" ("would you like?").

The municipal secretary is giving the hairdresser a ride, instructing her: "Mind your manners, talk proper Italian, he is a Prince, you know. Not just any old fellow. . . ." The woman makes her way hesitatingly across the lobby of the Grand Hotel and goes upstairs. To the notes of "Abat-jour," the hairdresser goes into the royal apartment where gentlemen surround the Prince (Marcello di Folco), drinking champagne. Left on her own, Ninola breaks into a sort of improvised striptease, striking poses usually seen in the sexy calendars hanging in barbershops. When the Prince reappears in nothing but a robe, the woman accompanies him to the bed, saying: "Sir Prince, *gradisca?*"

But the Lawyer never believed that story, just like he doesn't believe the tale the pumpkin seed seller Biscein (Gennaro Ombra) often tells.

A bus pulls up in front of the Grand Hotel. The Emir's thirty concubines come out, surrounded by scimitar-wielding warriors. Biscein is sitting on his tricycle, taking in the scene. The group of veiled women quickly crosses the lobby. There was a scene in which the Emir was drawn by the beauty of a Romagnola cook, but it was cut.

In the Lawyer's version of the tale, the Emir's women call out to Biscein and have him climb up a rope ladder made of bed sheets and into their rooms. Once he has climbed up, the pumpkin seed seller finds himself in a large Asian salon where the concubines await him, all dressed up as harem girls. Like a snake charmer, Biscein plays an Asian version of "Abat-jour" on his flute and some of the women perform a belly dance for him. We hear the Lawyer's voice, incredulous: "He claims that that very night, of ugly girls and pretty girls, he did twenty-eight of them. . . ."

Another, more concrete flock of females on the terrace of the Grand Hotel. Titta and his friends are outside spying on the efforts of Lello and the other vitelloni, who are busy hitting on the foreigners. They dance to the sounds of "La cucaracha." Pataca asks a German girl to accompany him on a romantic stroll along the beach, then comes back and brags: "She gave me the ultimate proof of her love, she let me take her in the behind." Even though it is late, one vitellone continues to dance, embracing his prey. Then the lights go out.

Titta's entire family heads out to the insane asylum to pick up Aurelio's brother Teo (Ciccio Ingrassia, voiced over by Enzo Robutti) and let him spend a little time outside the hospital walls. As they head down a tree-lined road, Teo eats some pasta and asks about a priest who has been dead for ten years. The grandfather claims that Titta's crazy uncle did much better in school than Aurelio. Teo shocks everyone by showing them his pockets full of rocks. When they stop to let him go the bathroom, he forgets to button his pants back up.

In the farmyard of the country house after finishing his meal, Teo seems calm. After a little while a young boy comes running up to tell everyone that their uncle has climbed up a tree. Teo is perched atop a leafy elm, shouting: "I want a woman!" His family tries to get him to come down, but he throws stones at them. Aurelio organizes a fake departure, but the attempt has no effect. The horse and carriage driver goes back to the insane asylum to get help. At sunset the grandfather is beside himself over his demented son, but the doctor and nurses finally arrive. The dwarf nun is with them (already seen in *The Clowns*) and she climbs up the ladder and orders Teo to get down, a command he immediately obeys. The doctor shrugs his shoulders and "with the opaque inevitability of a doctor in a Chekov play" reads the script and says: "What can you do? Some days he's normal, others he's not. But then that's just like the rest of us." Titta says good-bye to his uncle as the nurses take the man away.

At this point, the original script called for a scene with a waterspout, a sort of tornado from the sea. However, this scene was discarded because it would have cost too much. In it, the Lawyer tells the story of this meteorological phenomenon, an event that is often catastrophic, while a waterspout rams into the town. Winds come in from the sea and crash furiously onto the beachfront and streets. In order to keep from flying away, Titta clings onto Gradisca. Biscein tells one of his famous tall tales: during a bad storm, a boat carrying a lady from Ancona was washed all the way into the town piazza. When the storm passed, the whole town was turned upside down and inside out. There was sand everywhere, a bedside table standing erect in the town square, and countless fish, which Giudizio gathered up on the pavement.

Toward sunset, the entire town seems to be heading down to the seaside. Titta's family is there, too. Out on the boardwalk, we see the little orphan children led by Father Balosa. Other people arrive riding bicycles, in carriages, or by car. Pedal boats and fishing vessels of all kinds line the beach. Gradisca and her sisters sit down on a pedal boat. Giudizio turns to us and asks himself: "Where are all these people going?" Titta's friends are there, as well as the Lawyer, the vitelloni, Biscein, the municipal secretary, and many others. Out on the terrace of the Grand Hotel, the headmaster and teachers have gotten together to watch the event through a spyglass. They talk about the weight of the thing

for which they are waiting patiently. One says: "Two and a half times the Grand Hotel, plus the Arch of Augustus." The sea is full of boats and ships. Pataca, who wanted to go swimming, is dragged up onto a fishing boat. The Fascist party official joins the flotilla aboard a motorboat. Titta's father looks at the stars: "I wonder how he manages to put up with all this mess." Miranda is cold and starts to feel a little tired. Aurelio says: "They said around midnight. But even if it is a little bit late, after all it's coming all the way from America. . . ." The blind man, Cantarel (Domenico Pertica), plays a melancholy tune on his accordion. Gradisca is moved and says that now that she has turned thirty, it is time to get a husband, children, a family.

Everyone has fallen asleep. Suddenly, out on the sea, a black mountainous shape decked with lights appears. A siren calls and Titta shouts: "Daddy! Daddy! The Rex!" Shouts, excitement, and exclamations worthy of a miracle. Everyone celebrates the passing of the marvelous transatlantic vessel, each in his or her own way.

Titta's grandfather leaves the house and goes out into the autumn fog, though he gets lost right away. "It seems like I'm nowhere. If this is what death is like, then it's not much fun. . . ." The horse and carriage driver helps the old man back home, which is actually right in front of him. The little brother goes out into the heavy fog, headed for school, but he is afraid of the old, skeletal trees. There is an even

Below: *A drawing of the Fascist parade by Fellini.*

more frightening silhouette of a bull with big horns that seems like some kind of prehistoric monster.

"Do you guys get fog like this over in China?" At the café, Pataca is teasing the Chinese tie salesman. Fellini recuperated this scene, which was filmed and then subsequently cut, in *A Basketful of Fellini*. For the pleasure of the others present, they continue to discuss the differences between Italians from Romagna and the Chinese. Lello convinces the man to take his clothes off in order to prove that the Chinese have belly buttons just like everyone else.

The terrace of the Grand Hotel is covered with fallen leaves. The hotel has closed and the kids are spying inside through the cracks. Inspired by the magical atmosphere, Titta and his friends start dancing on the terrace as if they were holding the girls of their dreams in their arms.

Racecars from the famous Mille Miglia (One Thousand Miles) race roar underneath a banner in the middle of the night. Everyone tries to identify the drivers. Titta dreams of winning a Mille Miglia, while Pataca picks up the ear that one racer sliced off a dog.

In the tobacco shop around closing time, a mischievious Titta is helping the owner (Maria Antonietta Beluzzi) move a sack of salt. In order to prove how strong he is, he offers to lift the woman up, too. The woman proves more than willing, to the point that she takes out one enormous breast and then the other, but the boy is overwhelmed and seems suffocated by such forwardness. Disappointed, the woman gives him a *nazionale* cigarette as a gift and sends him away. Titta is so overcome that he can't even lift up the rolling storefront gate without the woman's help.

Sick in bed, Titta asks Miranda to tell him how she and his father met. Bright-eyed and feverish, the boy confesses that he would like to wear stockings and rambles deliriously about the problems in his love life.

A film is showing at the Fulgor. Giudizio comes into the Fulgor and announces that it is snowing. The kids run outside immediately and start throwing snowballs at one another. Standing at the café door, Pataca claims that snow doesn't stick. The Count of Lovignano tosses out grain in his courtyard to feed the birds. By sunset the snow is coming down heavily. At night men are out working to shovel it away. Titta and his brother throw open the window to watch the snow. Aurelio curses the heavy snowfall, which has been coming down for four days now. Out in the piazza, covered under a thick blanket of snow, the Lawyer announces: "This year will be remembered as the year of the blizzard." (In truth, the event took place during the winter of 1929.) He keeps reciting a list of the big snowstorms the town has experienced until a few guys start pelting him with snowballs.

Gradisca is crossing the piazza, followed by Titta. The motorcycle rider races among the mounds of snow that practically form a labyrinth. Titta gets lost among them and winds up in front of Father Balosa, who asks him about his sick mother.

Titta and his father head to the hospital. They find Miranda wearing a heavy jacket over her nightgown, staring out the window. Titta gives her some flowers. They say very little to one another.

In the piazza, the vitelloni and local boys are throwing snowballs at Gradisca, who throws them right back. The Count's marvelous peacock glides into the battle in the middle of the piazza and fans out its feathers in a splendid rainbow of color.

Waking up suddenly, Titta hears that they have come to pick up his grandfather in a car with some excuse or another. The boy gets up and finds the house filled with women dressed in black and people who tell him to "be brave." He starts crying and hides in his mother's room, which is now empty. Father Balosa presides over the funeral. Titta, his father, and others stand alongside Miranda's coffin. Pataca faints unexpectedly and Aurelio growls: "Take him to the brothel." When the coffin is taken out of the church, Pataca is desperate. Everyone files into procession behind the coffin, along with the band. All the townspeople say good-bye to the passing coffin in one way or another, including Fascist salutes, until finally the procession reaches the cemetery. At home, Titta can't stand his father's silent pain and goes outside, out on the dock. There he realizes that the *manine* are flying through the air again.

Spring has arrived and Gradisca is getting married to a policeman. All the characters from the film have come together at three large tables in the Trattoria Paradiso out in the countryside. There are toasts, friendly banter, and the blind man plays the accordion. The owner of the cinema tells everyone that Gradisca has "found her Gary Cooper." There are more friendly toasts from Father Balosa and the tobacco shop owner. The photographer urges everyone to hurry up because it is starting to rain. There is a struggle to kiss the bride, Calcinaz recites a new poem, and the policeman shouts "Hooray for Italy!" Biscein, Giudizio, and others come to pay their respects as well. Gradisca is already overwhelmed with nostalgia, and the groom practically has to drag her away, toward the car that will take them far from the little town. There are numerous good-byes, tears, the last few jokes and gags. It has stopped raining. The blind man continues to play: the wedding guests wander off and head home, leaving the man there alone. Night has arrived.

A MIRROR FOR EVERYONE

Fellini's movie couldn't have been more successful with critics and audiences alike. It was released just before Christmas, on December 15, 1976, and earned 3,333,450,000 lira. *Amarcord* was destined to be Fellini's last great success at the box office. On May 9, 1974 it was shown at the 27th Cannes Film Festival and on April 9, 1975 *Amarcord* won the Academy Award for Best Foreign Film. (Fellini was not present, but Cristaldi, who produced the film, was on hand to accept the Oscar and was absolutely overjoyed at the success.) It was Fellini's third Oscar after *La Strada* and *Nights of Cabiria*. And it would not be his last.

"Casanova is nothing more than an Italian male chauvinist, always chasing after women, as much of a scoundrel as possible. You might say he is a vitellone, even a super-vitellone, but dislikable. How dislikable? I'll tell you when I've gotten him out of the way, once the movie has been finished."

FELLINI'S CASANOVA

IL CASANOVA DI FEDERICO FELLINI

GIACOMO THE DISAGREEABLE

I n Italian, to work *contraggenio* means to work unwillingly or reluctantly, even hating the task at hand. For Fellini, it was *Casanova*. The interesting thing is that no one had ordered him to make it. But then Fellini never did anything under order; he did everything his way. In the name of personal and professional autonomy, he often ignored extremely appealing offers. So it is not unreasonable to wonder: Why did he agree to make a film that he was fed up with no sooner than he had signed the contract? The same thing had happened with *Satyricon*, only with *Casanova* the final result was much less satisfying.

Fellini's interest in Casanova's memoirs dated back at least twenty years and was related in part to advice from Pinelli, an attentive and refined reader. At the time, De Laurentiis had already produced Riccardo Freda's *Il cavaliere misterioso* (*The Mysterious Rider*, 1948), with an acrobatic swordsman Vittorio Gassman à la Douglas Fairbanks, while Gabriele Ferzetti had acted in Steno's *Le avventure di Giacomo Casanova* (*Sins of Casanova*, 1954) with yet another producer. Portraying the character in the cape and sword genre, De Laurentiis was more than happy to film Fellini's version, imagining a super-vitellone: a sort of macho, vital, powerful ladies' man. The producer was also happy to see that in the wake of their falling out over *Mastorna*, Fellini was rekindling their friendship, returning to the Venetian adventurer as a subject for their conversations about what movie to make in its place. This is what De Laurentiis was expecting: the picaresque travels of a vagabond moving about Europe in the 1700s, going wherever scantily clad beauties and the chance to draw a sword led him. As long as Fellini was manning the kitchen, this kind of filmed fricassee—a mix of love and dueling—was a guarantee for satisfaction. Thus a deal was quickly struck, followed just as quickly by disappointment, for each. Fellini discovered that the big book he was supposed to turn to for inspiration didn't inspire him in the least. Actually, it bored him, and to the horror of Casanova fans he defined it as nothing more than "a phonebook of names,

good only for lighting fires." De Laurentiis, on the other hand, quickly discovered that the filmmaker was taking a completely different course than the one he had expected. Nothing was a better indication of this than the fact that Fellini refused, once again, to work with the American star De Laurentiis insisted upon: Robert Redford. Redford was asking for a million dollars, but no matter: just having him in the cast would be enough to guarantee financing from the other side of the Atlantic. They forged ahead anyways, pretending to misunderstand one another for a year, during which names such as Marlon Brando and Al Pacino were presented and promptly rejected. Finally, on July 24, 1974, De Laurentiis abandoned the production. Fellini then turned to Andrea Rizzoli, son of the successful Rizzoli senior, known in Italy as the *Commenda*, who had only recently passed away. It was not difficult to convince "Junior" to pick up the project, and they immediately set October 30 as the deadline to start filming. On August 28, Fellini was in London and had practically decided to take on Michael Caine, but the British actor had other commitments. After having considered and rejected a number of Italian actors, including Marcello Mastroianni, Vittorio Gassman, Alberto Sordi, and a particularly quarrelsome Gian Maria Volontè, Jack Nicholson was considered for the part. But even Nicholson failed to convince the filmmaker. Fellini finally chose the Canadian actor Donald Sutherland, whom he knew well. Sutherland had already acted for him, playing himself in Paul Mazursky's *Alex in Wonderland*. Fellini went to visit the actor in Parma on the set of Bernardo Bertolucci's

Page 231: *Donald Sutherland*

Opposite: *Donald Sutherland and Margareth Clementi.*

Below: *Casanova with the mechanical doll (Leda Lojodice).*

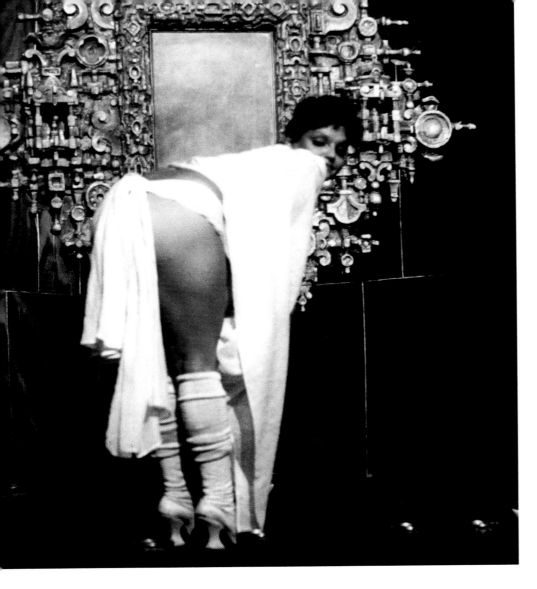

Novecento (*1900*) and they quickly reached an agreement. Sutherland accepted a "mere" 180 million lira for the role, and at the end of the meeting said: "I would have swum all the way to Italy to make this movie." But the production dates continued to be postponed for one reason or another, and people close to Rizzoli (headed by the producer's financial manager, Fulvio Frizzi), who had had a chance to read the complicated script by Fellini and Zapponi, fought the film tooth and nail. Finally, even Rizzoli decided it would be better to abandon the project. Once again Grimaldi saved the day, on the condition that they film in London where it would cost less. But Fellini preferred to stay on his home turf. He insisted they work at Cinecittà, and in the end, the producer gave in to the filmmaker's wishes. The project was approved on July 20. It would go way over its nine million dollar budget, with twenty-one weeks of production and 186 actors (although in truth almost all were unknown, as was Fellini's custom). On August 27, more than three years after discussions to make *Casanova* had first begun, Fellini shot the first scene in theater number five at Cinecittà, entirely filled with sets made by Donati based on Fellini's drawings. On the 27th

the rolls of film from shooting over the previous three weeks were stolen. There was a rumor that the thieves had requested a 500 million lira ransom, but at least part of what had been stolen was found almost a year later. On December 17, workers in Cinecittà went on strike to protest contract issues. An exasperated Grimaldi decided to throw in the towel, shutting down the film and firing everybody. The project was suspended for a month, with vitriolic accusations flying left and right (Grimaldi even went so far as to say "Fellini is worse than Attila"), but the good-hearted efforts of mutual friends managed a reconciliation toward the end of January.

Starting on March 23, filming resumed on scenes with an elderly Casanova in the Dux castle and at the oneiric carnival in Venice, after which in May (given that four years had passed since the project first began) the film could finally be considered complete. Throughout that period, Fellini worked at full steam, was constantly irritated, and brought his irritation to bear primarily on Sutherland. In the beginning, he was quick to declare that he was glad he had chosen Sutherland for the actor's "moonish" face (an adjective that would reappear for Benigni in *The Voice of the Moon*), as well as for "his baby-blue eyes," but things quickly changed. Generally speaking, Fellini was very understanding of and friendly with his actors, but as far as "Donaldino" was concerned, the filmmaker became implacable, temperamental, and pitiless. Later on, Fellini would explain that this attitude, one he was sincerely sorry he had adopted, was the result of his need to vent his deep dislike for Casanova. Sutherland just happened to be there, an easy target. (After all, who could possibly provide a better target than the actor who was playing the character?) Extremely heavy makeup meant Sutherland had to get up at dawn, constantly change in and out of forty costumes, deal with ten different wigs, three hundred noses and three hundred chins, as well as painful stockings and endless repetitions. The actor demonstrated that he understood the situation and approached his lot with an impeccably professional attitude: he did every single thing that was requested of him and never failed to respond "thank you" to a clearly unhappy director. Therefore, at the foot of the fake Rialto Bridge on the last day of shooting, the crew and those present were that much more surprised to witness a truly unexpected denouement: Fellini, his eyes full of tears, said good-bye to Sutherland, embracing him and whispering apologies in the actor's ear. They made peace with one another and Sutherland left satisfied. But an important issue remained: Would the film they had made together actually work?

THE SEX ATHLETE

The film credits play on the water of Venice's Grand Canal at nighttime. Masked revelers at the Venice carnival crowd around the Rialto Bridge carrying lanterns and torches. One person recites "Orazione a Venezia" ("A Prayer for Venice)" by Andrea Zanzotto, and the crowd responds in chorus. Chopping through a rope with his scimitar, the Doge brings an angel down from the bell tower, sending it splashing into the canal. Accompanied by trumpet peals, a giant female figurehead (a symbol of Venice? a symbol of the Great Mediterranean Mother?) is pulled up out of the water, while the coryphaeus recites an invocation of the "Mona ciavona" by Tonino Guerra. But the figurehead is too heavy. The rope breaks and the giant woman's head falls back into the canal. While fireworks light up the sky, we catch our first glimpse of Casanova (Donald Sutherland, voiced over by Luigi Proietti; in the French version, voiced over by Michel Piccoli, directed by Patrice Chereau) among the masked revelers. He is wearing a *bautta* (a typical eighteenth-century Venetian mask) and small red hat. A girl gives him a note.

On the banks of San Bartolo Island, at nighttime, Casanova takes off his mask and rereads the note. In it, a nun makes an appointment to meet him "with no servants and holding a candle in one hand." The nun (actually, she's not a nun) arrives in a boat and leads Casanova through a courtyard and into a hallway lined with erotic tiles. When the two reach the bedroom, Sister Maddalena (Margareth Clementi) checks to make sure the French ambassador is hiding behind a fish painting. (The goal of this encounter, which in the book takes place the night of "Saint Sylvester," or New Year's Eve, is to give the ambassador the opportunity to see the famed Casanova in action.) Not the least bit opposed to the idea, Casanova opens up a big case he always carries with him and takes out a golden mechanical bird that sings in synch with his carefully calculated performances as sex athlete. The protagonist dedicates himself to a sort of frenetic Kama Sutra, a series of acrobatic acts during which his passionless lust produces a lot of sweat, shortness of breath, and a sense of emptiness. After the orgasm, which takes place when their bodies have become detached from one another and at different times, the spectator on the other side of the wall comments on the performance with measured compliments. A braggart and pimp, Casanova seizes the moment to offer a vast range of services to his majesty the King of France. Then he leaves Maddalena.

There is a storm in Venice. Out in the waters of the lagoon, Casanova's gondola is approached by a big boat. On it, a man dressed in black announces that the adventurer is under arrest.

In the Piombi prison, the chief of police reads a list of the crimes Casanova has been accused of: black magic, possession of outlawed books, heretical writings, and disregard for religion. Casanova is locked in a cell so small that he cannot stand up. In order to pass the time, the prisoner reminisces about one of his love encounters.

The encounter takes place in an embroiderer's house. The women working there sing and joke with one another while they sew a round tablecloth. The Countess Giselda (Daniela Gatti) shows up in a gondola and the women put their heads under the tablecloth in order to keep from looking directly at her. Giselda and Casanova dine on oysters. At the height of a conversation rife with double entendres, the woman offers her bare behind to her seducer's whip. After he is through flogging her, Casanova is moved by tenderness. He embraces the Countess and calls her *cocolon*, or his "little darling."

But even Casanova's sweetest memories are not enough to make the cell in the Piombi prison bearable. He delves into other memories to return to the embroiderer's atelier, where the pale Anna Maria (Clarissa Mary Roll) faints during dance lessons and has to be bled. Casanova comforts her as well.

The following two scenes were cut. In the first, Casanova's maid Barberina (Chesty Morgan) comes to tell him the news that the affair with his patron, the marchesa, has been discovered. As she is telling him this, the maid uncovers her enormous breasts, inflaming the great lover's passions and leading to another seduction scene (this scene was later used for Fellini's television special, *A Basketful of Fellini*).

In Anna Maria's house, Casanova hears her moving through the courtyard at night and goes to catch up with her. Their romance is interrupted when the woman faints once again, leading to yet another bleeding session. Looking at her in bed, Casanova finds he cannot resist and jumps on top of her. The girl is shocked awake by this brutal contact. We see her back in her gondola, perfectly healthy and calm.

There is an escape from Piombi, running across rooftops during a moonlit night in which we can make out cupolas and bell towers against the dark sky. Casanova says: "My escape from Piombi was a masterpiece." It also marks his farewell to Venice for many years.

In Paris, in Madame D'Urfé's salon (Cicely Browne, voiced over by Lilla Frignone), Casanova is eating with a series of extremely important guests, including the Count of Saint-Germain, known as Cagliostro (Hatold Innocent), who claims he has lived for three hundred years. Madame D'Urfé loves to surround herself with magicians and swindlers: there is even a little girl who expresses wise confutations to the teachings of Saint Augustine. When the host gets up, Casanova follows her. In her private quarters, rife with cabalistic symbols, Madame D'Urfé shows her guest a small box of gold coins and takes him to bed. Under the rain, a carriage has come to pick Casanova up at the old lover's house. She accompanies him to the transom. Once he is alone in the carriage, the fundamentally provincial Casanova finds himself so happy to be in Paris that he masturbates excitedly. Between one jerk and the next, the carriage overturns in order to keep from striking a passerby, who is none other than Casanova's brother, an abbot. The protagonist is entirely uninterested in the reunion and takes advantage of the situation to carry off Marcolina (Clara Algranti), his brother's lover. Back in his hotel room, Casanova possesses Marcolina amid cries of pas-

Henriette (Tina Aumont). Two years earlier at an inn in Forlì, Casanova defended a Hungarian captain who was being threatened by papal officers because he was in the company of a girl dressed as a man. During a happy meal together in the carriage, Henriette ("Enrichetta") and her captain introduce Casanova to the delicacies of Parma: salami, prosciutto ham, and special cheeses. During a stop in their travels, the captain speaks to Casanova in Latin while Enrichetta sleeps, telling him that he is giving the girl to him. At a hotel in Parma, the captain takes his leave of his young lover, now dressed up again as a lady.

There is a big party taking place in the house of a hunchback, Du Bois (Daniel Emilfork Berenstein, voiced over by Oreste Lionello), a gay benefactor at whose table Spaniards and Frenchmen gather together. A "marvelous little opera" is performed (*La mantide religiosa*, or *The Praying Mantis*, verses by Antonio Amurri). The songs are sung by a pair of castrati, the lord of the manor dressed as a female praying mantis, and his lover, Giambruno, as the male mantis. Ending with a song dedicated to Cupid, the performance is about to earn a critique from Casanova, but the protagonist is distracted when Enrichetta starts playing the cello.

Wandering around the garden, restless and crazy in love, Casanova sees a mysterious and unknown man.

Everyone is applauding Enrichetta for her skill with the cello, but this mysterious Signor D'Antoine has come for her.

Casanova and Enrichetta lose themselves in a fit of passion while the mechanical bird goes haywire. The famed seducer pronounces the fatal word: "forever."

When Casanova wakes the following morning, Enrichetta is no longer there. Du Bois is present instead, advising him against chasing after her, because D'Antoine is taking the lady back to an unnamed European court, where she belongs. The chorus rising up from the monks in the convent on the other side of the

"Where do his voyages through women's bodies take him? Nowhere at all."

sion. His brother the abbot has provided further fodder for accomplishing his plans against the marchesa.

Back at Madame D'Urfé's, Casanova and a scantily clad Marcolina perform a ritual invoking various deities including Selene and Osiris. Once she has had her bath, the marchesa is brought to Casanova, who wears a crown of lit candles. After having been aroused by Marcolina, the Latin lover possesses the elderly lady in synch with the mechanical bird's fluttering wings.

Fleeing Paris with the marchesa's gold, Casanova tells his accomplice of his great love for the French woman

road invokes the death mirrored in the protagonist's mood. Casanova tells how "many years later" in London, he came close to committing suicide.

Back in another carriage, this time enveloped by the fog, an irritated and unhealthy looking Casanova is arguing with two women, a mother (Carmen Scarpitta) and her daughter (Diane Kurys). When the discussion starts to get out of control, Casanova has them drop him off on a bridge over the Thames. Bitter and unhappy, the famed lover has decided to put an end to it all: he dresses right then and there in his best clothes and heads into the river intent on killing himself, all the while reciting verses by the Italian poet Torquato Tasso. Suddenly he is distracted by the appearance of an incredible, gigantic female figure on the riverbank (Sandra Elaine Allen).

At a fair worthy of *La Strada*, one that looks as if it had come straight out of a Hogarth print, Casanova is searching for this giantess when a man invites him to enter inside the "great *mouna*" (in Northeastern Italian dialect, *mouna* is slang for "vagina").

È dalla mouna che è venuto fuori il mondo…
 The world came from the *mouna* . . .
Dalla mouna è venuta fuori anche la mouna…
 Even the *mouna* came from a *mouna* . . .

The verse was written by Tonino Guerra. Inside the mother of all whales, a magic lantern projects monstrous female images.

Casanova runs into his old friend Edgard, drunk and high in a local tavern, and chastises him: "You travel to worlds that don't exist." Edgard responds: "Oh yeah, well, where do your travels across women's bodies take you? Nowhere." The giantess is there, too, challenging anyone and everyone to an arm wrestle. Casanova accepts her challenge and loses. He discovers that his adversary, Angelina is a Venetian just like him. Angelina annihilates a few massive male champions in a wrestling

contest. Casanova gets the two dwarfs who manage the giantess to give him permission to see her bathe in a tub.

The next scene was cut, but is included in *A Basketful of Fellini*. During the scene, Casanova visits Ismail Effendi, with whom he engages in the only homosexual encounter of the movie in a refined parody of *A Thousand and One Nights*, Casanova accepts a kiss on the mouth from his host while they are together on a boat.

The scene after this was never filmed and can only be found in the original screenplay. In Maria Theresa of Austria's moralistic Vienna, Casanova anticipates Nabokov's masterpiece, *Lolita*, seducing a ten-year-old girl.

Below: *The Pope (Luigi Zerbinati).*

In Rome, we see the Pope (Luigi Zerbinati) surrounded by cardinals. There was a scene planned in the gardens at the Quirinale during which the Pope hears Casanova's confession, a sort of repeat of the meeting with the cardinal in *8 ½*, but the scene was never shot. Casanova experiences the excitement of *la dolce vita* lifestyle several centuries earlier, waltzing through orgies and erotic games at the English ambassador's house. Someone has the idea of provoking the famous seducer into a challenge against the coachman, Righetto (Mario Gagliardo), a poor man's Casanova who claims to have satisfied his lover seven times in a single evening. In order to have intelligence triumph over brute strength, Casanova chooses the Roman model (Veronica Nava) as his partner for the challenge, gulps down eighteen raw eggs, and tackles her in a frenzy. Meanwhile Righetto straddles a spoiled aristocrat with far less success. When the clock strikes the hour, Casanova is proclaimed the winner in an atmosphere of rascally excitement.

The next scene, during which Casanova was to visit Voltaire in Switzerland, was never filmed.

Next, Casanova tells the tale of his stay at the house of the famous entomologist Moebius in Bern. The scientist's two daughters take good care of the Venetian, who faints under their ministrations. Isabella (Olimpia Carlisi) and her sister (Silvana Fusacchia) put Casanova in a little bed, where they practice a sort of acupuncture on him and whip his toes to bring him back to consciousness.

After a few days, the guest feels more at ease, even though Isabella still does not like his way of mixing amorous discussions with funereal citations. On his way out the door, Casanova tells the girl to meet him in Dresden. While he is waiting in vain for Isabella at the Moor's Inn, Casanova runs into his ex-lover Astrodi (Marika Rivera), a Venetian singer who introduces him to a long-tongued, hunchbacked girl known as "the single most dirty pervert in the world." Casanova decides right then and there to stay the night.

A boisterous night ensues, complete with the chiming mechanical bird and a foldout bed that bounces and shudders beneath the chaos of Casanova and the two passionate lovers—the hunchback and the singer—while a crowd of entertained spectators comes and goes.

Astrodi's performance in *Orfeo e Euridice* (*Orpheus and Eurydice*) at the Dresden Theater earns her hearty applause. Once the audience has cleared the theater, Casanova is left alone in the large hall as the candle chandeliers are lowered down and blown out. A woman calls out to him from the stage: it is his mother (Marie Marquet, voiced over by Cesarina Gheraldi),

whom he has not seen in years. Casanova brags of his successes and apologizes for his long silence, but his mother won't hear of it. The son climbs up on stage in order to support his mother, who has difficulty moving around. "You're wrong, mamma, to say that I'm just a *cabron* [Venetian for "old goat, brute"]. I'm famous across Europe." But Casanova's mother continues to treat him like a liar and complain that he doesn't send her any money.

Outside a carriage takes his mother away before Casanova can get her address. The Venetian leaves on foot, while he tells us about trips to Holland, Belgium, and Spain. Then on to Oslo, then Würtenberg.

At this point, the screenplay calls for a scene in Naples that was never filmed. Casanova is attending the court of Ferdinand I, where he meets his old lover Lucrezia, who has given him a daughter, Leonilda. The seducer makes love to both the mother and daughter together, and is savagely beaten by Lucrezia's husband's thugs.

The court in Würtenberg, which according to our narrator is supposed to be the "most brilliant court in all Europe," seems more like a living hell of drunken officials; everyone is celebrating the Duke of Würtenberg's anniversary, but the Duke isn't interested in listening to flattery from his Venetian guest. Casanova turns his attention to the Duke's elderly sister, imploring her to nominate him ambassador to the Saxony court. A black, shiny tortoise wanders around while various court officials are pushed on extremely high ladders toward special organ buttons lined on the wall. "Orgelnoten wie kanonenkugeln!" ("Organ notes like cannonballs!"): musicians and singers perform a deafening tune for tenors and chorus, "Il cacciatore di Würtenberg" (or "The Hunter of Würtenberg," lyrics by Carl A. Walken). Seeing two buffoons molest a lady, Casanova takes out his sword in order to defend her, but the lady in question is merely Rosalba, a mechanical doll made in Nuremberg (Adele Angela Lojodice, wearing a porcelain mask).

Once the party is over, Casanova invites Rosalba to dance with him in the middle of the empty hall. After they reach Casanova's room, the two dancers slide into bed together. Casanova gives himself the extreme experience of seducing a doll.

At dawn the Venetian lover gets up, goes to the mirror, and puts on his makeup. He barely glances at the doll lying motionless on the bed, her legs and arms spread wide apart, and exits the room without looking back.

A carriage is moving through the snow toward Dux. The protagonist's voice warns us that the winter is long in Bohemia, where he has been living for many years in

Waldstein Castle, working as a librarian, "an important position that is a perfect fit for my studious nature." In the castle kitchen—a sort of military mess hall—a bent and bald Casanova asks in vain for a plate of his favorite pasta, only to be made fun of by the head butler Faulkircher (Reggie Nalder) and the other fellows present.

The librarian escorts a few noblemen to the bathroom, where someone has stuck his portrait to the wall with shit. Casanova points out that the image of him was ripped out of his "famous" novel, *Icosameron*, and after asking if any of those present had read the book, he repeats the name he used as a "famous Italian writer," but nobody recognizes it anymore.

During a meeting with the old countess, who ignores him, Casanova once again rails against his old enemies. The young Count of Waldstein presents Giacomo Casanova to those present, "an adventurer many have spoken of. . . ." Amid some absent-minded commentary

("I thought he was dead," and "Is it true he's insane?" "Oh, but he's a caryatid!"), Casanova starts to recite some verses by Italian poet Ludovico Ariosto. A girl laughs then apologizes, but the dejected Casanova bows to the assembly and takes his leave. The scene moves to his messy chambers, where we catch a glimpse of the mechanical bird, now battered and bruised. The wigless and exhausted Casanova says: "I am proud because I am nothing." All he has left is the memory of a dream.

Winter has Venice in its grip; its waters are frozen. A young Casanova dares to venture out to see a woman's head imprisoned in the ice. Women from his past appear behind him, all running toward Rialto Bridge. A golden carriage rides past, drawn by eight white horses. His father and mother are inside. Once again, this is an existential dream, like the one in *8 ½*, but the only female that Casanova manages to get close to is Rosalba, the mechanical doll. Together, they perform one last dance.

ONLY SIMENON, APPLAUDS

The film didn't seem to work, or it only worked in part. It was released before Christmas, on December 1, 1976, and earned 2,559,964,254 lira (a reasonably satisfying amount) at the box office. But the people who first ran to see the movie weren't particularly impressed: Fellini's antipathy was a bitter pill for his audience. Publicly some people applauded the film, as in the sincerely admiring interview Fellini was given by his friend Georges Simenon, appearing on the front page of *L'Express*, but many critics panned the effort and some (especially in the United States) blasted it outright. With only a few exceptions, Casanova experts, who constituted a true sect, condemned Fellini's unilateral and moralistic version of the Latin lover. Fellini was accused of failing to recognize the cultural accomplishments of his subject, as well as downplaying the value of Casanova's memoirs as a document of their times. Piero Chiara was an exception. Ever sharp-minded and direct, Chiara absolved Fellini despite his own love for all things Casanovian, claiming that he found the filmmaker's point of view "stimulating."

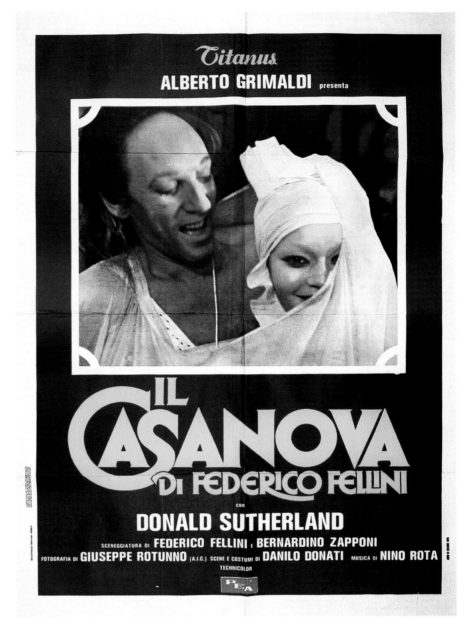

Above and right: *Federico Fellini and actors on the set.*

"I wanted to start the film with gunfire, explosions, shouts, police sirens . . . But you'll find none of this onscreen. At a certain point I realized I didn't need all that in order to make people understand the real facts that gave birth to this story, and the way we're currently living."

ORCHESTRA REHEARSAL
PROVA D'ORCHESTRA

UNBEARABLE YEARS

I n order to debunk his reputation as someone who always ran late, who in fact often forgot or ignored his appointments, Fellini adopted a special technique. He chose four or five people and carefully maintained an extremely close relationship with each of them, even going so far as to appear on time and complain about the tardiness of others. Then, when talk of his own failure to keep scheduled appointments arose, Fellini would quickly mention these four or five privileged people and bring them forth to testify on his behalf. Of course, they could not help but describe the filmmaker as a champion of punctuality. To the joy of producer Leonardo Pescarolo, Fellini employed the same trick for *Orchestra Rehearsal* (intended for distribution through RAI), promising to make the film in exactly four weeks. Even more amazing, despite the pitfalls that regularly await filming, Fellini was able to pull it off. As a result, Pescarolo went around proclaiming that Fellini was simply the fastest, friendliest, and most reasonably priced director on the planet. He also added, with the wisdom of someone who had worked for years in the business, that despite the excellent results he would never dare to make another film with Fellini out of fear that the second attempt would ruin his positive experience with the first.

This newly adopted respect for deadlines and schedules was joined by something much more important. Up until this point, critics and scholars all agreed that Fellini's films were entirely apolitical. *Orchestra Rehearsal*, on the other hand, was nothing less than a metaphor of Italy's political situation, viewed realistically with open eyes, and therefore resulting in an entirely bleak outlook.

Fellini felt he could see disturbing signs of chaos and destruction everywhere: the most troubling was the kidnapping and murder of the Christian Democrat leader Aldo Moro at the hands of Red Brigade terrorists between March and May 1978. This was most likely the episode that prompted Fellini to join the fray.

The explicit, powerful, and undeniable metaphor is that of an orchestra that can no longer play together, that refuses to try, that won't obey its conductor. In order to make the metaphor more believable, Fellini took care to meet and get to know as many musicians as possible: he invited them out to lunch one by one in his favorite restaurant, Celestina, and had them talk about themselves. He listened to their confessions and recriminations, jotting down details. Then he hired minor actors or walk-ons to interpret the musicians, having them learn the basics of how to hold and play their instruments for the film. Rota provided a majestic score that framed the entire movie.

Page 243: *Fights in the orchestra.*

Opposite: *Federico Fellini explains a scene to the actors.*

Right: *A drawing of the harp player by Fellini.*

A FAMILY DESTROYED

An invisible television crew (we only rarely hear Fellini's voice as the interviewer) enters an old oratory transformed several centuries ago into a concert hall. Some information on the place's history, an apology for the acoustics, and a variety of other digressions are amiably provided by the elderly Copyist (Umberto Zuanelli), who, in the meantime, is busy laying out the music on the musicians' stands.

Orchestra musicians wander in a few at a time, some curious about the presence of a television crew, others annoyed. We see First Violin, Pianist, Clarinetist, and others pass by in front of the camera. Interviews are interwoven with the same old conversations, nonsense, minor squabbles over this chair or that music stand. Some of the people discuss their private lives, another works on a crossword puzzle, someone else talks about an argument at a red light, a few listen to a soccer game on the radio. The First Violin measures the dampness in the air, which promises to be perfect. The Second Violin takes some anti-anxiety medicine, while the Trumpet player complains that somebody stuck a condom in his instrument.

When the conductor announces that there is a hidden television crew in the room, the musicians start arguing whether or not this unexpected "performance" should be provided free of charge. The group's union representative seems conciliatory, but several others are against the idea. The Harp player (Clara Colosimo, voiced over by Isa Bellini) grows angry because the same-old idiots welcome her arrival by playing a few notes from the marching tune associated with the television characters Laurel and Hardy.

The Pianist (Elizabeth Labi, voiced over by Angiola Baggi), the Flutist (Sibyl Mostert), and the Trombone player (Daniele Pagani) bare their souls in front of the television camera. The elderly Violoncellist (Ferdinando Villella, voiced over by Pietro Biondi) is fascinated with a spiderweb on the ceiling that vibrates with every pulse of music: "Isn't it wonderful that we are all here to let that little spider swing through life?" The Neapolitan Drummer talks about the friendships, competition, and petty dislikes that exist among instruments. Meanwhile the camera pans across the characters, creating a gallery of images worthy of Gogol. We get the impression we are witnessing a drawing set to life with real characters.

Each musician brags about his particular instrument, and finally one says: "The first violin is the brain and heart of the orchestra." Someone makes fun of him, adding: ". . . And the clarinet is the cock!" The film forges ahead amid loud cheers from the double bassoon and freewheeling nonsense from just about everyone: the Clarinetist plays a personal favorite, describing the compliments he once received from Toscanini; the Trumpet player complains because playing music makes his lips crack. With eloquence worthy of a workers' revolution, the union representative announces that he has saved the orchestra from a servile situation and has managed to transform the "slave musician" into a "fully integrated and accomplished worker, one who is well aware of his place in mass culture."

The sudden and unexpected appearance of a mouse in the room creates an exaggerated ruckus, and the characters behave like schoolchildren: a bunch of musicians chase after the rodent, killing it and proudly holding it up for the union representative to see ("Hey, you owe us a mouse finder's fee!").

The nervous, fidgety Conductor arrives (Balduin Baas, voiced over by Oreste Lionello). He is blond, has a German accent, and is immediately put off by the television lights. After declining a personal interview, he starts warming up the musicians, beginning with the string section. But the musicians interrupt him, complaining that they are not members of the same party; in other words, they don't play together. Things start up again, then are interrupted. There is more arguing. The Clarinetist begins laughing and the Conductor chastises him: "There's no point in your laughing!" During the warm up, the Conductor makes a phone call while the orchestra members keep chatting among themselves. The Conductor gets angry, shouting and throwing music sheets into the air. There is a certain amount of general irritation in the air.

Interrupting the general chaos, as the orchestra musicians take off their jackets and a few even go so far as to take off their shirts, the Conductor invites "Toscanini's clarinetist" to play a few notes. The musician cites the union rules that prohibit him from repeating a passage for the third time. The Conductor makes the mistake of inviting the musician to respect the music itself before bothering with the union rules. Everyone starts to protest and the room is filled with complaints and insolent remarks. Once again, the entire auditorium is rocked with violent noise as if there were a thunderstorm or earthquake.

There is another incident concerning the absence of the Flugelhorn player, who has refused to attend for union reasons. When the union representative and the Conductor start fighting, the head of the orchestra announces that the musicians are upset and have decided not to contin-

Preceding pages:
(top left) The Palazzo del Cinema set by Dante Ferretti; the big rehearsal room and other preparatory scenes.

Below: *Producer Leo Pescarolo.*

Above and left: *Federico Fellini and the actors.*

ue the rehearsal. Exasperated, the Conductor shouts: "What do you people want from me? . . . Do you want my ass in a sling? [He shows his behind.] Here it is, you've got it!" Amid indignant protests from the orchestra and the maestro's spectacular exit, someone announces a twenty-minute break, twice the usual time allotted.

Out at the bar, members of the orchestra comment on what has just happened. Others play cards or complain.

The Double Bassoon player gets angry at his own instrument, a "symbol of obtuseness."

Back in the auditorium, other musicians are still waiting. A violin player, the husband of another violin player, argues with his wife, who has started sipping from a bottle of whiskey. The Tuba player (Giovanni Javarone) confesses that he has gone to bed with his instrument because "it looks like me." The Oboe player (Andy Miller)

faithful become atheists." Music is always sacred, every concert is a holy mass . . . Now "we all play music together, but we're only united by our shared hatreds . . . We are like a family that has been destroyed."

Another rumbling sound, this time more threatening than before. The lights have gone out. The Copyist escorts the Conductor back to the auditorium by candlelight, but the orchestra members are outraged and ready to revolt. After having covered the walls with lewd messages (the most inoffensive reads: "Hooray for record players"), they start chanting slogans then breaking and smashing everything. The Double Bassoon player and the Pianist take advantage of all the chaos to hide under the piano and make love. Dust and rubble start raining down from the ceiling while the union representative and the head of the orchestra, no longer allies, blame each other for everything that is happening. Even the other members of the orchestra start to fight with one another. Something disgusting and slimy starts dripping from above. Even though she has been injured in the mouth by a broken teacup, the Harpist, insists on declaring her love for her instrument in front of the television camera.

"Orchestra / terror / death to the conductor!" chants the chorus of rebel musicians. An enormous metronome is brought into the auditorium, but the most violent musicians knock that down as well. There are more blows on the walls, the rubble raining down from the ceiling grows more intense, and an old, exasperated orchestra member fires a few pistol shots into the air. The confusion reaches its peak and we hear a tremendous blow. A crack opens up in the wall in the back. Beyond it, we can see an enormous steel wrecking ball.

There are cries of terror, everyone scrambles to escape, and the room is upset as if during an earthquake. Overrun during the chaos, the Harpist is carried away in someone's arms. The Conductor takes advantage of the situation to tell everyone to pick back up their instruments: "We'll save the notes." The only way to make sense amid all the chaos is to start playing music again: "We are musicians, you are all musicians . . . And we are here to rehearse together." The Copyist offers him the baton, the Conductor takes it in his hand, and the orchestra musicians play standing up, gathered close around the podium.

For a few minutes their music, played with conviction, reverence, and fear, seems as if it will be enough to save them all. But no sooner than the piece is over, the Conductor starts railing at them again and shouting, and while the scene fades to black he continues his tirade in German with an aggressive eloquence that is a clear echo of a much more (in)famous German leader.

brags about his own sound. The Organist reads tarot cards for the union representative and head of the orchestra, drawing out a threatening omen: the roofless house.

While they wait for the Conductor to finish taking a shower in his chambers, the Copyist sighs and reminisces about the hardworking ethic of past maestros, when musicians had to rehearse all night long. He is indignant at the sight of two musicians who are writing things on the wall against the Conductor, but it's time to take the television crew to the dressing rooms for an interview. The maestro's monologue is an outburst railing against the public's ignorance and the death of music: by now the head of the orchestra, who many people consider a king, has degenerated into nothing more than a poor sergeant devoid of even so much as the right to scold the lazybones in the orchestra. Democracy has flattened the scale of values: all that is left to do is horde money and buy houses all over the place. "You say the 'head of the orchestra,' but these words don't make sense any more. The head of an orchestra is like a priest who needs a church full of believers, of the faithful, when the church crumbles and the

"Music is always sacred, and every concert is a Catholic mass . . . Now let's all play music together, but united by nothing more than our shared hatred."

A GREAT DEAL OF APPREHENSION, BUT NO LESSON

Orchestra Rehearsal was produced by Pescarolo's Daime cinema company for RAI, with the German company Albatros Filmproduktion. It was broadcast in October 1978, preceded by a screening at the Palazzo del Quirinale (the official residence of the president of the Italian Republic) that Sandro Pertini, then president of Italy, insisted on holding. Numerous government authorities were there, and Italy's main newspaper, *Corriere della Sera*, decided that instead of having its film critic comment on the evening, the paper would publish a piece by Giulio Andreotti, a prominent politician at the time. Amid widespread admiration for the movie, each politician offered different opinions of Fellini's creation. Rightwingers interpreted it as the "call to order" Italy needed most, while the left insinuated that it was best understood as the opening salvo of a reactionary. As always, Fellini kept himself out of the debate, believing he had already said what he needed to say and did not consider distributing messages to be one of his responsibilities. The film was later released in the theaters, but as is the case when a film is shown first on television and then in the theaters, its box office earnings were disappointing.

Below: *Federico Fellini and president of the Italian Republic, Sandro Pertini.*

"In order to shoot this film, the most tormented of my career, I had to cross from one anteroom to the next for years. And then all hell broke loose, starting with the ferocious opposition from feminists."

CITY OF WOMEN
LA CITTÀ DELLE DONNE

A MANHUNT

We have now come to the film that had the single longest gestation period of any of Fellini's projects: it took nearly a decade to come to fruition, starting in 1969 when the initial idea for the story appeared as Fellini's *Duetto d'amore* (*Love Duet*) project with Ingmar Bergman, a movie that never got off the ground. In the spring of 1975, Fellini was in contact with the producer Franco Rossellini, a relative of his friend Roberto Rossellini who had once graciously accepted to play an aristocrat in *La Dolce Vita*. The younger Rossellini had a reputation as being a playboy and owned a production company he had named "Felix" in honor of his dog. Fellini liked the young Rossellini because he didn't feel rushed. While

Fellini muddled through the screenplay together with Zapponi, who was given credit for the initial idea, he also set things moving in the United States, where at a certain point Bob Guccione, the Croesus of *Penthouse* fame, appeared interested, apparently drawn by the libertine aura that surrounded the project. Nothing came of it, however, and as often happens in the film industry, weeks and months continued to shuffle past. Preparation for the film had been initiated with Dante Ferretti as the art director and Gabriella Pescucci in charge of costumes, but all work on the project came to a halt during the spring and summer of 1978 once Fellini decided to focus his time and talents on *Orchestra Rehearsal*. Franco Rossellini decided to turn the project over to his son, Renzo Rossellini, who managed to cover the entire budget for the project through the French company, Gaumont. Starting in November 1979, preparations in Cinecittà intensified.

On March 3, 1979 Rota passed away unexpectedly, and it was as if Fellini had lost an intimate part of himself. His collaboration with the great composer had existed for so long and been so close that the filmmaker was understandably devastated. In order to continue work on the movie, Fellini called in the maestro Luis Enrique Bacalov. The gloomy mood that surrounded the project grew even

Page 253: *Federico Fellini on the set.*

Opposite: *The rebellious women.*

Below: *Federico Fellini directs Marcello Mastroianni in a scene from the film.*

worse for Fellini when he became afflicted with an insistent bout of insomnia. Unsatisfied with the script, he set about rewriting it together with Rondi, but everything moved forward so slowly; he was affected by the same alienation he had experienced years earlier when working on *Casanova*. He was not particularly attracted to this film, either, and could already feel the project weighing down upon his shoulders. It had become little more than a job he had to get done, a contract he had to respect.

Filming began in the spring and was almost immediately criticized by feminists, who were bothered by its satirical aspects. The countless women who took part in the film were ceaselessly attacked, estranged, and targeted. Fortunately, some of the tension was alleviated by Mastroianni, who knew how to put Fellini back in a good mood. Right from day one on the job, Mastroianni man-

aged to add a measure of lightness and good humor to the project.

Shooting took place in the movie sets built at Cinecittà, then in the pinewoods outside Fregene. Unfortunately, a fatal mistake had been made: the choice of Ettore Manni, now far from being the "handsome man" of Italian cinema, to play the grotesque role of the horny male chauvinist Katzone. ("Katzone" is a pun, almost identical in pronunciation to *cazzone*, or "giant penis.") The actor showed up drunk on the set nearly every day, in a worse state than Broderick Crawford had been in during filming of *The Swindle* and undoubtedly less convincing as an actor. He couldn't remember his lines, messed up his movements, and seemed lost in space. Nothing worked to pull him back into line. It was a disaster that ended tragically on July 27, when the actor took a pistol into his hands and aimed it at himself. Some said his death was an accident, while others believed it was an act of desperation.

Fellini, too, was desperate. The entire project had been an overwhelming affair, and now this tragedy threw a wrench into the film itself. Katzone was supposed to appear in various scenes, and most importantly in the finale, during which he was to stand alongside Mastroianni as they fly up in an aerostatic airship. They would have to find another solution: film whatever they could with a stand-in shot from behind, cut, edit, and make changes to the script. It was a major problem. And, in fact, on August 10, Gaumont, undecided about whether or not to cancel the entire production and write the investment off as a loss, suspended filming and fired the entire staff. It was the second time something like this had happened to Fellini, the first being with Grimaldi during the filming of *Casanova*.

Once the production company realized that it would cost more to declare the project a failure, especially in light of the fact that most of the budget had already been spent, filming resumed on September 24. The movie was finally completed on November 29 at Cinecittà after seven months of tormented and chaotic effort. Fellini, with one broken arm locked in a cast, drew his final conclusions on the film with growing dissatisfaction. But despite the filmmaker's unhappiness with the result, he had managed to impress a level of coherence on the movie that ultimately made it a new, incomplete chapter in the self-analysis he had initiated in *8 ½*. This time his theme was relationship with women, developed on three different levels: youthful erotic fantasies; singular dependence on a wife; and the irresistible attraction for a femininity the essence of which continued to escape him amid the turmoil of contemporary feminism (at turns laughable, irritating, or indicative of vitality).

MARCELLO IS GAME

What does Snàporaz (Marcello Mastroianni), the handsome man napping on a train in the opening scene of *City of Women*, dream about? Since Freud has taught us that "the driving force of dreams is the desire to satisfy," it is not difficult to interpret the image that opens and closes the movie: a locomotive steaming its way into a tunnel. Hitchcock concluded *North by Northwest* with the same image in order to let his audience know that Cary Grant was finally going to bed with the blonde. But in Fellini's film, the metaphor doesn't take on equally consolatory characteristics.

Opening his eyes in the train car, Snàporaz (at first Fellini wanted Dustin Hoffman to play the role, considering him "a funny, bewildered little man à la Buster Keaton") realizes that outside the glass door, like in *Matrimonial Agency*, some children are busy making fun of him. But he is immediately intrigued by the blonde woman he discovers seated opposite him (Bernice Stegers, voiced over by Adriana Asti). Dazzled, he follows her to the bathroom, where he attempts to seduce her on the spot: the first coitus interruptus. The train comes to a halt in the middle of the countryside near Fregene, the woman gets off, and Snàporaz goes running after her. Mastroianni is as irresistibly attracted and pliant as he was back when he chased Ekberg into the Fontana di Trevi. At the foot of a large tree, just when it appears that they will finally get down to business, the signora (the second coitus interruptus) orders the clumsy Casanova to close his eyes in order to better appreciate her passionate kisses. When he does, she abandons him on the spot: "lost in an unknown forest, alone and without any food."

We see a sign for the Grand Hotel Miramare, presumably where the signora has fled. Unfortunately, the hotel has been invaded by a tumultuous group of women of all shapes, sizes, and ages. Snàporaz wanders through this grotesque antimale inferno, within which Fellini has added every imaginable irony on the excesses, mythomanias, and exuberances of modern feminism. The pilgrim wanders in and out of meetings and debates, coming to a stop before a mime (Alessandra Panelli) performing an act on a housewife's toils for a monstrous husband wearing a Frankenstein mask. There is also a foreign woman who demonstrates the advantages of polyandrous relationships, showing off her six happily cuckolded husbands. Snàporaz has no choice but to move cautiously forward while the hullabaloo continues unabated around him, like an explorer delving deeper into an unknown jungle. He makes an attempt to join the assembled Furies by chanting with them "matrimony is for the insane!" but his efforts prove futile. In passing we can see a large cardboard head with Fellini's eyes (either painted on or photographed), staring down upon everything, watching everyone.

Suddenly the woman from the train reappears. She launches into a verbal attack against Snàporaz, bringing the ire of the entire female community down squarely on his shoulders, insulting and threatening him. A pair of girls, Donatella (Donatella Damiani) and Loredana (Rosaria Tafuri), push Snàporaz into an elevator and lead him to a large gymnasium. His two companions get him to put on a pair of rollerskates in order to make him even more uncomfortable and off-balance amid a crowd of irate females.

Fortunately Snàporaz, rolling down a flight of stairs, winds up right in front of the stoker from Trieste (Jole Silvani), who offers to save him by carrying him away on her motorcycle. On the way, the horrible virago draws him into a plastic greenhouse and tries to take advantage of him, when suddenly (the third coitus interruptus) the sex-starved woman's elderly mother shows up and starts kicking her daughter, freeing the poor fellow. Snàporaz continues his travels, picked up by a car full of strange folks—a group of slightly drugged-out punk rockers who stop near Rome's Fiumicino Airport in order to watch the jets drop down like birds of prey out of the dark night. Snàporaz is frightened half to death upon seeing one of the punk rockers take out a pistol and make as if to shoot at one of the planes. He runs away, but is chased by three cars full of screaming feminists. The protagonist makes his way to the old castle owned by Sante Katzone (Ettore Manni, voiced over by Marcello Tusco), a diehard macho man who chases off the women hunting Snàporaz with rifle shots. Snàporaz and Sante recognize one another: they are old schoolmates! The man

Preceding pages: *Federico gives instructions to Alessandra Panelli.*

Below: *Composer Luis Enrique Bacalov.*

launches into a long-winded monologue about the threat of demolition his manor is currently under, bragging that he has had no fewer than ten thousand women in his lifetime (precisely what Simenon once told Fellini about himself), and that very evening has plans to celebrate his record with a giant cake and candles. While he is waiting for the party to start, Snàporaz takes a look at the erotic curios around the castle. He is amused and a little shocked when he visits a sort of phallu-cratic mausoleum where his old friend keeps giant photographs and recordings of his most memorable bedroom escapades (mostly voiced over by Solveig D'Assunta). Lacking any form of logic as is the way with dreams, at the back of the crypt Snàporaz discovers his wife Elena (Anna Prucnal, voiced over by Livia Giampalmo), in her usual unhappy and recriminating self.

The party celebrating Katzone's ten thousand conquests takes place in a funereal atmosphere. While his latest girlfriend is busy demonstrating that the female sex organ has enough prehensile strength to draw in coins and pearls, Katzone laments his forthcoming adieu to sex. Suddenly a squad of policewomen arrives, with the female stoker in full uniform, and starts questioning whether or not the party has gone over its allotted time. They have come in with the aim of annoying Katzone, and even go so far as to kill his beloved dog, Italo. They also ransack his laboratory, the place where the horny man was busy constructing his ideal woman (the mechanical doll from *Casanova*?). Katzone expresses his deep pain by clinging to a marble bust of his mother.

Once his superphallic alter ego has disappeared, Snàporaz sees the surprise his host has prepared for him: a pair of scantily clad dancers—once again Donatella and her companion, who entertain themselves and Snàporaz by imitating Fred Astaire in a sort of "coming soon" from *Ginger and Fred*. It seems like a good idea to continue the game underneath the covers of the broad, comfortable bed they have led him to, but just as things are starting to get interesting (the fourth coitus interruptus), the girls melt away. His wife appears to the sounds of "Amami, Alfredo" ("Love Me, Alfredo") and is clearly in the mood for lovemaking, but between her heavy makeup and beauty creams the woman has become anything but appealing. This clownish Elena leaps onto her husband with obscene desire. Snàporaz himself performs the fifth coitus interruptus, running away beneath the bed, where he finds an actual water slide as an escape route.

He likes letting himself slide down the twisting chute, into an amusement park decked out with countless

lights, behind three old men dressed in tailcoats (Armando Paracino, voiced over by Lionello; Umberto Zuanelli, voiced over by Gianni Bonagura; Pietro Fumagalli, voiced over by Vittorio Congia) who are shouting. Snàporaz returns to the women of his childhood and adolescence. In portraits that turn on and off one after the other, we see a beautiful servant, a fishmonger (Gabriella Giorgelli) with some eels, a saucy nurse from the spa, two blonde, leather-clad motorcyclists, a stall on the beach complete with a tiny spy hole for which boys wrestled with one another for a chance to catch a glimpse of female bathers getting undressed, images of film divas from the past (silver screen vamps including Greta Garbo, Brigitte Helm, Marlene Dietrich, and Mae West), together with an audience of boys lying down on a big, broad mattress and collectively masturbating beneath the sheets in a relatively tasteless

Above: *(from top to bottom) Ettore Manni as Katzone (with Carmen Russo below on the right); additional scenes from the film.*

scene. The subsequent scene is rather questionable as well: a legalized Italian bordello with a *maîtresse* talking and moving around like a mechanical doll, as well as a bespectacled prostitute with a gigantic behind.

Even the sexual experience in Snàporaz's hall of memories is interrupted (we have now reached the sixth coitus interruptus) when the protagonist reaches the end of the water slide. The feminists, as ferocious as ever, are once again hot on his heels: Snàporaz remains caught between the shame of his own impotence and his fear of castration. He is locked up in a cage and taken into a horrible hangar where shady homosexuals make deals with feminists hooded à la members of the Italian terrorist group, the Red Brigade. The time has come to put Man on trial, to brutally and systematically annihilate what little is left of his personality. But Snàporaz remains incorrigibly curious and can't help but ask what lies "back there." They tell him that there is an arena where, before an all-female audience, some gladiators battle with the ideal woman and come out of the experience in rather poor shape.

> *"I was, like never before, on the edge of disaster. I don't know how I managed to make it out."*

Snàporaz wants to give it a shot, too, and heads down a long, narrow corridor and out into the spotlight: our hero is assailed by flowers, whistles, and firecrackers worthy of a Kafkian antihero. Two women dressed like Laurel and Hardy invite him to climb up a rope ladder, at the top of which he finds Katzone's old servant waiting for him. The servant helps him climb up into the cabin of a blimp shaped like a very buxom girl with a halo of little lights like those used to crown a statue of the Madonna. For Snàporaz, flying up into the night sky aboard this marvelous ship proves to be a magical moment: but suddenly a female terrorist wearing a heavy coat puts an end to the experience (now the seventh coitus interruptus), shooting a machine gun from the empty arena down below, thus deflating the blimp and sending Snàporaz's airship plummeting to the ground.

Our protagonist abruptly awakens in his seat on the train. His wife, who has been keeping a kind eye on her husband, is sitting in front of him. On one side he sees the woman he first chased after in his daydreams, on the other the two friends, Donatella and Loredana, who are actually two students with schoolbooks tucked under their arms. It is a finale not unlike the one that was discarded for *8 1/2*: life is a journey that everyone takes together, so we might as well be friends and get along. Meanwhile, the train rolls into a dark tunnel and no one knows what lies inside.

ZERO TO ZERO

P roduced by Opera Film with coproduction from Gaumont Paris, *City of Women* was released on March 28, 1980 and took in a total of 1,002,157,000 lira at the box office. Most people panned the film and it received relatively negative reviews. This time, the match between the filmmaker and his audience ended in a tie, zero to zero. The movie was heavily criticized at the 33rd Cannes Film Festival on May 19, earning Fellini some of the worst reviews of his entire career. Fortunately, not all critics reacted as harshly, but media around the world (including in the United States) did not labor particularly hard to understand or appreciate even that which was admirable in the film, since such elements were invariably within rather questionable contexts. Instead, most members of the press found it easier to pan the entire production.

FEDERICO FELLINI
LA CITTÀ DELLE DONNE

con
MARCELLO MASTROIANNI

Gaumont

e con
ANNA PRUCNAL   BERNICE STEGERS
DONATELLA DAMIANI   IOLE SILVANI
e con
ETTORE MANNI
soggetto e sceneggiatura FEDERICO FELLINI BERNARDINO ZAPPONI
collaboratore alla sceneggiatura BRUNELLO RONDI
musica di LUIS BACALOV

edizioni musicali (Cam)

ANNO DI EDIZIONE 1980

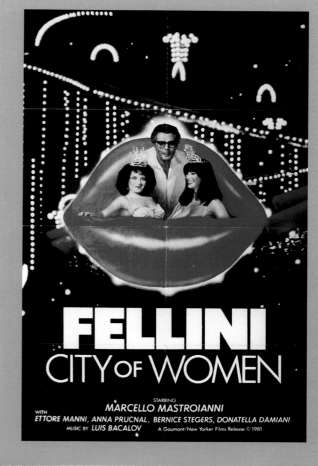

FELLINI
CITY OF WOMEN

STARRING
MARCELLO MASTROIANNI
WITH
ETTORE MANNI, ANNA PRUCNAL, BERNICE STEGERS, DONATELLA DAMIANI
MUSIC BY LUIS BACALOV

A Gaumont/New Yorker Films Release © 1981

FEDERICO FELLINI LA CITTÀ DELLE DONNE

"Once again, I wrote a screenplay a century before actually starting the film . . . Today people expect a filmmaker to continue to be inspired forever, but how is that possible? The years go by, you change and turn into someone else, you start to think about different things."

AND THE SHIP SAILS ON

E LA NAVE VA

WHERE IS IT HEADED?

Things were slowing down for Fellini, and the filmmaker would take months and even years to finish each new film. This situation grew worse with Fellini's indecisiveness, as he was assailed by many short-lived temptations. Apparently, the filmmaker's genius was best suited to "ready-made" moviemaking, where decisions had to be made on the fly even amid contradictory impulses, forcing him to think quickly and on his feet. A series of ideas were discarded, including a number of offers from the United States, where one person in particular insisted on doing a version of Dante's *Inferno*. More to the point, Fellini's old friend De Laurentiis had turned into a Hollywood mogul and was keenly interested in resuming their longstanding collaboration. But Fellini was dead set on sticking to his familiar settings between Via Margutta and Cinecittà. Talking about different projects with Tonino Guerra, they remembered a short script they had patched together some years earlier: *L'attentato di Sarajevo* (*The Attack in Sarajevo*). Although it was unusual for Fellini to set out to do a historical film, the plot quickly took on all the trappings of a fable built upon numerous current events—a looming war, the blessed ignorance with which everyone bore down on catastrophe, the weight of destiny in tragedies. Franco Cristaldi, a producer Fellini had never worked with before, was immediately attracted by the project and put the trusted Pietro Notarianni alongside Fellini to make sure things went smoothly. Notarianni had been a part of the famed Vides production company for years and had been the deceased film director Visconti's trusted collaborator. To everyone's surprise, Notarianni found another Visconti in Fellini, and quickly made himself fully available to the filmmaker. From that moment, Notarianni became Fellini's main assistant, just as Fracassi had been twenty years earlier.

Incredibly enough, the stars all aligned to bind Fellini to a project even he considered ephemeral. RAI, the Italian state television company, agreed to come on board. Thus, while the screenplay moved forward thanks to Guerra's fervent and fertile imagination, Fellini began to check out studios and potential locations, traveling among other places to Genoa in April 1982 to see the *Guglielmo Marconi*, a ship that was at the time dry-docked in Ligurian shipyards. The *Marconi* would provide useful inspiration for the work that Ferretti eventually conducted, building the ship to be used in the film directly in the studio. At a certain point, the idea of having the imaginary voyage reflect the actual ship that transported Maria Callas's ashes, spread out over the Aegean Sea, began to take shape. There would be numerous passengers, including a guide: a bizarre reporter named Orlando (taken from the name of a famous RAI correspondent, Ruggero Orlando). Mastroianni silently hoped he would be picked for the part, but this time Fellini would disappoint him. The filmmaker traveled all the way to London to screen a vast number of actors, all of whom proved well prepared, well mannered, and professional. But when it came to the protagonist, Fellini tried a host of actors and ultimately chose Freddie

Page 267: *The rhinoceros is lowered into the hold.*

Opposite: *Federico Fellini during filming.*

Below: *Federico Fellini and Peter Cellier on the set.*

Above: *Federico Fellini on the deck.*

Opposite (from top to bottom): *Sara Jane Varley and Fellini, Freddie Jones and Fellini, Fiorenzo Serra and Pina Bausch.*

Jones, a relatively minor character actor who was sure to do at least a decent job with the part. The filmmaker's sudden and unexpected predilection for actors who had different habits, rigorous training, and most importantly thought and communicated in a different language surprised everyone. Some people in Fellini's inner circle worried that a cast mashed together in this manner (though not without a few "gems," including extraordinary choreography by Pina Bausch), would ultimately prove un-Fellinian and therefore would not be able to express that natural, merry, and rascally complicity that Fellini had always managed to draw out of his actors.

Shooting began on November 15, 1982 and was the object of intense speculation in newspapers and mass media throughout its production, which lasted four months. Rotunno worked to achieve a particular coloring in the original film, giving the movie a refined patina of yesteryear. Unfortunately, as often happens over time (and as often happened with Fellini in particular), Fellini's longstanding collaboration with his cameraman began to sour: *And the Ship Sails On* would be the last film they would make together. There were no battles between them; their relationship deteriorated in a way that seemed, at least on the outside, painless for both.

A MOVIE STAR'S ASHES

To the droning whir of a movie camera, like in old silent films, we see a few jittery images of dock number ten in the port of Naples, where the ship *Gloria N.* is still anchored. It is July 1914. Passengers start to arrive aboard cars from the turn of the century, moving among the Neapolitan wharf boys and climbing up on board the ship. A few captions accompany the reportage Orlando (Freddie Jones, voiced over by Ferruccio Amendola) is putting together. An enormous wagon full of dead bodies appears. A burial urn is taken off the wagon and carried up onto the ship. It contains the ashes of the great singer Edmea Tetua (Janet Suzman was photographed for the part). In the meantime, a band plays and the images on the screen shift to color. Soloists and the chorus perform a piece composed for the occasion:

Seguiamo sui flutti	Let's follow the flow
di gioie e di lutti	of joy and pain
la rotta più ardita	the most challenging route
la nave che va…	the ship's off again . . .

As everyone onboard, including the engine room workers, continues to sing, the ship is unmoored from the dock. And the ship sails off. Now the music we hear is taken from Tchaikovsky's "Nutcracker Suite." Down in the kitchens, people are frenetically at work; up in the restaurant, passengers are sitting down at their tables. We catch a glimpse of Orlando's camera (even more imaginary than the camera in *Orchestra Rehearsal*) and characters cross the screen: Ildebranda Cuffari (Barbara Jefford, voiced over by Rita Savagnone), the deceased singer's main rival; the tenor Sabatino Lepori (Fred Williams) together with his petulant Argentinean wife; the comedian Ricotin (Jonathan Cecil); the impresario of Covent Garden, Sir Reginald Dongby (Peter Cellier, voiced over by Lionello) along with his wife, Violet (Norma West), who is more than a little drawn to the waiters' Latin looks.

Orlando is laboring over his silent documentary, behaving much like a modern television figure, asking himself the rhetorical question: "Where are all these beautiful folks headed?" Hindered by the constant back and forth of the waiters, the journalist ticks off a list of the celebrities: the directors of all the most important

theaters, the *enfant prodige* Von Rupert, and the bearded tenor Aureliano Fuciletto (Victor Poletti, voiced over by Alessandro Haber). This last character teases a seagull, showing the bird tasty mouthfuls of food as it flies outside the ship's window. At a certain point the gull manages to find its way into the restaurant, provoking panic and sending people knocking about left and right.

To the sounds of a triumphant marching tune, the Grand Duke of Herzog (Fiorenzo Serra) enters the scene, together with his blind sister Lherimia (Pina Bausch), the Prime Minister (Philip Locke), and Signor Tutz (Colin Higgins), the chief of police. The journalist doesn't stand a chance of getting close to such illustrious individuals, and to keep from feeling too embarrassed, Orlando reveals that this voyage is actually a funeral: a trip to fulfill the last wishes of Edmea, who asked that her ashes be scattered in the Aegean Sea off the coast of her native island, Erino, at the first light of dawn. The blind woman Lherimia lists the colors she imagines she can see, linking each one to different musical notes.

Inside the Captain's cabin, Orlando is showing off the funeral urn and introduces the Captain in his usual bumbling manner. After having dryly dismissed the interviewer, Sir Reginald goes on deck to look for his wife. Orlando points out a very rich Egyptian, the deceased singer's ex-lover: "Apparently he has an enormous, purplish penis . . . At least that's what I've heard."

Down in the kitchens, the two elderly maestros (Umberto Zuanelli and Vittorio Zarfati) are playing Schubert's "Musical Moments" with some glasses.

Up on deck, illuminated by the light of sunset, guests and officers are entertaining one another. Both the sun and the moon are visible in the sky, shining down on the ship. We hear casual conversation, often referring to the legendary legacy Edmea has left behind. Orlando is struck by the sudden appearance of Dorotea (Sarah-Jane Varley), who looks like she has stepped straight out of a Botticelli painting.

At night, while the ship sails along, people are at the bar talking once again of Edmea. Aureliano, who worked

with the famous singer, is not all that interested in joining in: "Whatever she had in her hand she'd throw right at you." Orlando is getting drunk. Only the Count of Bassano (Pasquale Zito, voiced over by Massimo Giuliani) is on deck, basking in the beautiful moonlight.

A lot of people are in their cabins, still awake. Sir Reginald's wife has just bid her waiter lover good-bye when her husband begins to make a scene.

Meanwhile, the Count of Bassano watches an old film of Edmea, and Orlando runs into Lherimia in the hallway.

When it is time to go to bed, the journalist, alone and exhausted, gathers up his paperwork and notes and says: "These are just some notes I was jotting down . . . for my diary . . . I write and tell people things, but what do I really want to tell you about? A voyage across the sea? The voyage of life? You can't tell people about that: you do, and that's already more than enough . . . It's banal, isn't it? Everything has already been said before! And better! . . . But everything has already been said and done before."

A guided tour of the ship. Drawn by the sudden appearance of so many famous stars from the world of opera, the macho engine room workers ask them to sing. Ildebranda hesitates, but Aureliano and Sabatino launch right into a performance, dragging their colleague into an unusual singing duel.

Down in the hold among piles of hay, we see a rhinoceros that has been entrusted to a Turkish guardian. The animal is headed for a zoo in Amsterdam. Dorotea sighs: "He's in love, poor thing."

Despite the lively reaction of the bodyguards, in the ship's theater the journalist has managed to get an interview with the Grand Duke. They talk through a German interpreter and amid lengthy discussions on the actual meaning of his oracular words, the Grand Duke comments on the international situation: "We are all sitting on the brink of disaster."

On the second day of the trip, the passengers pass the time chatting on the deck, drinking, and taking snapshots. The chief of police notes that the Prime Minister is spending some time alone with the princess. Down in the kitchens, the Russian singer gives a practical demonstration of his ability to hypnotize a chicken with song. Unfortunately, he makes Orlando faint as well.

In the bar, the conductor is once again rehearsing with all the singers. Out on deck Orlando is delighted at the chance to exchange a few words with Dorotea. A terrible stench rises out of the hold where the rhinoceros is kept, creating a few misunderstandings and protests. The big animal is tied up, brought on deck, and

"English actors have won me over: punctual, as rigorous as if they were headed into the office."

washed with great blasts of water. Then they put him in one of the lifeboats.

From Orlando's reporting we learn that during the third night of the voyage everything gets a little stranger. In the library, the secretary to the conservator of La Scala opera theater holds a séance, acting as a medium, and goes into a trance. People try to get Edmea's spirit to talk, but the guests who have come together are frightened by the arrival of the ghost: the Count of Bassano wearing one of the deceased's costumes.

A little gypsy girl appears on deck, at night, and an enormous horde has gathered behind her. They are all Serbian refugees who have fled their country out of fear of Austrian reprisals following the murder of the Archduke Ferdinand in Sarajevo. After having picked them up at sea, the captain decides to take them all to the closest port, but it does not seem like it will be easy.

When it is time to eat, the hungry refugees watch the passengers dining from behind the glass windows. Attracted by the handsome, virile-looking men, Violet goes out boldly among them, bringing them food and drink. The chief of police protests with the captain: the refugees are a threat to His Majesty's safety. The Serbians start to make their way into places that are supposed to be off limits to them, including the bar. A series of ropes are set up to keep them out. One of the old maestros, Ruberti, offers cookies to a Serbian girl. His intentions seem more than a little sleazy: in fact, he is giving her cookies in order to get closer to her. People in the Grand Duke's chambers are nervous, and the Grand Duke tries to distract himself by playing chess with his sister. But the blind woman checkmates him.

After dinner the passengers hear Serbian singing on deck. Lherimia and the Prime Minister hold a secret meeting: they are lovers and are planning a coup d'etat. After they finish singing, the Serbians start dancing. Some of the more curious passengers join in. The party becomes a social event. Orlando is dancing with Dorotea (although she more than willingly longs for the attention of young Mirko), and the ship sails through its last night as a gigantic dance floor.

At dawn, once the dancing is over, the ominous silhouette of a battleship appears on the horizon. It is the flagship of the Austrian navy and its officers want the Serbians to be turned over immediately. While people on the ship become increasingly restless, the captain refuses to hand over the refugees. Officers on the battleship threaten to open fire, but out of respect for the memory of Edmea Tetua, they are willing to grant a truce so that they can proceed with the funeral ceremony.

The sea burial ceremony gets underway off the coast of Erino Island. The ship chaplain reads the Psalm of David. The dead singer's voice issues forth from the broad, trumpet-shaped speaker of a phonograph while her ashes are scattered in the wind. Everyone present is deeply moved. When the ceremony is over, the chief of police arrests the Prime Minister for political conspiracy.

Right: *A drawing by Fellini.*

25 Feb. 82. La nuova nave buia *grandissima* ~~elettrica~~ (venata di nascosto all'insaputa di tutti) ~~eeeeeeee~~ gigantesca sul mare solcandolo impetuosa e potente. Può anche immergersi e nessuno in profondità come un immenso sottomarino

Above: *A drawing of the ship by Fellini.*

The next scenes take place to music and singing, like in a melodrama.

No, no, no non ve li darem…
    No, no, no we will not give them to you . . .

The officials and passengers aboard the *Gloria N.* are all singing their rebellion against the Austrians in defense of the Serbians. The battleship draws closer in order to allow the Grand Duke to get on, while the refugees are sent to the lifeboats. In the midst of an amorous fervor, Dorotea decides to go with her beloved Mirko.

It seems like one of the Serbians aboard the first lifeboat has thrown a hand grenade into the battleship (but the specific details of the event are never clarified). The warship responds with cannon fire: everyone panics, chaos ensues, and the ship is wrecked. Water crashes into the hallways of the "Gloria N." Everyone dashes toward the lifeboats. Hypnotized by the images of an old film of Edmea, the Count of Bassano decides to go down along with the ship.

At this point, we suddenly become aware of the presence of cinema: the audience discovers that we are not actually onboard the *Gloria N.* but in Studio 5 at Cinecittà, amid a host of film sets, spotlights, and a large film crew. The camera is set up on a crane, filming the entire scene, and the narrator (Orlando? Fellini?) has one eye glued to the lens.

Orlando's story ends with the reassuring news that many of the passengers were saved. We see a colorless image like in the initial scenes of the film in which the journalist is floating along on a lifeboat with the rhinoceros. "Did you know that rhinoceroses make excellent milk?" We hear the whirring of the camera once again.

IT SEEMED LIKE PEOPLE COULDN'T WAIT

The film was produced by Cristaldi under the auspices of RAI and coproduced by Gaumont and SIM (Società Internazionale Milanese), owned by a Libyan-born Italian of Milanese descent, Aldo Nemni. The film debuted at the Venice Film Festival on September 10, 1983. As always, Fellini unwillingly attended, avoiding the press conference and giving only a few interviews. Interest for the new film had never been greater, and initial reactions to the screening were positive. Everything seemed to presage considerable success at the box office, but it was not to be. The film was released in theaters on October 7 and earned 1,002,157,000 lira. There was a clear incongruence between the vast media coverage of the film and its ad campaign with the all-too-modest earnings in theaters. Furthermore, the most significant earnings came right at the beginning and then disappeared shortly thereafter. The movie earned a cruel comment from the critic Pauline Kael that reflected the changed level of interest that now existed for Fellini the man and Fellini the filmmaker: "At this point, he is the real film, so much so that all he need do is show up, and forego actually making the movie."

Franco Cristaldi presenta

Federico Fellini
E la nave va

una Coproduzione RAI Radiotelevisione Italiana
e VIDES Produzione S.r.l. (Italia) GAUMONT (Francia)
Produttore associato Aldo Nemni per la SIM
Realizzata dalla VIDES Produzione S.r.l.
Gaumont

Above and right: *Scenes from the film.*

"All things abnormal, monstrous, delirious, or exceptional are served up on television as if they were the most obvious, normal, familiar, and banal events of everyday life."

GINGER AND FRED

GINGER E FRED

GIULIETTA IS BACK, DANCING

After *Juliet of the Spirits,* Fellini had not made a film with his wife for over ten years, and at a certain point the issue of offering her another opportunity became paramount. Her career began parallel to that of her famous husband (in truth she started earlier, with her memorable performance in *Senza pietà,* or *Pitiless,* for which Fellini wrote the screenplay), and Masina had become a star with *La Strada* and *Nights of Cabiria.* But in *Fortunella* the attempt to entrust her talents to someone else (even an experienced and capable man like Eduardo De Filippo) did not work. In general, most of the work the actress did separate from her husband was as unfailingly professional as it was disappointing. To make matters worse, even in *Juliet of the Spirits,* she and Fellini were not able to establish a perfect working relationship despite their best intentions. The two TV specials *Eleonora* and *Camilla* (written by Pinelli) had proven more successful, but television is not cinema, and the programs were not broadcast enough to satisfy a vast international audience that wanted to see an important new performance from an actress who may well have been more popular outside Italy. In any case, Fellini and Masina had always taken pains to keep from conditioning one another. Therefore it is correct and inevitable that Fellini and Masina would work parallel to one another, each trying not to get in the other's way.

Fellini felt a certain urgent desire to renew Masina's artistic reputation, which, if truth be told, even Masina had neglected somewhat in favor of her obligations as the wife (and erstwhile ambassador) of a great filmmaker, not to mention her adopted crown as regal queen of house and home. At RAI headquarters, a great deal of time was spent considering a proposal for a series dedicated to Masina and directed by important filmmakers (one movie for each), including Antonioni. Of the various movies proposed for this series, the only one to survive was an idea of Fellini's: a duet between two former tip-tap dancers famous in the past for their imitation of Ginger Rogers and Fred Astaire. Grimaldi,

who in the meantime had made peace with Fellini following their argument over *Casanova,* agreed to produce the film and willingly set about scraping together the nine billion lira necessary to pay for the project.

For this film, Fellini decided to reunite his wife with Mastroianni, thirty-seven years after the two had first performed together in the play *Angelica* by Leo Ferrero, presented at the Teatro dell'Università in 1948. The idea was to create a glittering megaspecial for television that they would be called upon to participate in after so many years far apart. In order to make the screenplay work, there was no better partner than Fellini's old collaborator, Pinelli. Fellini was happy to turn to his trusted friend, and they picked back up where they had left off. It was a new start for the celebrated partnership, and they would remain together right up until Fellini's final film.

While work moved ahead at breakneck speed on the screenplay (which began to show the first signs of Fellini's protest against the decline of commercial television), Ferretti installed a big, marvelously make-believe

Page 279: *Giulietta Masina and Marcello Mastroianni: Ginger and Fred*

Opposite: *Federico Fellini, the cameraman Tonino Delli Colli, and Giulietta Masina.*

Below: *A drawing of Fred by Fellini.*

Above: *Two scenes from the film.*

Below: *Nicola Piovani who wrote the music for the film.*

TV studio inside Studio 5 at Cinecittà. Donati made more than one thousand costumes. Stand-ins of all shapes and sizes marched through Fellini's offices on a daily basis as the filmmaker searched for the faces he needed. At first the cameraman was Ennio Guarnieri, but as had happened other times in the past, he was unfairly fired after just a few weeks on the job. His replacement was Tonino Delli Colli, a sharp-minded and good-humored man who was quick to crack a joke and would become a key player in everything else Fellini produced. The deceased Rota was substituted with Nicola Piovani, another collaborator who would stick with Fellini from then on out. Prematurely aged by the heavy makeup he had to wear for the film, Mastroianni entertained himself by going out and frightening people with his fake physical decay. Mastroianni and Masina found themselves in perfect harmony, and when they danced as Mastroianni had to perform his silly, clumsy fall, they immediately insisted on filming another version (where on earth has it gone?) in which they did the same dance as perfectly as if they really were Ginger and Fred, just to show people they could. Fellini was tempted to bring Sordi back into the fold (more than thirty years had passed since they had worked on *I Vitelloni*) for the extremely important role of the television host, but in the end he decided that his old companion had become too set in his ways. Fellini held a number of auditions, including one with Alberto Lionello (whom he would bring back as the "voice" for Franco Fabrizi). Curiously enough, Lionello had gotten his start as the dance hall presenter in Antonioni's *Cronaca di un amore* (*Story of a Love Affair*), a role for which he never received onscreen credit.

Filming began on February 12 at Cinecittà and was completed by the end of spring so that the film could be released at the end of the year. The final result was at once ironic, festive, and melancholic: a meditation on life, on the way to face living without becoming overwhelmed, on the onset of senility, on love that comes and goes, on the capricious nature of success, and on oblivion. Various important events took place during production. On June 10, Fellini had to fly to New York City to take part in one of those events that made the filmmaker as embarrassed as he was flattered: a tribute to him at Lincoln Center. During *ferragosto*, the traditional Italian vacation period in the middle of August, he suffered a slight ischemia, fortunately without consequences. On September 6, the filmmaker (a little tired and slightly bored) received the Golden Lion for lifetime achievement at the Venice Film Festival. Meanwhile, he even filmed a commercial for the Italian pasta company Barilla.

Fellini could sense that there was even greater hope and expectations than usual for his new film; the realization made him happy and, at least at first, he would not be disappointed with the final result.

MELANCHOLY AND MUSIC

Credits at the beginning of the film are accompanied by the sounds of "The Continental" by Magidson and Conrad, including photos of Ginger and Fred in front of a drop curtain of skyscrapers. In other words, the way the world was back in 1939, the year Fellini moved to Rome and started to spend time in the world of entertainment. Now, in the present, we see Amelia Bonetti, aka Ginger, arrive on track five at Stazione Termini. A rather rude girl is there waiting for her, carrying a sign that reads "Ed ecco a voi" ("Now Over To You"), the name of the popular television program Amelia is about to debut on, dancing once again—thirty years later—with her erstwhile partner Pippo Botticella, aka Fred.

It is Christmastime and the train station feels more than ever like a Persian market. There is an enormous *zampone* (pig's leg stuffed with seasoned mincemeat, a traditional Northern Italian dish during winter holidays) hanging in the middle of the entrance. People everywhere are pushing and shoving, complaining out loud in the middle of all the chaos. Ginger is put onto a little bus together with some other "victims": and for anyone who has yet to figure out that we are on Charon's ferry, an ad with a Dante puppet recites the opening lines of the famous poem on the television. The bus crosses the city, passing by absurd billboards and big bags of abandoned, disgusting garbage. Passengers aboard the bus include a garrulous Neapolitan transvestite (Augusto Poderosi), a pair of Lucio Dalla (a famous Italian singer) impersonators, and a gold-medal admiral who is a total fool (Friedrich von Ledebur, voiced over by Corrado Gaipa). Imitators are one of the main acts of the television show. We will see many others, from Claudio Villa to Bette Davis, Marlene Dietrich to Adriano Celentano, Ronald Reagan to Michele Sindona, with the overall effect that we become convinced we are living in a secondhand society, crowded with imitations.

The Manager Palace Hotel, a modern cathedral erected in the desert that is the outskirts of Rome, is filled with shouting from stadium images broadcast on television: the staff at the hotel are all busy watching a soccer game and ignoring the guests. In the solitude of her own room, Amelia bursts out: "Why on earth did I do this?!" Depressed and hesitant, in order to escape the sleazy company of a Clark Gable impersonator who is wandering around with an equally improbable Marcel Proust, after dinner Ginger goes out for a walk in front of the hotel. In a self-ironic turn of events, her good

Right: Several participants on the show "Ed ecco a voi" (Now Over to You). On the bottom is Moana Pozzi.

mood returns and she starts to dance alone just as Cabiria did years before. But she has little to feel good about: the motorcycle-riding barbarians from the final scenes of *Fellini's Roma* show up and form a threatening carousel around her. One man goes up to Ginger and frightens her, asking for one hundred lira. Fortunately just then the same bus she rode on returns with yet another busload of people destined for the show. But Fred is not on the bus. Instead, Ginger sees a group of dwarves get out, the "24 Los Liliput 24." Later on, a cow with eighteen udders will appear as well.

More than the director's arrival in *Fellini's Roma* or the newlyweds' arrival in *The White Sheik*, this unloading in the Eternal City is reminiscent of *Toby Dammit*: the signs of the Apocalypse, a *dolce vita* that has degenerated into visions of hell. Here we see what Pasolini referred to as the "Afterhistory": a catastrophe has occurred and Ginger and Fred are two survivors. Then something rather comical takes place: she has trouble sleeping because someone is snoring loudly on the other side of the wall, and in order to get the person to stop, Ginger bangs on his door. When the door opens, we discover a yawning, sleepy-eyed Fred.

We can tell right away that life has been rougher on Fred. We already know that Ginger has a daughter and grandchildren, and owns a small business in Santa Margherita Ligure. Poor Fred, on the other hand, has had nothing but bad luck and earns a living by selling encyclopedias. Even his wife has left him. Bewildered and a heavy drinker, right now he is still half asleep. When he realizes it's Ginger he laughs: "I didn't even recognize you."

"Ginger and Fred are part of our collective memory. I don't understand why Rogers wants to block the film."

The next day they meet by the piano, but there is no question of actually trying to dance together. The television show will run in a postmodern chaos of amateurishness and superficiality. Ginger is worried; she wants to rehearse their act a few times. Fred spouts nonsense as he is apt to do, and seems to be thinking of nothing more than the 800,000 lira they have been promised for their performance. On the bus that takes them all to the television studio, a pair of nutcases—a mother and son—let everyone listen to a message from the afterlife that they have recorded. The faint voice, they say, is call-

Opposite: *Fred Astaire and Ginger Rogers in* Carioca *(1933).*

Below: *Giulietta Masina and Marcello Mastroianni dance in a scene from the film.*

Above: *Giulietta Masina,
Toto Mignone, and Federico
Fellini on the set.*

Below: *A drawing of Ginger
by Fellini.*

Opposite: *Federico Fellini on
the set at Cinecittà.*

An old colleague of theirs, Tot ò (Toto Mignone, the brother of the singer MillyMignone), tells Ginger that back when she separated from Fred, the old dancer took it so hard that he wound up in an insane asylum. The couple rehearse their dance act in an out-of-service bathroom where the mirrors are covered with plastic. Between old age and misplaced kicks, we have stumbled into something straight out of Samuel Beckett. But there is still magic between Ginger and Fred, and we can feel it as soon as she, wearing a white dress that is perfect for the performance, sees her partner in a coat and tails in the mirror. Nevertheless, the rehearsal is a disaster. Fred is out of breath and threatens to insult the audience: "I'm going to tell sixty million Italians they're all just a bunch of sheep!" Ginger believes that the time has come to abandon the whole thing, but she changes her mind when the television host begins to compliment her. The character of Lombardoni, the studio president (Narcisio Vicario, voiced over by Oreste Lionello), is a clear imitation of the actual god of Italian commercial television at the time.

Out in the hallway, the gloomy parade of guests for the program marches toward the studio, warned to come in "on tiptoes like you would in church." Now the host is Franco Fabrizi (voiced over by Alberto Lionello), who is cursing left and right behind the curtain but is all smiles once the camera is turned on. Meanwhile the guests show up onstage amid triumphant applause: the young man who has married a venerable elderly lady; a man on a hunger strike to protest fishing; the inventor of flavored ladies' underwear; a housewife who has accepted cash in exchange for living for an entire month with no television. Fred is visibly nervous. The dancers go out, surrounded by applause, but suddenly there is a blackout in the studio. Fred wants to make a run for it, while Ginger is so angry she starts to cry. In the darkness, they sit down in the middle of the dance floor "like in a dream, far away from everything else." Somewhere in the studio the cow with eighteen udders starts to moo. Fred mentions the insane asylum and Ginger confesses that she came because she wanted to see him again. Finally they agree with one another and are about to leave the studio when Fred gives in to the temptation to poke a little fun at the "tele-holics" the way Sordi did at the "asphalt workers" in *I Vitelloni*, but the lights come back on right as he is making his impertinent gesture.

After "The Continental" we hear a medley of Irving Berlin songs. Fred is confused and cannot remember anything, and right in the middle of the *claquettes* for "Cheek to Cheek" he gets a terrible cramp. There is some con-

ing Fred. Fred's face darkens: "It's like strange things have been happening to me for some time now . . . As if life wants to say good-bye . . . Good-bye, Pippo, goodbye." But at the metal detector located at the entrance to the TV studio, Fred's good humor returns when the machine alarms go off, bringing policemen and guards running just to see the old dancer take his lucky horseshoe out of his pocket. The policemen are there to escort the big mafia boss Catanzaro, who has been given special permission from the Italian Ministry of Justice to participate in the show and sing a short song.

In the enormous bar, among dancers and brawny men, we continue to get a better look at the characters who will be seen on "Now Over To You": a friar on his way to sainthood who can levitate; a woman who claims she is an extraterrestrial's lover; a successful writer with ties to politics and certain politicians; an ex-priest who will kiss his bride. Fred makes a good impression, telling one reporter how tap dancing was invented as a Morse code for black slaves kept on plantations in the American South—a language of love and death—and Ginger agrees that tap dancing is unquestionably "something special." But Fred's conversation quickly degenerates when he starts reciting a few of his favorite aphorisms such as:

Donna senza culo   A woman with no butt
è come alpino senza mulo   is like a mountaineer
                              without a mule

solatory applause, the host stirs everyone up with a "but wait, he's going to continue!" and the mobile martyrdom continues. An old violinist pays Ginger an affectionate tribute; he has recognized her. Ginger whispers, "I think I'm going to cry." Now "Top Hat" and "White Tie and Tails" come on. The rhythm comes alive, their feet move around on the floor more agilely, and Ginger and Fred give new energy to their performance. It is as if, just for a moment, the two poor imitators have actually become the real-life Ginger Rogers and Fred Astaire; as if there really exists "something else, something more" in the tap dancing they used to perform in their youth. They barely have time to realize this when the dance comes to a close. The audience breaks into applause and Ginger happily murmurs: "We did it." But the navy march strikes up immediately and the admiral comes stepping out in full uniform, accompanied by a girl from the Red Cross and an assistant.

Back at Stazione Termini (which has made its way into Fellini's films ever since *Variety Lights*), Ginger and Fred are saying good-bye. A few people saw them on television and somebody asks them for an autograph: some children, a boy who wants "a signature." Ginger gives some money to Fred. They kiss and promise to see one another again (but when?). As she is getting on the train, Ginger takes one last look at her old partner. Fred is on the other side of the window, in the bar, surrounded by a group of Africans. The train takes off, the lights on the great big *zampone* display disappear, and the TV keeps right on going.

SUCCESS, BUT NO CALLS

An entire constellation of international companies presided over the production of *Ginger and Fred*. Grimaldi's P.E.A. company was joined by RAI as an associate producer, and coproduction from Films Ariane Paris, FR 3, Raiuno, Revcom Films Paris, and Stella Film Muennchen. There was an initial, solemn showing at the Palazzo del Quirinale, just as had happened with *Orchestra Rehearsal*. The president of the Italian Republic Francesco Cossiga approved the film, and it earned public applause from other important politicians present. The minister Giulio Andreotti was asked to replace the *Corriere della Sera*'s usual movie critic and write a review. The film's official debut was held at the Palais de Chaillot in Paris on January 13, 1986, prompting some Italians to complain about the perceived snub to Fellini's native country. The film debuted in Rome shortly thereafter, on January 22, followed by a festive evening gala ceremony at the Sistina. On February 14 the film officially inaugurated the 37th Berlin Film Festival. Fellini presented the film in person and proved unusually willing to meet with people for the occasion, attending even the press conference he so abhorred (which actually proved to be an entirely enjoyable experience, punctuated by warm reviews for the film, smiles, and plenty of laughter). It would be the last press conference of his long career. On March 28 the film debuted in New York, with both Fellini and his wife in attendance. It was an auspicious start, but the movie did not do particularly well in the theaters. Even back home in Italy it failed to make much headway with the general public, earning a disappointing 1,650,600,000 lira (placing *Ginger and Fred* at the twenty-eighth position in the list of most viewed films). On both sides of the Atlantic, people began to form a general opinion that Fellini continued to be interesting as an individual, while his films had grown less appealing.

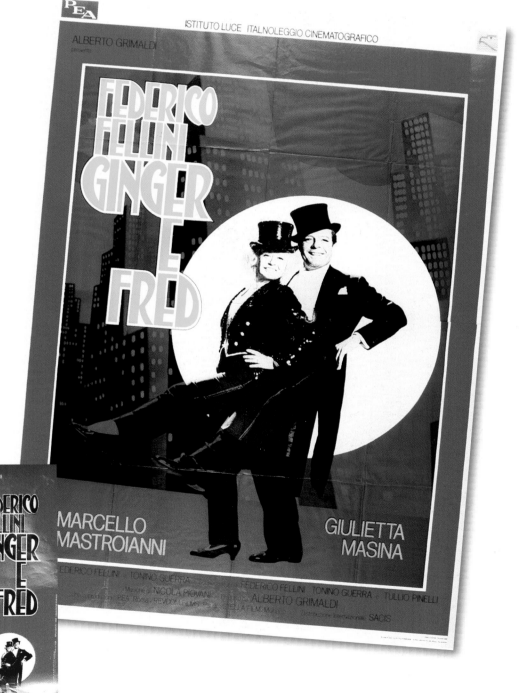

"I don't really know why I made this film rather than another. But I have discovered that at my age, what really drives me is the dignity of work itself, the pleasure I get from creating. I've learned to leave judgment of the final product to others, especially to the general public."

FELLINI'S INTERVISTA

INTERVISTA

A HOME FOR HIS WORK

In the middle of three different projects Fellini took on for RAI—a special on Cinecittà, another on opera, and yet another on a work trip to the United States that he never actually took—the filmmaker still wanted to make a movie about the film studios at Quadraro. In the meantime, Ibrahim Moussa, a junior producer and former agent for various actors, had taken over the project. But Moussa was complicating things by requesting a full-length feature to be distributed like a regular movie. Fellini had never denied the fact that he considered Cinecittà "the home for my work," and had come to realize that "the city-home where films are made extends to all of Rome as well." It was something of an addendum to his rhapsodic relationship with the Eternal City. He never failed to remind people, and made a point of doing so again for this project, that his mother was from Rome and that his mother's ancestors had been Romans for at least seven or eight generations. He proudly flaunted his love for "a city that is gloriously and comically ill-mannered," a familiar place "where it seems like Romans walk around as if the whole city were their own apartment." For Fellini, Rome was a place that "doesn't judge you, but welcomes you with open arms and lets you leave the moment you want to escape," except that the filmmaker had never been tempted to abandon Rome, and never would.

Work on the movie began in August 1986 and finished on January 22, 1987. At first, the filmmaker wanted a troupe made up only of clowns for his "non-story," but he later got Mastroianni, Ekberg, and other longstanding collaborators involved. Despite the usual difficulties that always accompanied a Fellini production, on the whole it was a happy time in the filmmaker's life; perhaps the last period characterized by a surprising and unexpected lightheartedness.

Page 291: *Anita Ekberg and Marcello Mastroianni during filming.*

Opposite: *Federico Fellini on the set of* Intervista (Fellini's Intervista).

Below: *Anita Ekberg in her villa.*

Nighttime in Cinecittà. A few cars drive through the gate and among the studios. Here and there, dogs jump around and bark. The members of the film troupe get out of the cars while the camera arrives on a wagon covered with black cloth. A secretary dressed as an elderly clown gets to work, shouting orders and advice. The lights are turned on, including the first big spotlight. Tonino Delli Colli is bustling about among his electricians while Fellini keeps an eye on things from the steps of the director's building. A small woman appears in one corner. She is lit from behind and introduces herself with a bow. She is the interpreter for the Japanese, a small group that has come to do a news report, an interview

with the Italian maestro. They were supposed to arrive tomorrow, but they have appeared earlier than expected: Can we ask a few questions right away? A dialogue (or nondialogue) begins with the Japanese and with it the film gets underway. Two extremely tall cranes face one another like gigantic machines in an atmosphere reminiscent of Ariosto. The filmmaker confides to the interviewers: "I'm shooting the opening scenes of this film, and I thought I'd begin with a dream, a typical dream of flying. People in Japan dream of flying, too, don't they?" As part of what the filmmaker defines "a prisoner's dream," we see his hands groping in the dark. Back in the days of $8\frac{1}{2}$ it was easier to fly away, now it takes twice as much effort and it seems that he might not manage to pull it off. But finally the dreamer works his way free, rising up to a great height. He contemplates Cinecittà from way up in the sky, small and spread out far below him.

After this magical night view of the studios, we see Cinecittà in full daylight. The assistant Maurizio Mein gives a little speech about the tools necessary for any director's assistant: a whistle and a megaphone. Being a director's assistant, he claims, may be a way to avoid becoming a real director; in other words, a way to avoid growing up. By the time Fellini arrives there is a crowd of walk-ons as well, of whom Chiodo proves to be the most annoying and unfortunate. We can also see some kids who are there for the role of Karl Rossmann in the film scheduled to be made from Kafka's *Amerika*. Some commercials are being shot on the streets in Cinecittà. Seven male dancers in tailcoats and top hats are performing an act that represents a gigantic typewriter (the playback music: "Tea for Two"). A parade of majorettes (moving along to the song "Dove sta Zazà?," or "Where Is Zazà?") escorts a golden cannon that fires a reddish projectile against a billboard with two big female lips.

The Japanese insist on interviewing Nadia (Nadia Ottaviani), whom Fellini introduces as "the vestal virgin of Cinecittà." She oversees the film library in which Cinecittà preserves the memories of itself. They follow her to the bar while Fellini attempts to answer their questions in the middle of a disrespectful hullabaloo. Then there is a calmer conversation with Nadia, held on a grassy field while the interviewer gathers some herbs. The Japanese ask if they can taste the chicory, only to find it is not to their liking. Nadia points out where the swimming pool used to be before it was destroyed, as well as the new construction sites that are creeping closer and closer to Cinecittà. Little by little, the real world is moving in and consuming the world of fantasy.

Below: A drawing of an elderly Snàporaz as Mandrake by Fellini.

Fifty years from now there may be nothing left. There won't be any more moviemakers, just building owners.

The Japanese are curious to know what this "city of cinema" looked like when Fellini saw it for the first time. This marks the beginning of the main episode of the film. The troupe surveys the Casa del Passeggero (a low-cost hotel) near Stazione Termini, from which the sky-blue transept for Cinecittà departed. They also visit the warehouse where the old tramcars are kept. The general director for the film shows up in a car, immersed in his copy of the newspaper *l'Unità* (*l'Unità* is a traditionally left-wing, Communist Italian newspaper). Fellini introduces him to the Japanese as "the legendary Notarianni," explaining that their relationship is based on "a complete and utter mistrust for one another." They start to evaluate the state of the cars, which are all falling apart. The most likely candidate under consideration to play Brunelda arrives, a beautiful dark-haired woman that Maurizio saw on the street.

The Casa del Passeggero is re-created next to the old tramcar warehouse and the makeup room is installed

Above: *Sergio Rubini from the film, and in a drawing by Fellini.*

Left: *Federico Fellini at the time of the affair being re-created.*

Above: *Federico Fellini and Danilo Donati, the production designer for the film.*

Right: *Federico Fellini and Pietro Notarianni, the production supervisor. In this film, Notarianni plays a Fascist party official.*

Opposite: *A drawing of his dream by Fellini.*

his profession lies in trying to plan for the unexpected.

The general director of the project suddenly emerges from the Casa del Passeggero dressed in an immaculate Fascist uniform. In addition to the obvious political inappropriateness of his new role, Notarianni appears to be embarrassed about his boots, which hurt his feet. Laughing, Fellini goes over to him, clearly satisfied with this ad hoc solution, and accompanies the man to the tramcar. The tram has been cut down and mounted on a platform on two trucks.

The feverish efforts to get the tram sequence ready is underscored in play-back by the two Nino Rota songs used in Nicola Piovani's soundtrack for the film: the marching tune from *The White Sheik* and the song that accompanies the cheats in *The Swindle*. When asked why he chose this particular music, Fellini responds: "What else do movie people do, if not swindle?" Other music for the film would also be selected from Rota's repertoire.

Fellini's odd parade of vehicles gets underway with two motorcycle police driving along at the front. The filmmaker's car follows immediately after with the Japanese crammed in, then the truck with the front half of the tramcar on top, then the camera truck, and finally the third truck with the rear half of the tramcar. It looks a lot like a guided tour through Rome's traditional sights: San Giovanni, the Appia Antica, the Roman ruins. Two children on the tram ask the journalist if he is an actor. There is a very attractive blonde girl (Antonella Ponziani) and a man who is on his way to an audition. But soon, just like in Fellini's Campari Bitter commercials, strange landscapes start to appear outside the windows and the trip is transformed into an entirely fantastical event.

Out in the open countryside a small crowd of housewives in costume is walking down a hill, holding up a large white tent. The tramcars stop to celebrate, amid loud cries and Fascist salutes, the grape festival. Notarianni pays homage to these "grape laborers" as bunches of ripe grapes are distributed to everyone and only the journalist has the courage to ask, half whispering: "Have these been washed?"

When it is time to move on, a donkey is blocking the way and they have to wait while it is chased off. A monk dressed in white and holding a butterfly net passes by. Through the windows, we can see the Marmore Waterfalls. The young man and the girl talk to each other. Indians appear up on a rock high above the tram. Then we see a river filled with bathing elephants. The Fascist party official points out that this is a sign that Cinecittà is near.

inside. Fellini decides to put a big pimple on the actor Sergio Rubini's nose. Rubini will be playing Fellini as a young man, and the filmmaker wants him to feel more ill at ease when he will have to interview, during a scene set in 1940, a beautiful film star from the era. What does *Amerika* have to do with any of this? Evidently, the filmmaker has established a parallel between his own arrival in Rome and young Karl's discovery of America.

Everything is ready for the crew to shoot the trip aboard the tramcar when they suddenly get news that the actor selected to play the Fascist party official is no longer available. Fellini is infuriated, but is inspired with a new idea when he sees Notarianni, who is at that moment talking to the Japanese about how the best part of

"I was shooting the beginning of this film, and I thought I would start with a dream, a typical dream of flying. Here in Japan you dream you can fly, don't you?"

Fellini and the crew are camped out in front of the entrance to Cinecittà. The filmmaker talks about his travels many years before, admitting that maybe they did not exactly take place the way he has depicted them; perhaps they were even more of an adventure.

Once they have arrived we discover that the beautiful girl has a brawny, vain boyfriend. There is an intense handshake with the journalist, but the "I" character's voice comes on to inform us that he would never hear from that girl again. Going into Cinecittà behind the elephants, the journalist is held back briefly by the uniformed doorkeeper. As soon as he is inside, he finds himself overcome by a whirlwind of white confetti: an extrovert film director, high up on a lift, is filming a scene of the embrace between a bride in white (Lara Wendel)

and an elegantly dressed groom (Antonio Cantafora). The film lingers over this scene from another period, with the director nearly in a swoon and the orchestra playing on the podium. When it is time to take a break, the journalist goes over to get a better look at the camera; then a seamstress asks him to get the star's basket and offers to escort him back to the camper.

Walking down the corridors of Studios 1, 2, and 3, the costumer and the journalist sneak a peek inside. Two painters up on cabled scaffolding are painting a celestial panorama for a new big-budget film. This poetic atmosphere comes to an end when they exchange a few off-color jokes, like in a vignette.

In order to get to the star's camper, they have to cross paths with Egyptian priests, Nazi SS officials, and

sansculottes. They meet a group of girls in bathing suits and a farmer who offers them a fresh egg. The interior of the camper has been rebuilt inside a theater.

This is a memory that the director had already planned to make room for in *Fellini's Roma*. Inside the candybox camper (accompanied by the play-back of "Il tango delle capinere," or "The Songbird's Tango"), the atmosphere is the same as Suzy's party in *Juliet of the Spirits*. A couple of ugly fellows are discussing the Kama Sutra. A number of banal remarks accompany the interview and everyone present struggles to get his or her two cents in. The makeup artist underlines the importance of eyes in cinema. The most audacious question the journalist can muster is: "How do you manage to look so beautiful?" Displaying downright regal vulgarity, the star finishes her conquest of her young interviewer by blowing him a kiss.

Quite interested, the young man trails after the movie star, dressed up as a *maharani*. The woman walks down the hallway in the studio along a carpet that is rapidly unrolled at her feet. They are shooting an adventure film set like in one of Emilio Salgari's novels, the temple of the Elephant God. The producer rambles on, while the director makes the actress cry, argues with the producer, and becomes enraged when an elephant's trunk snaps off. He shouts, "Goddamn this shitty production! I'm going to Germany!" and knocks over an entire row of elephants. Fellini intervenes to give him a hand and help complete the catastrophe.

When the Japanese ask: "Where do you find all these particular faces?" we head down into the subway to take a long look at a rich sampling of humanity. Maurizio identifies eight potential Bruneldes and escorts them back to Cinecittà. While they are all sent into the makeup rooms for auditions, a brief episode takes place that is reminiscent of the tense atmosphere in *Orchestra Rehearsal*.

Inside a studio in Theater 2, the general director Gino Millozza receives an anonymous phone call announcing that a bomb is about to go off. As professional as any patriarch of the cinema could be, Millozza clears everyone from the building and courageously stays behind until he is sure he is the last one to leave. The police arrive and search for the bomb in vain. Maurizio comments: "They looked everywhere, but couldn't find a thing. I felt bad, even disappointed." The chaos typical of the preparations for a Fellini film starts back up again, and potential walk-ons are kept in line, interviewed, and photographed one after the other.

In the director's office there is a discussion underway

to evaluate the costs associated with producing *Amerika*. Building a New York street set is going to cost one billion lira. The walk-on Chiodo tries to sneak in but is sent away. While they are arguing, there is a surprise: as they open the window they see Marcello Mastroianni appear in a Mandrake costume, lifted up by a crane in the middle of an artificial whirlwind.

Called over by this Mastroianni-Snaporaz, at the moment given the name Callaghan, Fellini goes down to talk to his friend, who is filming a commercial for the stain remover, Smack. Fellini decides to take him to the Castelli Romani, a series of small towns outside Rome, to visit Anita Ekberg's villa. He invites Rubini to

Opposite: *Scenes from the film.*

Below: *A drawing of the 1930s film star by Fellini.*

come along, too. (By strange coincidence, this young actor playing the "I" character has the same last name as Mastroianni in *La Dolce Vita*.)

Once they are in the car, their conversations are light-spirited and rambling until Mastroianni finally falls asleep. It is hard to find the road that leads to Villa Pandora and they have to ask a priest on a scooter for directions. When they get there, Fellini happily says his name into the intercom, but Ekberg is standoffish ("Federico who?") and reluctant to open the gate. However, once she has, she is happy to see her old friends again, and finally the car can enter, surrounded by ferocious dogs. The film diva and Mastroianni embrace.

Fellini has asked Mastroianni to help him convince Ekberg to come and audition for the Brunelda character. But the real reason for their visit is quickly forgotten as the group organizes an impromptu party. The Japanese offer to cure Mastroianni of his smoking habit with a simple *kiuli* massage, but the Italian film star would rather stay faithful to his beloved cigarettes. Mastroianni draws on his Mandrake superpowers and speaks the magic formula:

Bacchetta di Mandrake,	Mandrake wand,
il mio ordine e immediate:	my order is immediate:
Fai tornare	Bring back
i bei tempi del passato!	the good times of the past!

A white bed sheet appears and images of *La Dolce Vita* start to materialize on it: Marcello and Sylvia's dance at Caracalla's and the Fontana di Trevi, with Rota's music playing in the background. The two actors watch their legendary performances play out on the sheet-screen, repeating their lines along with their characters. In the end, everyone there feels serene and melancholy, and there are smiles on everyone's faces. The scene seems to be a cinema verité repetition of *Ginger and Fred*, but it is clear that at least Mastroianni has been willing to compromise (for example, in reality Mastroianni only accepted working in television commercials in Japan). Outside the dogs are listening to the music, sitting as motionless as statues.

What is an audition? Maurizio is trying to answer this question during the screen tests for the Brunelda character going on at Theater 14, but everything is in an uproar in part because Sergio is banging away on the piano while Santonella is playing the saxophone ("Stormy Weather," "Yes Sir That's My Baby," and some of Rota's songs.) The other potential Bruneldas are dancing the Charleston.

Outside they are taking down the gravestones in the cemetery because Fellini, to Nadia's disappointment, has decided not to shoot the scene where the Cinecittà "vestal virgin" pays homage to the film industry's great figures of the past. It is raining harder and harder. Everybody runs for cover under a plastic tent, a sort of defense against the end of the world. With "Stormy Weather" on play-back, the entire troupe has gathered to await an unspecified extraordinary event, like the appearance of "Rex" in *Amarcord*.

At dawn the elderly production inspector announces: "I think they are going to attack." All around them, the television antennas have turned into spears: Indians on horseback are getting ready to charge cinema's last stand. All hell breaks loose around the plastic tent, but it is soon over.

The end. Thanks all around, it is Christmastime, toasts to everyone, and the troupe breaks up. Everyone starts to leave, almost saddened by the event.

We find ourselves once again in Theater 5, now dark and empty. We hear Fellini: "There, the film is supposed to end here, in fact it has already ended. . . ." The dream of a winged escape has finished with a return to the studio, this time full of light. Seeing as how producers in the past asked specifically for "a ray of sunlight," we can make them happy and provide an artificial ray using spotlights. It is time to turn on the camera for a new film: "Ready, action."

MONTAND AND DE NIRO TOGETHER FOR·THE AWARD

Intervista had a grand international debut at the 1987 Cannes Film Festival, with Fellini escorted to the gala ceremony by the producer Moussa's companion, Nastassja Kinski. The film was a success, so much so that Yves Montand (president of the Jury for that edition of the festival) invented an award specifically for the occasion (the Festival's Fortieth Anniversary Prize) even though the film was not officially entered in the competition. The prize was awarded to Fellini on May 19. At the Moscow Film Festival the following July 17, where the jury was presided over by yet another established star of international cinema—Robert De Niro—Fellini's film earned the grand prize. It was his second gold prize at the festival, following the one he had received twenty-three years earlier for *8 ½*. All the elements were in place for a great box office success, but unexplainably the film failed to meet expectations. The movie debuted in Italian theaters on September 18 and was presented along with a wonderful billboard created by award-winning Italian artist Milo Manara, but despite these efforts, the earnings for *Intervista* were disappointing. But there was no one to blame; c'est la vie, especially in show business.

Left: *Fellini and Robert De Niro at the awards ceremony for* Fellini's Intervista *in Moscow.*

Above: *Yves Montand, president of the jury at the 1987 Cannes Film Festival.*

"Benigni and Villaggio are the umpteenth reincarnation of classic clowns: the White Clown and Augusto. One is as much of a buffoon as could possibly be, while the other is presumptuous, arrogant, and ridiculously severe. Put together, the two guarantee a good time."

THE VOICE OF THE MOON

LA VOCE DELLA LUNA

TWO INSPIRED NUTCASES AMONG THE OBTUSE

Page 303: *Paolo Villaggio and Roberto Benigni.*

Opposite: *Roberto Benigni in a scene from the film.*

After he had finished working through the enthusiasm and disappointment of his experience with *Intervista*, Fellini made no public announcements about what he planned to do next. There were the usual special projects he had with RAI, first and foremost *L'attore* (*The Actor*) and another on Venice that got lost in the usual bureaucratic red tape. Strangely enough, there were rumors that the filmmaker was searching for something he could put on a movie screen. There had been talk of doing *Amerika*, a project that had even gleaned some interest from De Laurentiis all the way on other side of the Atlantic, until Fellini explained to him that he was imagining a film shot entirely in Cinecittà rather than in the United States, not to mention the fact that his original idea had already been reduced to a fleeting bit of fiction included in *Intervista*. In any case, this return to the written word was as unexpected as it was interesting. Fellini had drawn inspiration from stories just three times in his life: from Edgar Allen Poe for *Toby Dammit*; from the *Satyricon* for the film of the same name; and from Casanova's memoirs for the film *Casanova*. Furthermore, each time he did so, the filmmaker translated the story into "beautiful and unfaithful" images. Something must have inspired him to riffle through what he read at night, during his long battles with insomnia, studying first and foremost the works of young Italian writers. This is exactly how Fellini chose Ermanno Cavazzoni's *Il poema dei lunatici* (*The Moody People's Poem*), picking the publication off a bookstore shelf after having read a lengthy article about it in a weekly magazine. Fellini discovered that the book was written by a professor from Reggio Emilia. He called the author, they met, and they got along right from the start. Flattered that he had aroused the interest of such an important reader, Cavazzoni was more than happy to grant Fellini free reign with the text: if the filmmaker wanted to use the professor's characters simply as a starting point, then he should feel free to do so. Cavazzoni was happy to let Fellini work his magic and admire the result without asking for anything in exchange. The writer and the film director agreed on the personal use of literature:

each enjoyed the right to find in different books the things that were most congenial to each, developing and elaborating them as each saw fit. Day after day, Fellini found among the pages of his new friend's writings the calm folly of the Italian countryside, something that brought him back to his own childhood memories of Gambettola, the silence that existed years ago and that had now been swallowed up by the infernal noise of the modern world. Attracted to the vast Padania plains, which he would visit again for the occasion, Fellini was tempted to shoot in different locations, the way people did half a century ago. But once again the irresistible allure of fiction, in other words exerting total control over that which appeared before the camera, got the better of him. Perhaps in reference to the modest nature of the real landscapes he was considering, Felllini continued to speak of shooting a "little film"; but when all was said and done, his willing producers Mario and Vittorio Cecchi Gori estimated that Fellini's "little film" was going to cost them at least 15 billion lira.

An entire village was built in the studios of the former Dinocittà, now renamed "Empire," where a few set pieces

Below: *A drawing of the prefect Gonnella by Fellini.*

Below: *Tullio Pinelli receives the "Premio Fondazione Fellini 2008".*

Opposite: *Federico Fellini explaining a scene to Roberto Benigni on the set.*

made for *Mastorna* still survived. Fellini's long-standing designer Donati was tired of working and had turned construction of the set over to his trusted colleague, Ferretti. Their job was to create an entirely imaginary town, not to re-create an actual location—something that had to be invented *ex novo* and which would in turn inspire Fellini to invent even more.

At the center was the couple from the book, the Clown and Auguste: the so-called Signor Salvini and the prefect Gonnella. In order to provide the right faces, Fellini had two comics he had never worked with—the rising star from Tuscany Roberto Benigni and the well-known Paolo Villaggio from Genoa—undergo a series of auditions. Although each actor arrived with his own professional tricks and tics of the trade, both Benigni and Villaggio were more than willing to put themselves in Fellini's hands and do exactly what the famed filmmaker wanted. They immediately established good working relationships and understood one another perfectly. There was even talk with Benigni of making a film version of Pinocchio, which Benigni would eventually shoot on his own after Fellini had passed away. The rest of the cast was composed more or less of the usual foreign legion Fellini was accustomed to.

Fellini and Pinelli disagreed to a certain extent over the script, and especially when, once the plot was complete, Pinelli wanted to proceed the way they always had when writing in tandem. But during the many years they had worked independently, Fellini had changed his method: he no longer needed a screenplay in hand when making a film—actually, he found the idea oppressive and restricting. All he needed now was a list that he could run through daily and modify as he saw fit. Pinelli, on the other hand, thought this kind of attitude was like setting out on a journey without a compass, and while it might be advantageous in terms of freshness and creativity, it could lead to unforeseeable costs and other disadvantages. Nevertheless, despite Pinelli's opposition, the director stuck to his ideas. In the end, even Pinelli had to admit Fellini had been right once he saw the extremely beautiful scenes the filmmaker's new method produced. But when all was said and done, Pinelli still thought that it was a shame they couldn't have thought them up together before bringing them to the silver screen.

Shooting for the film began on February 22, 1989 and continued until halfway through June with only a few brief interruptions. For the wrap-up party, Benigni wrote a poem in ottava rima especially for the occasion.

EVERYONE BE QUIET, SELENE IS TALKING

As the opening credits roll, we hear a whip cracking, strange noises, and a voice whispering: "Salvini, Salvini!" It is night and we are on a moonlit moor. Ivo Salvini (Roberto Benigni) is standing in front of a well, his face white like a clown's. Is the noise from the well really the moon's voice? Salvini asks us: "Did you hear that, too?" Then he tags along at the tail end of a group of rough-looking fellows from the town, marching toward a cottage, where a man is offering people the chance to pay for a glimpse of his aunt's breasts through the window. Inside, the woman is performing a striptease to the tune of "Abat-jour." Salvini doesn't have enough money to pay for a ticket and a fight ensues, but the gravedigger Pigafetta (Giovanni Javarone) shows up on a bicycle and drags Salvini away for their usual tour around the cemetery grounds. A woman passing by warns the young man to "stay away from the wells." Down in an empty urn, the oboist (Sim) answers a reporter's question, claiming that "music should be officially outlawed." In a flashback, he explains how the furniture in his house started dancing whenever he played the notes "sol-la-do-me," in other words, what medieval texts referred to as the *diabolus in musica*. Exasperated at continually seeing music "make promises that it doesn't keep," the little man buried his instrument in the garden. But his efforts were in vain: "I plug up my ears, but I can still hear the music." Salvini locates his grandfather's grave and is sad that he can no longer communicate with the old man, or with any other dead person: "Where are you all?" he asks in desperation. Seeing that there is a hole in the roof, he slips in with hope, but there is nothing but rain "on the other side."

The thunder reminds Salvini of the fears he experienced as a child, and now we see his grandmother (Uta Schmidt) come running up to get him and take him back home. She calls him "Pinocchietto," or "my little Pinocchio." But the restless young man climbs through a window and goes back into the stormy night in order to visit Aldina Ferruzzi (Nadia Ottaviani), a girl he has fallen in love with. Making his way around her sister's (Syusy Blady) defenses, Salvini slips into his lover's bedroom. He contemplates her face, pale as the moon, while she sleeps. A poem by the famous Italian poet Giacomo Leopardi (the "Canto di un pastore errante," or "Song of a Errant Shepherd") comes to mind and he recites it softly to her. But the girl wakes up and is extremely angry, throwing a silvery shoe at her admirer. In a sort of variation on the Cinderella story, Salvini runs away clutching the girl's shoe to his chest.

Now we are introduced to another crazy person, Adolfo Gonnella (Paolo Villaggio), a former prophet who uses an abrupt authoritarian attitude to hide his secret pathological persecution complex. Gonnella is the victim of paranoid obsessions. He categorically refuses help from a doctor who follows him by car, and barricades himself in his own home. However, just like in *Juliet of the Spirits*, Gonnella's house is invaded by imaginary, unwelcome guests that the poor man has to battle with until finally, when dawn arrives, he realizes that he is actually all alone.

It is market day and Salvini is wandering among the merchants and Japanese tourists taking pictures. Some men are taking a plaster statue of the Madonna off of a truck. Salvini meets the Duchess of Alba (Lorose Keller), a lady

who has fallen on hard times, and talks to the doctor who used to take care of him at the insane asylum, confessing that he feels increasingly anxious to understand something "that there isn't much time left for."

He meets the eldest of the three Micheluzzi brothers (Vito), then the plumber Giuanin (Nigel Harris) pops up out of a sewer manhole. He assures Salvini that down there he never saw any fires, torments, or devils, then confides in him his family's greatest ambition: to capture and eliminate the moon because "she's worthless anyhow." While practically the whole town looks on in curiosity, the saucy Marisa (Marisa Tomasi) is packing up her furniture because she is separating from her husband Nestore (Angelo Orlando) to run off with a butcher, who carries

her away on a motorcycle. When Nestore calls out to him, Salvini goes into the empty apartment, where he listens to the abandoned husband's sad and painful tale of the day he first met Marisa, who insisted right away on reading his palm, and the wedding banquet in Las Vegas where they danced cheek-to-cheek to "Fascination." Nestore's brief illusion of happiness was immediately followed by stormy nights: the relationship became a living hell because of Marisa's nymphomania. Nestore describes his estranged wife as a "sex locomotive."

Nestore tells this story, in keeping with a time-honored tradition, on the roof of his house, where he has invited Salvini to join him. But after a little while, Nestore realizes that Salvini has crawled away in order to steal a glimpse

Above: *Federico Fellini and Paolo Villaggio on the set.*

through the window of Aldina's room. The people down below mistakenly think he is trying to commit suicide and our protagonist is saved by Terzio (Dominique Chevalier), the third Micheluzzi brother, who has been lifted up to save him with a gigantic construction crane.

By chance, Salvini runs into Gonnella, who at first mistakes Salvini for one of his persecutors but then shares with him his knowledge of an imaginary plot. To the sounds of "Stars and Stripes Forever," the band announces the traditional *gnoccata* festival, or potato dumpling festival. Aldina and the other girls competing for the "Miss Farina 1989" ("Miss Flour 1989") title are parading around in front of the entire town. Everyone applauds the attractive young beauties while Salvini, who has snuck underneath the stage, finds himself trapped. While the dumplings are being passed around, the Duchess of Alba offers a plateful to Gonnella, who was once her lover. Aldina wins the competition, and when Salvini sees her dance with another man he dumps an entire plate of pasta on his rival's head. Gonnella helps him escape.

It is nighttime again. The two new partners in crime are sitting together in the middle of a field, talking with one another while fireworks explode in the sky. Salvini talks about the sounds he always heard when he was alone in his room, while Gonnella tells the story of his secret love affair with the Duchess of Alba. Gonnella is in the middle of his tale when he suddenly realizes that his companion has disappeared. Salvini has climbed down inside a well in an attempt to find an answer to the mysteries that plague him, and is once again saved by the Micheluzzi brothers. He catches back up with the prefect Gonnella who, although he deplores Salvini's fantasies, nevertheless orders him to kneel and nominates him his lieutenant.

Out on a mission to explore the limits of their prefecture, the two nutcases reach an abandoned factory that opens up like a spaceship, revealing an enormous discotheque full of young people. Salvini tries to put Aldina's shoe on a bunch of different girls, believing each time that he has finally caught a glimpse of the shoe's legitimate owner. Irritated by the noise of the disco music, Gonnella cries out for silence: "Haven't you people ever heard the sound of a violin?" Then he adds that "dancing is a hymn

sung for life." He dances a classic Johann Strauss waltz—"The Blue Danube"—together with the Duchess, who is wearing an elegant evening gown. The waltz is followed by "Trink, Trink," and everyone present comes to a stop for a moment, enchanted by the performance like the audience was in *Ginger and Fred*. After a chaotic, deafening round of applause, the rock 'n' roll starts up again.

We see Salvini, happy to find himself surrounded by so many women, at the disco exit, where he is picked up by his sister Adele and his brother-in-law Osvaldo. They take him back home, where he is moved by family memories and shocked to see his sister's children staring numbly at the television set. The neighbors recognize Salvini and welcome him warmly, then he goes to his old room where there is a giant wooden Pinocchio underneath a portrait of Giacomo Leopardi. But the thing that attracts Salvini the most is the nearby room of mysteries, although straddling the window is Nestore, who has come to announce "They've pulled it off. . . ."

A parade of bicycles is heading towards the town piazza, where a pair of giant television screens have been set up. A television reporter is presenting various civil and religious authorities. The big news of the day is that the Micheluzzi brothers have managed to capture the moon ("It's a woman, she wanted to be caught!"), which is now firmly anchored to the Gregorini farm building, as we can see on the giant television screens. The people assembled in the piazza pray fervently to their newly captured celestial prisoner, the way the characters did in the temple of Divine Love in *Nights of Cabiria* or out on the field of miracles in *La Dolce Vita*. A man in the crowd interrupts a debate between illustrious commentators that includes participation from an ambiguous high prelate like the one in *8 1/2* and starts shouting embarrassing questions on life, death, and the meaning of it all. Exasperated by the evasive answers he receives, the man pulls out a pistol and shoots at the moon on the screen, causing all hell to break loose. Gonnella takes advantage of the uproar to slip into the minister's car, but he is immediately kicked out.

Back in the empty piazza, the heavenly moon has begun shining once again and Salvini can finally hear her voice. Now she looks like Aldina, and keeps telling him, "You have to understand . . . You just have to listen, just listen to those voices and hope that they never get tired of calling out to you." This is followed by an ironic singing announcement: "Commerciaaaaaaal. . . ."

Just like at the beginning of the movie, Salvini is left alone at night, facing the well. We hear him say: "If only we could all be quiet for a little while, then we might be able to understand something. . . ."

> *"The voice of the moon? We're not supposed to understand those voices, and let's all just hope they never stop calling out to us."*

A TESTIMONIAL FILM

ario and Vittorio Cecchi Gori, who had been extremely understanding and anything but impatient with Fellini, produced the movie through various companies, and the Cecchi Gori Group and Tiger Cinematografica had additional coproduction help from Films A 2 Paris, La Sept Paris, Cinemax Paris, and RaiUno. The film was first shown on February 1, 1990, shortly after Fellini had celebrated his seventieth birthday. Its overall box office earnings totaled 6,494,402,000 lira, which was no worse than any other movie had done in a moment of serious difficulty and turmoil for the film industry. On May 18, *The Voice of the Moon* was presented at the 43rd Cannes Film Festival. It was not part of the competition, and for the first time ever Fellini did not attend. The film was well received, but enthusiasm was nothing like it had been for *Fellini's Intervista*. *The Voice of the Moon* earned what Italians referred to as "grudging respect," but little else. For the rest of that year, without any new noteworthy projects on the horizon, Fellini busied himself with various activities: on September 15, he stood alongside his alter ego Mastroianni as the Italian actor won a Golden Lion for lifetime achievement at the Venice Film Festival; he flew all the way to Tokyo with his wife to receive an Imperial Prize that was given to him directly by the Japanese Emperor in person. But the height of his Asian tour was a memorable evening spent with Akira Kurosawa, one of the few filmmakers that Fellini had always and sincerely admired.

Right: *Mario Cecchi Gori and Federico Fellini on the set.*

COMMERCIAAAL

"It's true. I agreed to shoot some TV commercials. But not so that they could debase and damage the films broadcast on television."

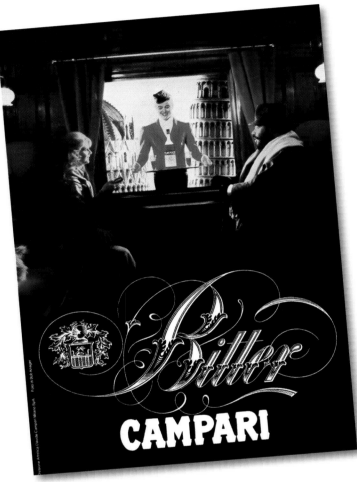

Above: *Silvia Dionisio, Antonella Barchiesi, and Victor Poletti in the Campari commercial.*

Right: *Scenes from the Barilla commercial, with its protagonist Greta Vaillant in the foreground. (Archivio Storico Barilla).*

When You Can't Say No

"Commerciaaaaaaal . . ." says the moon at the end of a film dedicated to her. Fellini, who had always proven entirely indifferent to job offers that arrived on his desk from that part of the industry (which generally for filmmakers constitutes fertile terrain to be harvested during the downtime between one movie and the next), would accept three specific commercial commissions over a nine-year period–from 1984 to 1992. It was precisely what would happen when, as he himself said, he was faced with one of those offers that "you can't say no to," although often for different reasons. He was tempted by the opportunity to create a well made and short joke, *Oh, che bel paese* (*Oh, What A Beautiful Country*), honoring Bitter Campari, a popular drink. Immediately after that he received a request from a friend, the industrialist from Parma, Pietro Barilla, to do a TV spot for Barilla pasta that Fellini would entitle *Alta società–Rigatoni* (*High Society–Rigatoni*). In the wake of the hard times of the entire Italian film industry, more than two years after he had finished *The Voice of the Moon*, Fellini was given an opportunity to return to the set. Naturally, the filmmaker was completely unaware that this would be his last time behind the camera, and he chose to use the opportunity to shoot three commercials for the Banca di Roma, each of which was inspired by a different dream he had written down and illustrated in his secret diaries. For the Campari and Barilla commercials, the cameraman was Ennio Guarnieri, while for the Banca di Roma com-

mercials Fellini brought back Peppino Rotunno. Thus Rotunno had a happy ending for his long and fruitful relationship with the filmmaker.

Prominent members of Italy's right-wing political parties created some moronic controversy over these short films, taking the field in order to defend television companies, which were interested in creating more commercial breaks in order to earn money from advertising. Fellini and others who created films and television programs opposed this move, proudly defending the integrity of movies viewed uninterrupted from start to finish. In truth, Fellini took a particularly strong stand with regards to the issue, seeing a threat to his own work and the cinema in general in this new and upsetting trend. He denounced the development as a foolish idea, and thanks to the professional authority he wielded, helped mitigate its effects. But then Fellini had already made his own personal opinions about television perfectly clear to everyone with *Ginger and Fred*.

Fellini adapted his skills to fit the needs of commercials. For example, he refused a tempting Japanese offer from Honda and turned down an enormous sum of money offered to him in return for personally playing the role of the psychoanalyst in the Banca di Roma commercials (the part would be played by Spanish actor Fernando Rey). It has never been clear whether Paolo Villaggio, the protagonist of the commercial, brought Fellini in as the director or if things happened the other way around. Whatever the case, once he was asked to take part, Fellini accepted with the utmost seriousness and professional rigor, writing banker Cesare Geronzi a letter/program that made it clear the filmmaker had studied at length the aims and methods of television communication and could most likely teach a better lesson on the subject than most established experts.

An Aperitif, a Plate of Pasta, and Three Scary Dreams

In *Oh, What A Beautiful Country*, we find the tenor Fuciletto (the Italian actor Victor Poletti) from *And the Ship Sails On* sitting on a train and facing Silvia Dioniso. The bearded gentleman tries to make a pass at the beautiful Silvia, but the woman wants none of it and nervously presses buttons on a remote control in order to change the landscapes flashing past on the other side of the window. Death Valley is followed by deserts, the medieval era, the ruins at Petra, a barren high plain, and finally—when Fuciletto puts his own finger on the button to change the landscape—the

Left: *Anna Falchi, Federico Fellini, and Paolo Villaggio (his back to the camera) on the set for the Banca di Roma commercial (Sogno del déjeuner sur l'herbe or Dreami of Dining on the Grass).*

Above: *A drawing of the déjeuner sur l'herbe dream by Fellini: a little meal is taken out on the grass.*

Piazza dei Miracoli in Pisa, where a gigantic Bitter Campari bottle stands at its center.

In *High Society – Rigatoni*, a lady (actress Greta Vaillant) sits at a table for a sumptuous dinner in a luxurious hotel restaurant and orders, to the maître d's horror, "Rigatoni!"

The three commercials (each of which had about a two-minute run time) Fellini shot for the Banca di Roma on June 2, 1992 amounted to the filmmaker's swan song. He died one year later. In the commercials, we see Paolo Villaggio grappling with dreamscape misadventures. In *Sogno del "dejuneur sur l'herbe"* (*Dream of Dining on the Grass*), Villaggio is eating with Anna Falchi on train tracks, terrified by the sound of a train that is approaching. In *Sogno del leone in cantina* (*Dream of a Lion in the Basement*), Villaggio is frightened by the sudden appearance of a beast. In the *Sogno della galleria* (*Dream of a Tunnel*), Villaggio drives into a tunnel, inside which he can hear the roof begin to crumble and is afraid he will never make it out alive. In each of the commercials, the finale is a shot of the psychoanalyst Rey, who reassures and advises his patient that in order to live safely Villaggio should put his trust in the Banca di Roma.

Audience

Fellini's debut as a director of television commercials was greeted by experts in the industry with vague approval. When people saw the shifting landscapes outside the train, many of them asked: "Is that all?" But people's reactions began to change after the pasta commercial, which although fundamentally simple was immediately hailed as an incredibly direct and perfect method for getting the message across. Even today, the rigatoni commercial remains a classic example of commercial television in the history of Italian advertising. The commercials for the Banca di Roma were well received and popular, thanks above all to the general popularity of their protagonist, Villaggio.

In Rimini, Europa Cinema 1984 ended with the screening of the Campari commercial. Fellini did not attend; he had passed through his hometown briefly just a few days earlier when his mother had passed away. On September 9, 1992 the commercials starring Villaggio were presented at the Venice Film Festival, but they were rather absent-mindedly scheduled and failed to elicit the least bit of interest, with barely twenty-five viewers showing up to see them. It was a melancholy ending for Fellini's relationship with Venice, which had begun in turmoil back in 1952 with *The White Sheik* and been through ups and downs during the filmmaker's life. It was yet another confirmation of the Italian axiom that no one is a prophet in his own country, not even a cinema genius such as Federico Fellini.

Above: *Paolo Villaggio in the Banca di Roma commercial (Sogno della galleria, or Dream of a Tunnel).*

Right: *Fernando Rey in the Banca di Roma commercial.*

Opposite: *Paolo Villaggio in the Banca di Roma commercial (Sogno del leone in cantina, or Dream of a Lion in the Basement) and several drawings by Fellini.*

INDEX

Films by Fellini cited in the text are indicated with the following abbreviations:

Variety Lights – *Lig*
The White Sheik – *She*
I Vitelloni – *Vit*
Matrimonial Agency – *Ag*
La Strada – *Str*
The Swindle – *Swi*
Nights of Cabiria – *Cab*
La Dolce Vita – *Ldv*
The Temptations of Doctor Antonio – *Tem*
8½ – *8*
Juliet of the Spirits – *Jul*
Toby Dammit – *Toby*
Fellini: A Director's Notebook – *Note*
Fellini Satyricon – *Sat*
The Clowns – *Clo*
Fellini's Roma – *Ro*
Amarcord – *Am*
Fellini's Casanova – *Cas*
Orchestra Rehearsal – *Orc*
City of Women – *Cit*
And the Ship Sails On – *Ship*
Ginger and Fred – *Gin*
Fellini's Intervista – *Int*
The Voice of the Moon – *Moon*